Advan.

FROM CONFLICT TO CONNECTION

"In this profound yet practical guide, John Kinyon and Ike Lasater show us that within every conflict lies the seed of transformation. *From Conflict to Connection* doesn't just offer a better way to resolve conflict, it provides a means of using conflict to deepen our connection to others and to ourselves."

—CHRIS KRESSER M.S., L.Ac
author of *NY Times* bestseller *The Paleo Cure*
chriskresser.com

"*From Conflict to Connection* gives you the ability to develop valuable and effective skills for dealing with conflict in personal and work relationships. When you apply what John and Ike teach in these pages, you'll move closer to the life and relationships you most want."

—MIKE ROBBINS
author of *Nothing Changes Until You Do*
Mike-Robbins.com

"Written with tender precision, this book is a complete guide to navigating interpersonal engagement. A happy by-product is how these external practices inexorably move us to a greater capacity for inner peace."

—LEE GLICKSTEIN
founder of Speaking Circles International and author of *Be Heard Now!*
Tap Into Your Inner Speaker and Communicate with Ease
speakingcirclesinternational.com

"This amazing book is like having a GPS for navigating conflict. It offers step-by-step, concrete tools to get you to where you want to be—in a place of harmonious, peaceful, and meaningful relationship with yourself and others. A true roadmap to happiness."

—KRISTIN NEFF, PH.D.
author of *Self-Compassion: The Proven Power of Being Kind to Yourself*
self-compassion.org

"Kinyon, Lasater, and Stiles describe a concise and thorough path for anyone seeking to transform the habitual cycles of conflict that plague our culture, families, organizations, and selves. Walking this path gradually frees us up from habits that otherwise undermine our lives and our work; instead, we develop our capacities and abilities for greater freedom, clarity, creativity, and service to others. Thus, these practices are crucial to building a better future for us all."

—JEFF BARNUM
Magenta
magenta.fm

"From Conflict to Connection is a beautifully and thoroughly written offering that can provide clear and powerful support to everyone in a relationship. The clear, everyday examples that illustrate the concepts make this an eminently practical book. I am happy to know that John and Ike are in the world sharing NVC in such an accessible way. I feel a partnership in their work and believe this book will go a long way to giving people a way through conflict to real communication. A wonderful and important enhancement to the legacy of Marshall Rosenberg."

—ROBERT GONZALES
author of *Reflections on Living Compassion*; CNVC certified trainer
living-compassion.org

"John and Ike offer a unique approach to responding effectively in difficult and crucial conversations, in personal life and at work. Their work is a valuable contribution to how human beings are learning to create peace and resolve conflicts compassionately and collaboratively."

—CORT WORTHINGTON
faculty, UC Berkeley Haas School of Business
cortworthington.com

"They've done it again! Written a book that is engaging, stimulating, thought provoking, and potentially life-changing for those who are willing to do the exercises and apply the principles to their lives. *From Conflict to Connection* is a winner!"

—SYLVIA HASKVITZ, MA, RD,
CNVC certified trainer; author of *Eat by Choice, Not by Habit*

"Systems thinkers teach that in any system there is one touchpoint that will yield the greatest amount of influence while requiring the least amount of effort. In this refreshingly clear and accessible book, Ike Lasater and John Kinyon demonstrate that in all human systems—family, friendships, community, business and political—that point just might be conflict itself. Full of learnable, practical, and doable skills, this book is a how-to guide for anyone who wants to be an agent of peace and happiness."

—MITCH ANTHONY
idea wrangler, design and brand strategist for Clarity
clarity-first.com

"A wonderfully satisfying evolution of John and Ike's previous volume. The authors' engagement with conflict through embodying Mediator Mind reminds us to cultivate our distinguishing characteristic as human beings: self-awareness. Awareness coupled with observation can allow us to successfully guide ourselves to positive, compassionate resolutions that can transform our individual and collective lives. John and Ike's work is a true gift of love in service!"

—SHIRA MARIN, PHD
developer of Intentional Life Design for Couples;
co-founder, The Hekate Institute for Leadership Communication;
author of *Shards of a Broken Mystery: The Restoration of Hekate*

"It is rare to find a book about human relationships that offers both transformative insights and well-articulated practices for applying those insights in real-world situations. It is even rarer for such a book to be clear, compelling, and enjoyable to read. *From Conflict to Connection* is that book and is a graceful distillation of John and Ike's years of developing Marshall Rosenberg's work of Nonviolent Communication to a new level of understanding and practical application. Throughout the book, their commitment to peace shines through, illuminating the path to a world where everyone's needs can be met through compassionate giving."

—JESSE WIENS AND CATHERINE CADDEN
Center for Nonviolent Communication certified trainers;
founders of ZENVC and Play in the Wild!
zenvc.org, playinthewild.org

"The historical complexities of the relationships within a family-owned business are rife with conflict. *From Conflict to Connection* offers step-by-step mapping to help advisors and individuals navigate the predictable challenges that come with mixing family and business. Ike and John provide a roadmap to help us recognize what our role is within conflict and how to take responsibility to initiate change within ourselves to resolve conflict and choose peace."

—RICCI M. VICTORIO, CSP, CPCC, ACC
managing director, Mosaic Family Business Center;
president, ICF San Francisco Bay Area Coaches
mosaicfbc.com

"How much conflict do you navigate on a daily basis with your spouse, children, friends, neighbors, colleagues, store clerks, etc.? It's a major part of our lives, yet we spend so little time improving our skills. John Kinyon and Ike Lasater's book is radiant in its ability to simplify conflict —its symptoms and demonstrations—and clarify the road to peaceful resolution. They don't offer pie-in-the-sky theory. Instead, they offer concrete, practical tools that you can integrate into your life *today*. It's brilliant and easily applicable. I'm certain it will transform the way you perceive and navigate conflict and therefore every person with whom you come in contact."

—MARY MACKENZIE, M.A.
author of *Peaceful Living: Daily Meditations for Living with
Love, Healing and Compassion*; co-founder, NVC Academy
nvctraining.com

"Being human, I am subject to conflict. It not only threatens my dreams and desires, but I am robbed of peace and well-being as soon as my heart experiences alienation from others. I am grateful to John and Ike for applying their profound grasp of Nonviolent Communication principles in offering us a comprehensive framework to effectively move us through all manners of conflict. I appreciate their clear, thorough, and methodical guidance and the timely appearance of this manual in a world riddled with ruptured relationships. I'll be keeping this book close to hand!"

—LUCY LEU
CNVC certified trainer;
founder of Puget Sound Network for Compassionate Communication;
author of *Nonviolent Communication Companion Workbook*

"*From Conflict to Connection* isn't intended to provide 'the answer' to solve your problems. It goes beyond that. The authors offer concepts and principles to change your mind about what causes conflict and what resolves it. They make a clear case that peaceful resolution of conflict is not only consistently possible, it's 'learnable.' Put their potent and time-tested tools into practice and discover your own answer to the essential question, 'How can I endeavor to live the life I imagine?'"

—CHRISTINE FLAHERTY
healthcare executive; CNVC certified trainer

"What I like most about John and Ike's new book, *From Conflict to Connection*, is it includes lots of examples and many practical ways to deal with power dynamics. Their tools help us do our own internal work, which is crucial in shifting from the power-over mentality to creating relationships where power is shared."

—MARTHA LASLEY,
author of *Coaching for Transformation*
LeadershipthatWorks.com

"*From Conflict to Connection* goes step by step in offering a clear and doable roadmap to resolving conflict and hearing others more deeply. It addresses crucial skills—self-management, responding to triggers, fight or flight, and power differentials—from the powerful lens of Nonviolent Communication. This is a significant book, further developing the legacy and vision of Marshall Rosenberg."

—DIAN KILLIAN, PHD
CNVC certified trainer; co-author of *Connecting Across Differences: How to Connect with Anyone, Anytime, Anywhere*

"John and Ike touch on most of the challenges that anyone attempting to mediate will encounter. Finding inspiration to keep yourself 'on your toes' is crucial as a mediator—whether it is in a formal setting or informal mediations in the family or amongst friends. This book is a gift to everyone wanting to help people connect."

—LIV LARSSON,
mediator, CT NVC trainer;
author of *A Helping Hand: Mediation with Nonviolent Communication* and *Anger, Guilt and Shame: Reclaiming Power and Choice*
friareliv.se/eng

"With *From Conflict to Connection*, John Kinyon, Ike Lasater, and Julie Stiles continue to expand on their already impressive body of work in the fields of mediation and conflict resolution. Rooted deeply in the tradition of Marshall Rosenberg's Nonviolent Communication, this beautiful, creative book offers a roadmap for anyone interested in learning how to turn painful conflicts and disagreements into deeper connections with self and others. Easy to read, well organized, and based on decades of firsthand experience, this handy guide promises to be a dog-eared, well-worn staple in my collection of 'go to' resources."

—OLI MITTERMAIER
mindfulness teacher; CEO of Pollinate.life

"Yes yes yes, *From Conflict to Connection* is a gift to the world! With the visionary and radical goal of using each situation of conflict to make connection with ourselves and others, John and Ike have offered us detailed tools to help us make it so. The examples of how easily misunderstandings and conflicts arise (as we know so well) and how, using the tools and skills offered, connection can ensue, bring me hope and courage to keep trying. I'm done being a 'martyr of niceness' and on to being honest and considerate of my own needs and the needs of others. What a relief!"

—MARCIA MILLER,
co-owner of Yoga on High
yogaonhigh.com

"From a peace-building perspective, John and Ike's book essentially calls into question the very foundation of conflict transformation. By understanding on the deepest level the impact of our actions upon another and ourselves, we come to a choice point of healing and connection or prolonged pain and isolation. *From Conflict to Connection* is a foundational guide to living in 'right relationship.'"

—JEFFREY WEISBERG & HEART PHOENIX
founders of River Phoenix Center for Peacebuilding
centerforpeacebuilding.org

MEDIATE YOUR LIFE:
A GUIDE TO
REMOVING BARRIERS TO COMMUNICATION

VOLUME 2

FROM CONFLICT

TO

CONNECTION

FROM CONFLICT TO CONNECTION:

Transforming Difficult Conversations
Conversations
into
Peaceful Resolutions

JOHN KINYON & IKE LASATER

with JULIE STILES

GLOBAL REACH BOOKS

Published by
Global Reach Books
4425 Meadowbrook Dr.
El Sobrante, CA 94803
connect@globalreachbooks.com

For more information about the work of Mediate Your Life, please visit:
mediateyourlife.com
To inquire about bulk orders or special programs:
connect@mediateyourlife.com

ISBN: 978-0-9899720-3-1
Library of Congress Control Number: 2015956972

Book design by Stacey Aaronson

Printed in the United States of America

We dedicate this book to Marshall Rosenberg, 1934–2015, for his insights into human connection and compassion through communication. We believe his work has contributed significantly to the advancement of human well-being and humanity's capacity to respond to the challenges we face.

TABLE OF CONTENTS

INTRODUCTION

YOU LIVE IN A WEB OF RELATIONSHIPS. THERE ARE THE PEOPLE closest to you—those you live with, the family you grew up in, and your closest friends. Then there are the people you interact with often, sometimes even daily, but who are not in your inner circle, such as people you work with, other family and friends, and people you encounter in living your daily life. Finally, you have the fleeting relationships with strangers that are not meant to last—on public transportation, with service folks, and with people you pass in going about your day.

As in a spider's web, a disturbance in any part of this network of relationships can reverberate throughout the entire structure. How much a difficult situation with someone intrudes on your life and well-being depends to some extent on how close the relationship is to the innermost part of the web. If you have an ugly interaction with a stranger on a street corner, it might reverberate through the web and affect your day, but likely less so than if you have a fight with your partner one morning. The ugly interaction becomes a story you tell coworkers when you get to work ("Can you believe what just happened to me?"), whereas you might find yourself ruminating on the fight for the rest of the day, upset and unable to focus on your work. Both situations, however, can trigger the stress response, the ancient fight-flight-freeze mechanism in the body that protects us from perceived danger.

It's surprising, considering the impact relationships have on people's overall well-being, that more attention is not paid in education to learning how to have relationships that work. People tend to learn through example (parents, siblings, teachers, and friends), piecing together as they grow up a way of dealing with others when they do not agree, often based on their particular fight-flight-freeze response. These piecemeal methods have varying levels of success, and the cost across all areas of well-being—health, finances, overall satisfaction, and relationships—can be quite high when these methods don't work.

Yet being able to cope with the stress response, disagreements, judgments of others, misunderstandings, and outright conflict is learnable. It's possible to create ways of being in a relationship with yourself and others—even in the worst of times when you think there's no hope—that lead you from conflict to connection.

The first book in the Mediate Your Life series, *Choosing Peace*, laid the foundational skills for this new way of being in a relationship. In that book we outlined the tools necessary to be able to respond to situations rather than react to them. We covered the four components of communication—Observations, Feelings, Needs, and Requests—from Nonviolent Communication (NVC) that form the basis for our work. *Choosing Peace* includes techniques that help you embody this new way of communicating so that fresh possibilities emerge in your relationships. We do recommend that you have either read *Choosing Peace* or are already familiar with the four components of NVC and the distinctions they represent before reading this book. We include a brief review in the following pages, but your ability to use the skills and tools in this book will be enhanced greatly if you have the foundation already in place.

In this second book of the Mediate Your Life series, we begin to introduce you to our various "maps"—specific steps you use to navigate conflict situations in any area of your life. Maps direct the focus of your mind and the actions to take in moments of uncertainty, especially when you are experiencing a stress response. Focusing the attention of your conciousness and engaging in conduct are, after all, the only two things you can do to affect your future. In these pages, we concentrate on the maps for navigating interpersonal conflict, meaning any situation in which you and another person are in disagreement.

How This Book Is Organized

The chapters of this book roughly follow a timeline that flows from maps and exercises you can do before a difficult conversation, to what you do during the discussion, to what we find helpful afterward. Following this order helps you learn how to prepare to have the conversation, actually have it, and then learn from it. Mastering these maps and skills in this order also supports you when you unexpectedly find yourself in a conflict with someone else. Similar to *Choosing Peace*, we use examples throughout the chapters of our fictional family as they handle various difficult situations that arise at home and at work. In addition, we link to videos throughout the chapters of the authors demonstrating the maps and exercises in this book. Use these videos to deepen your understanding and see concrete examples of how the steps of each process unfold in an actual conversation or practice session.

CHAPTER 1 sets the stage with an exploration of what interpersonal conflict is, how people wind up in conflict, and how to get out. Power is a central concept in conflict, so we investigate how your relationship to power affects the course of the conversation and the importance of shifting perspective. The three-chair mediation model and "mediator mind" set the stage for all the maps and exercises in the book, providing a powerful way to embody a part of you that will help you create connection between opposing viewpoints.

CHAPTER 2 opens where connection begins: with yourself. The first map, the Self-Connection Process, is the go-to map anytime you begin to feel the stress response, sense yourself becoming disconnected, or simply want to feel more in harmony with yourself. This process provides the jumping-off place for nearly every other map we offer, and practicing it regularly will help you to quickly and effectively reconnect to yourself and return to feeling centered and grounded, hence more readily connecting with others.

CHAPTER 3 continues the self-connection theme with an exercise designed to help you learn to use that process in the most difficult situation—when you become triggered into the fight or flight response. Using a safe role-playing situation and three-chair mediation model, you learn more about your physiological response to stress and practice coming back to a centered state so that you can choose a response you like. If you practice this exercise, you will find that you begin to embody "mediator mind," a place within that allows you to more easily connect with yourself, even in the midst of stress. You will also find that you become less triggered by the same stimulus in your everyday life.

CHAPTER 4 introduces a powerful map to use when you notice judgments—or enemy images—of another person. The Enemy Image Process prepares you to have a difficult conversation by neutralizing your judgments through connecting with your needs and the needs underlying the other's challenging behavior. When you can go into the conversation without these enemy images, you are more open to connecting with the other person and working with them to come to a resolution.

CHAPTER 5 covers the core process of this book, the Interpersonal Mediation map. This map outlines the common challenges people encounter in conflict conversations and the steps to go through when you are in one, and it covers the skills that help you navigate the conversation successfully. Since being able to apply this map "in the wild" can be challenging when you are actually in a difficult conversation, we discuss various ways to practice the map and skills so that you are able to remember them when you need to, giving you access to your mediator mind even when faced with a conflict situation.

CHAPTER 6 focuses on making agreements with others that are more likely to result in your own and the other person's needs being met. Agreements are more than just a crucial part of being able to successfully mediate your own conversations; they form the backbone of being in an ongoing relationship with others in a way that encourages mutual growth and peaceful coexistence. We discuss the types of agreements to make, how to handle agreements that are broken, and how to think about agreements so that you are able to be in integrity and be with "what is."

CHAPTER 7 acknowledges that after a difficult conversation, you are likely to have a variety of thoughts and feelings about it that may include judgments of yourself, recriminations, "should haves," and analyses of the situation. The map in this chapter, The Mourn Celebrate Learn process, allows you to work through all that you feel about what happened, connecting to the needs that were met and not met in the situation. This helps you escape from destructive recriminations and learn from what happened so that you can better meet your needs.

CHAPTER 8 expands the focus so that the whole cycle of difficult conversations becomes clear. Navigating the cycle is easier when you can identify where you are and which map is appropriate to use. We show you how to choose a map when you feel uncertain or stuck, and how to move through a spiral of conversations that revolve around a single conflict, always guiding you toward staying connected with yourself and the other person and finding strategies that work for both of you.

How to Use This Book

As in all of the series, this book asks you to do more than read it. You will learn a lot by reading, but you will learn even more—and will begin to embody what you learn—by putting it into practice. Throughout the book we give practice pauses that will help you take the concepts and apply them in your own life and in the relationships you find most difficult.

We also have exercises and practices that we recommend you do with a partner. Practicing with a partner takes the learning out of your mind and allows you to try out the skills in the situation where you're going to need them—when you're actually talking to another human being. Though you might imagine yourself successfully mediating a conflict or having a difficult conversation with someone, until you practice out loud with another person, you're likely to find you will be better in your imagination than in reality. Ideally, someone close to you is also interested in learning these skills, and you can practice with them. If not, you can visit the book page on our website at mediateyourlife.com/from-conflict-to-connection, where we have resources to help you find a practice partner.

We recommend that you first read through the entire book so you get a picture of the landscape of difficult conversations. After that, you can use this book as a guide and reference that you return to anytime you are in conflict. The maps and exercises are explained in depth in the chapters, but we have also included the steps for each map and exercise in the appendices for easy reference. What's more, you can visit the book's website at mediateyourlife.com/from-conflict-to-connection for printable versions that you can keep handy for practice sessions and as you live your daily life.

We also encourage you to use what you learn in these pages "in the wild," whether you feel ready to or not. Between this book and *Choosing Peace*, we have given you the foundation, tools, and skills you need to be able to work through situations in which you are in conflict with another person. We've also given you the tools and skills to deal with what comes up when you are not as successful as you would like to be, and how to then reconnect with yourself, learn from what happened, and move ahead to continue to work through the situation.

So don't merely read this book—live it. Use these skills in your daily life. Allow them to help you create a web of relationships so strong that it supports you through any challenge, and so beautiful that it enhances your well-being. Let every situation be the fodder for more learning, and allow every mistake you make to be an opportunity to make amends, improve your skills, build your confidence, and, ultimately, create more connection with yourself and others.

1 | FROM ARGUMENT TO AGREEMENT

Conflict is the beginning of consciousness.
—M. ESTHER HARDING

———∿∿∿———

SALLY RUSHES INTO THE KITCHEN AT 7:30 IN THE morning, giving Maggie, who is eating a bowl of cereal at the table, a quick kiss on the head. James smiles at her over his coffee.

"Want some?" he asks as he pops a piece of bread in the toaster.

"I'd love some but I've got to run," Sally says, grabbing a container of yogurt from the refrigerator. "I have a client meeting first thing this morning. You're taking the kids to school, right?"

"Yep, I'm on kid duty this morning," James says, ruffling Maggie's hair as he picks up the newspaper. "The train leaves in twenty minutes!"

Maggie rolls her eyes. "Who's picking me up to take me to soccer tryouts this afternoon?"

Sally smiles and claps her hands together. "Oh, that's right! They're today! I know how excited you've been about soccer starting up again." She squats down to her daughter's level. "I hope you won't be disappointed, but I'm in meetings all afternoon so your dad will have to take you."

James looks up from the paper. "Whoa, wait a minute, I'm taking the kids to school. I can't just leave work in the middle of the afternoon and stay with her through tryouts."

Sally stands up and squares her shoulders toward James. Her voice comes out hard as she says, "I told you yesterday that I have meetings all day today. We also need a few things for dinner tonight—and I was hoping you could pick them up on your way home."

James throws the paper down on the table. "What? You want to go back to work so I have to turn into Mr. Mom and risk my job in the process? Remember it's my job that's been supporting this family for the past ten years!"

"Yeah, and I've been raising our kids!" Sally counters. "You think that isn't work? You try it for awhile."

James stands as Sally continues.

"I'd like to contribute to supporting this family, and that means some of the things I usually do are now things that someone else is going to need to help with. We talked about this when we talked about me going back to work. Or maybe you've conveniently forgotten that?"

Maggie grabs her bowl and runs out of the kitchen. She passes Corey in the hallway, who is headed toward the battle-ground. "I wouldn't go in there if I were you," she whispers to him.

Back in the kitchen, James throws his arms up in the air and sits back down. "Fine. Whatever. I'll take them to school, and I'll get Maggie to her tryouts. No problem. And when I lose my job, and we can no longer afford this house or activities for the kids, maybe you'll come to your senses." Fuming, he picks up the paper again and buries his head in it.

Sally stands rigid for a moment staring at James as he pretends to read the paper, then grabs her keys and storms out of the house without even saying goodbye to Corey and Maggie. Seething, she gets in the car and slams the door. Her mind swirls with anger and irritation at James. "What the hell?" she says to herself out loud. "We talked about this. He knew he needed to step up more around the house and help me out. But when it comes down to it, can he just do it? No. I, of course, am supposed to be superwoman, balancing a new consulting business like it's nothing and still picking up the kids and doing all the household chores, cheerfully greeting my husband when he comes home from work with dinner ready and the house clean, like some 1950s commercial." With her jaw clenched and heart racing, she jams the key into the ignition and pulls out of the driveway.

—⚬⚬⚬—

Of all the conflicts you might encounter, disagreements with people closest to you—whether at work or at home—can be the most triggering and disorienting. Perhaps everything seems to be going along fine, then suddenly you are embroiled in an argument you did not see coming. Or, if the relationship is long-term, conflicts begin to fall into familiar patterns, and you recognize that you are in the same argument you've been having for months or even years.

These interpersonal conflicts—where you are in conflict with someone else—are often the most difficult to solve. Why is that? Conflicts with those close to you can bring up old hurts from your family of origin, hurts that have created patterns that dictate how you relate to power and control. In these situations, you can easily become embroiled in habitual patterns and triggers, and pulling out of them can feel like a monumental, if not impossible, task.

Yet, it is possible to change even the most entrenched conflicts and well-established patterns of relationships. When you learn to navigate these conflicts, you can make the biggest impact in your life and on the people around you.

After all, interpersonal conflict is inevitable. When two people try to live or work in harmony with each other—whether as co-workers, intimate partners, or parent-child—their different agendas and desires will unavoidably lead to clashes. The following examples may sound all too familiar:

+   You want to go to the mountains for vacation; your partner wants to go to the islands.

+   Your work colleague always leaves the breakroom coffee pot empty; you would like it filled.

+   Your boss makes a decision that impacts you directly, and even though she had promised to do so, neglected to seek your input.

+   Your child wants to play video games; you want him to do his homework.

+   One of the people on your team at work fails yet again to meet the deadline for their contribution to the project.

+   You catch your teenage daughter sneaking back in through her bedroom window after having been out with her boyfriend after curfew.

+   Your teenage son is rude to you and to his grandparents.

+ Your sister, who blogs about her strident political views, insists on provoking members of the family into acrimonious arguments at family holiday gatherings.

The people you live and work with are often the focus of relationship difficulties, yet even people you encounter less frequently, including strangers, can provoke a thorny situation:

+ The police officer stops you for what seems to you to be no good reason, and then is rude when he orders you out of your car.

+ You work in a retail store and one of your customers acts in a way you consider completely out of line.

+ Your community is debating an issue you feel strongly about and you would like to influence the city council's decision.

+ As part of your job, you regularly deal with irate customers.

+ You are an elected political official and in an open meeting, one of your constituents verbally attacks you.

How do you respond, both within yourself and with others, when people want something different from you? Do you try to get your way, negotiate, or give in to them? Your response can either enhance and strengthen your connection to others and your overall happiness, or it can undermine the relationship and set the stage for future conflict.

This book is about you in relationship to others. Within these pages, we will give you the tools to become aware of your own patterns when you get in conflict. As you go, you will learn new ways to connect with yourself and with the people around you, as well as understand how to use "maps" that will help you navigate interpersonal conflict so that it leads to connection and resolution.

In short, we will help you go from argument to agreement.

The Cost of Interpersonal Conflict

Disagreements with others can be insidious. The cost of conflict may be obvious to you when it boils over into an angry fight with both parties yelling. You might cut that person out of your life, with consequences for yourself, and often, for other people. If a conflict causes you to lose something—a job, an opportunity, a marriage, a friendship—then you are likely to notice that cost, and probably believe there's little that can be done about it.

Not all disputes are so conspicuous, however. James and Sally are nowhere close to a divorce, yet they are caught in an ongoing disagreement that has to do with shifting roles as Sally takes on more work. For many people, these kinds of quarrels are even less pronounced, with one or both parties choosing to not say what they are really thinking, trying to smooth things over.

Still, even less subtle arguments carry a significant cost; small resentments build up over time and turn into big ones. The lack of connection from each small disagreement can grow into a general feeling that you don't even know the people with whom you live or work. Disconnection from others can also drastically affect your connection to yourself, since you might blame yourself or wonder why you don't get along as well with them as you used to.

When people don't have the skills and knowledge to be able to do something about the conflicts they find themselves in, they tend to downgrade the cost or ignore it completely. Since it's painful to be aware of a cost, or if you have no hope that you can create change, the tendency will be to pretend the cost doesn't exist.

Yet the cost can also provide the motivation to change, to go through the growth process of shifting how you are in conflict, so that you can begin to reap the benefits of more harmony and connection with yourself and the people you are close to.

PRACTICE PAUSE

What is the cost of conflict for you?

———

James stares at the paper, not even seeing the articles in front of him, aware of Sally's glare as she grabs her keys and stomps out of the house. The door bangs behind her, and James feels the weight of the silence, as if all of the emotion and expectation their exchange unleashed was pressing down on him. He drops his pretense of reading the paper and rests his head in his hands.

I really don't need this right now, James thinks to himself. *As if there isn't enough pressure already at work, now suddenly I'm having to take time off? With all these changes in healthcare, I can't be seen as "slacking off" or not up to the task, especially with my team relying on me. And with Dad coming down on me too about Corey ...* He rubs his head.

As Corey comes into the room, James stands up. "We're leaving in a couple minutes for school. Are you almost ready?"

"Yeah. Mom left already?" he asks. "You guys fighting again?"

"No, everything's fine. She just had a client meeting this morning." James puts his coffee cup in the sink, missing the skeptical glance Corey sends his way. James feels a sinking sensation in the pit of his stomach as he reflects on the last thing he said to his wife. *I shouldn't have said that*, he thinks.

———

The problem with conflict is not that we have it. In our own life experience and in working with thousands of people, we have come to know that conflict is actually a profound opportunity to deepen our connection to ourselves and others, and to embrace what's alive in us at each moment.

So what is the problem?

Most people do not know how they get into conflict, or how to effectively get out of it in a way that feels satisfying. As such, let's take a look at the two main elements of this problem: how people get in conflict, and how to effectively get out.

GETTING INTO CONFLICT

You might be thinking, *Of course I know how I get in conflict! So-and-so does such-and-such even though they know I don't like it and that's how we get in conflict.* Or *Well, we're in conflict because he refuses to listen to me!* When people are in conflict, they often have a litany of explanations for the disagreement that focus on what the other person did or did not do or say.

In our work, we prefer to focus on things that we can actually change. We find that efforts to change other people generally don't work, and that they often create more conflict when the other person resists our well-meaning efforts to "make them a better person." The focus we suggest, therefore, is to look at what is going on in *you* that leads to you getting into conflict (and out of it), rather than focusing on what someone else may or may not be doing.

With that in mind, we find that people get into conflict because:

+ They have habitual patterns of thought and behavior that keep them disconnected from themselves and others.

+ They are taken over by the stress response.

+ The stress response and habitual patterns lead to behaviors that create and further conflict.

When James and Sally react to each other across the kitchen table, both are entrenched in their own point of view. In James's interpretation, Sally is being inconsiderate and unreasonable in her demands. Sally, too, is caught in her perspective, thinking James is selfish and obtuse. Remember, it is your *interpretation* of what has happened or what someone else says or does that determines your reaction to it. That interpretation is your point of view.

Most people get locked into their particular point of view, based on their interpretations of what has happened. It can be particularly difficult to escape your own point of view when emotions are running high—when needs of yours are not being met. It is likewise normal to be caught in your point of view, especially since being able to "stand in another's shoes" is a skill most people are not taught. We do not want to suggest here that it's somehow bad or you are wrong if you find you are stuck in your viewpoint about a situation. What we do suggest is that being stuck there is likely to cause or continue conflict.

Why is this?

When people are in conflict, it is their strategies that are in conflict, not their needs. When you are locked into your own perspective, you are also locked into the strategies you think will meet your needs. You see the other person in opposition to you, instead of as another human being who shares the same needs.

You are also likely to be caught in your judgments of yourself and the other person, another habitual thought pattern that leads to conflict. Judgments can be insidious; they are those limiting diagnoses and analyses of who we are or who the other person is that seem to arrive automatically. In conflict with someone else, you likely have a list of judgments of them, and you might also have judgments about yourself for how you handled the situation or for getting into it in the first place, piled on top of whatever judgments you have about the other person. Judgments are often based on interpretations, and they keep you from being able to connect with yourself and the other person.

The other habitual thought pattern that leads to conflict is a mindset about power that assumes there are two options: *power over* and *power under*. We will discuss this habitual pattern in depth shortly.

When any or all of these habit patterns get triggered, you become overtaken by the stress response, otherwise known as the fight-flight-freeze response. All the typical thoughts that get people into conflict will tend to trigger the fight-flight-freeze response, which is based on perceiving a threat in the environment. Evolutionary history has created neurochemical and biological pathways to help humans adequately respond to life-threatening events. Unfortunately, these pathways similarly get triggered when you perceive threats that are actually not life-threatening. So, if you perceive that someone has power over you or that you must make someone else give way to get what you want, that can trigger the stress response. Being locked into your own perspective with your judgments of yourself or the other person can also cause you to perceive danger that sets off the fight or flight pattern.

Once the stress response has taken over, it is as if you are no longer in control. More primitive parts of the brain are in charge, trying to protect you from the perceived threat. While in fight-flight-freeze, you will act in ways that tend to create and sustain misunderstandings and quarrels.

In summary, people get into conflict because they have habitual thought patterns that lock them into their own viewpoint, keep them in judgment of themselves and others, and prompt a mindset about power that assumes someone must have power *over*. These patterns lead directly to triggering the danger signal internally that causes the physiological fight-flight-freeze response to take over. When this happens, people act in ways that lead to more conflict, not less.

How to Get Out of Conflict

So if that's how people get into conflict, how do they get out of it? Better yet, how do they learn to connect so effectively that they don't get into conflict in the first place?

There is certainly no shortage of well-meaning advice about how to interact with others to minimize conflict. Religious traditions for eons have instructed followers to be kind and compassionate; self-help books advise readers to practice understanding of others; parenting books suggest that acceptance and approval are important for happy children. Even research on interpersonal relationships suggests that couples are more likely to stay together if they show respect for one another, even while arguing.

While we don't disagree with any of this advice, where we find most of it fails miserably is in the *how*.

- *How* can you be kind and compassionate when you are angry and upset?

- *How* do you show understanding when you don't feel understood?

- *How* do you give your kids acceptance and approval at the times you most want to throttle them?

- *How* do you show respect to your partner in the midst of seemingly irreconcilable differences?

In this book, we attempt to answer those questions, and, more importantly, give you the means to be able to act on that millenia-old sage advice, to put it into practice in specific situations in your own life when you most struggle to follow it effectively.

From our perspective on how people get into conflict, the following list outlines the keys to be able to act out of kindness, compassion, understanding, acceptance, and respect, even in difficult situations:

- Shift your mindset about power to *power with*.

- Be willing and able to take on perspectives other than your own, even in emotionally charged situations (embody "mediator mind").

- Know how to connect to yourself in any situation.

- Learn how to deactivate the stress response in particular situations.

- Change the habits of interaction with yourself and others.

✦ Become aware of judgments of yourself and others and
   learn how to shift them.

✦ Use a proven process to be in difficult conversations that
   will help you focus on being in the conversation in a way
   that leads to connection and resolution.

✦ Become adept at learning from a difficult conversation so
   that you increase your skills and capacity for the future.

This might seem like a long list, but in fact, if you practice
what's in this book, you will have the understanding and strategies
to apply each of the above points in your life. We will begin by
talking about power and perspective, and the maps and exercises in
the rest of the book will help you embody the above-listed shifts in
understanding so that you can find your way through sticky conflict
situations and emerge with integrity and relationships intact.

WHO HAS THE POWER?

Power is central to interpersonal conflicts, which often boil down
to a power struggle. Learning to be in difficult conversations means
being able to see your current relationship to power and to be open
to another way. Most people tend to have a particular approach
when in conflict: is your tendency to try to overpower the other
person, or are you the one who feels like you are being over-
powered? In ongoing relationships, it can become a predictable
pattern whether you are the one who pushes your agenda or always
gives in to the other person. If you tend to feel either way, you are
approaching the conflict with a *power over* or *power under* mindset.
Consider these two scenarios:

SCENARIO 1

Your partner asks you to go to the company event. You've had a busy week and long to curl up with a cup of tea and a book in front of the fireplace and have a quiet evening. You suck it up and go anyway, telling yourself that your partner's position is important, and because it's the work that's paying most of the bills, you ought to be supportive. The event feels like it goes on forever, and you strain to keep a smile on your face and be pleasant to your partner's colleagues.

SCENARIO 2

Glancing into your daughter's room, you notice she is playing a game on her computer instead of doing her homework. You feel angry as you walk into the room, ordering her to stop playing games and get to work. Her sullen look says it all as she slowly finishes the level she's on and stops the game.

The first scenario indicates a *power under* relationship: you go to the company event because you perceive your partner has more power and it's up to you to be supportive. In the second scenario, it's a *power over* relationship, using your role to exert what you want.

How do you know if you have a *power over* or *power under* mindset in relation to a conflict? Some indicators include if you:

+ have already decided the outcome in your mind

+ think that if you give in at all, the other person will "win"

+ are not willing to hear the other person's needs and take those into account

+ feel like the other person doesn't care about your needs

+ believe that the only way to get your needs met is to extract what you want from the other person

+ think the other person is trying to force something from you

+ think you have to give in to keep the other person happy or to be loved

+ aren't sure it's worth the energy to try to ask for what you want

The Mediate Your Life approach to conflict resolution focuses on finding the motivation behind what you want—what we call Needs. Needs are one of the 4 Components of Communication that Marshall Rosenberg delineated in creating Nonviolent Communication (NVC). Using these four components in your thinking and speaking creates a level of clarity that supports communicating and connecting with others. Here's a quick refresher of these four components:

+ **Observations** are what you observe about the external or internal world that are the stimulus for your experience, and are distinguished from the judgments or interpretations about what happened.

+ **Feelings** are bodily sensations that arise from your unconscious assessments about what has happened, assessments regarding whether your needs have been met or are being met. In addition, feelings can be, and often are, the direct consequence of the thoughts that ebb and flow through your mind.

+ **Needs** are the fundamental qualities that all humans require to survive and thrive, and are separate from the strategies for how to meet them.

+ **Requests** (as opposed to demands) are what you might ask
  of yourself or others to meet those needs.

All four components help people connect with each other, and
Needs are particularly powerful for creating connection because
they lie beneath the strategy—they are why people want what they
want. Everyone shares needs; everybody wants love, respect, food,
shelter, autonomy, meaning, and so on (see Appendices A and B
for a list of Feelings and Needs).

Conflicts are over strategies, and when people focus on strategies, the discussion can easily become about who gets their way,
rather than how to work together to meet the underlying needs.
Each person in the conflict advocates for what they think should
happen because they believe that their strategy is better or correct.

For example:

+ You want to stay home (meeting needs for rest and care)
  and your partner wants you to go to the company event
  (meeting needs for companionship and support).

+ You want your child to do her homework (meeting needs
  for care and support) while she wants to play video games
  (meeting needs for fun and play).

+ You would like your family to rinse their dishes
  immediately instead of leaving them in the sink (meeting
  needs for cleanliness and order), while they would prefer to
  leave them for later (meeting needs for efficiency).

When people think, even unconsciously, that someone doesn't
care about their needs, they tend to dig in and not want to give
anything up. With a *power over* or *power under* mindset, the question
becomes: Will I get my strategy (and therefore be the one to have

my needs met), or will I have to give up my strategy (and my needs)? When we don't address *why* the other person wants what they want, the conflicts continue or regularly recur. The kitchen, the calendar, and the household to-do list become battle zones, resentments simmer, and conflicts threaten to erupt from ever-smaller triggers.

If two people in a disagreement can uncover the needs they are each wanting to meet with their strategy, they can find a new sense of understanding and commonality. Since needs are unattached to strategies (any number of strategies can meet a need), focusing on needs not only helps people connect with each other, it opens up the conversation to creativity and collaboration in considering new ideas for ways forward to meet everyone's needs.

ESCAPING POWER STRUGGLE

You might be wondering, *What about relationships where one person does have power over the other?* Certainly there are situations in which power differentials play a part, especially when the power in a relationship follows from roles. When you and your boss have a disagreement, it might come with an automatic sense that he or she has power over you. In a conflict with a child, you might operate from having power over him or her.

In other relationships with coworkers or family members, who is perceived to have power can simply become a pattern in the relationship: an overbearing husband with a quieter wife may end up in a consistent pattern where the husband has power over her and the rest of the family. Power might also shift by situation: a husband with expertise in accounting might wield power over his wife when it comes to financial decisions, but she exerts *power over* when it comes to the household or the children.

While interpersonal conflict might be inevitable because everyone has different strategies for meeting their needs, the power struggle of a *power over/under* relationship is not. Even if you are in a longstanding relationship that has its set patterns around the use of power, you can shift these patterns. In this book, we present a model that shows you a way out of the power struggle that often ensues around each person trying to get what they want. The central question of interpersonal conflict is:

Can you stand in your power in a way that works for everyone?

In our method, this shift is from conflict to becoming connected and, out of that connection, finding a way to get your needs as well as the other person's met. It means co-creating strategies that work for everyone. It's a shift from *power over/power under* to *power with*.

—⁓⁓—

Sally pulls into a parking spot at her potential client's office, still angry and ruminating on her conversation with James. Glancing at her watch, she sees that she has a few minutes to spare and thinks, *This meeting is too important. I can't go in there like this.*

Sally relaxes the white-knuckle grip she has on the steering wheel and takes a deep breath, thinking back on the conversation and why she is so upset. *I want to make sure my family is cared for and that things get done there, but I also want care around my own dreams and desires to make a difference in the world through the work I'm doing.*

A wave of sadness rises from underneath the anger. Sally knows how powerless she had felt as a stay-at-home mom, both because she wasn't bringing in any income and because she wasn't contributing to the world outside her home. Even though she felt that raising her kids the best way she knew how was making a positive impact, it was hard to stand confidently in that contribution when society didn't recognize it, and when there was more she wanted to contribute professionally.

But going back to work has had its own challenges, and Sally feels the underlying fear that has been plaguing her ever since she started her new consulting business. *Does going back to work mean I'm not a good mother?* The thought brings tears to her eyes. *I'd really like to trust that it's the best thing for all of us, and that it will be a positive influence on my children for them to see me doing what I love in the world.* She takes a few deep breaths as she connects with her desires to be a good mom and to be fulfilled professionally.

Being in touch with what is going on for her, Sally feels her gut clench remembering how she had reacted to James. Going back to work was a major change in their household routine, which up until then had been in a nice rhythm. Sally feels responsible and guilty for disrupting that ease, which is at war with her desires and at times causes her to lash out, trying to force her way anytime she thinks James resists. True, she feels disappointed by how James responds, especially when she thought she had his support in going back to work. She sighs, wondering, *How can we stop being at loggerheads with each other over these things? It's all push and pull between us now. I'd really like some consistency and predictability when I have work commitments. What do we do to create a shared reality and a new possibility of working together to manage things on the home front while I go back to work?*

Though Sally doesn't know the answer to that question, thinking of it in terms of underlying desires and working together to meet them feels a lot better than the anger and hurt she had felt a few minutes earlier. She takes another breath before gathering her things and steps out of the car. Aware of her new perspective, she notices the crispness of the air and the way the sunlight plays off the windows of the building as she walks to the door.

THE POWER OF PERSPECTIVE

Making the shift to *power with* is rarely something people can do by *trying* to make that change; however, it comes naturally if you merely shift your mindset. The way we suggest doing that is through broadening perspective and embodying a "mediator mind." In order to explain this, let's first look at what we mean by the term *mediation*.

If James and Sally found over time that they were unable to work through their disagreements, they might ask someone to help them. This person would help them hear each other and work together to resolve their conflict—as a third party in the role of a mediator.

Mediation has emerged over the past few decades as a powerful alternative to the court system for resolving conflicts. People tend to think of mediation only in the context of a professional setting, perhaps as an alternative to going to court and involving lawyers and massive expense.

We offer instead that mediation is a part of everyday life. You can take the same basic idea of a mediator helping two people in conflict and apply it to every aspect of conflict in any area of your life.

You can approach every conflict you experience from the perspective of mediating connection between yourself and others.

Even if you think you avoid conflict, that doesn't mean you don't have any. If you are in relationships with others, you will experience disagreements with them, and those disagreements can trigger conflict within yourself. You also witness others in conflict, which you might react to in some way. Learning the skills we offer in this book and the rest of the series will enable you to be more effective in *any* interpersonal situation where there is conflict—or even potential conflict—which means that you can be more effective in *every* interpersonal situation.

The basic model of mediation can be represented by three chairs. The two chairs facing each other represent the two people in conflict, and the third chair at a 90-degree angle represents the mediator.

While these chairs represent people in a formal mediation scenario, they also represent *perspectives*. The two chairs facing each other are the two different perspectives in the conflict, and the third chair is the perspective of someone outside the conflict, one who has the space to be able to essentially hold both of the conflicting perspectives with the intention of bringing connection and collaboration. When thought about this way, it becomes clear that you can sit in any chair, taking the perspective of either side of an argument, as well as sitting in the mediator's chair where you can hear each side and help the other two people hear each other.

For example, suppose you are in conflict with your mother, who wants more contact with you. You can easily imagine sitting in your own chair—that's your perspective, the part of you that gets "triggered" and reacts. You might think, *She's so annoying. She calls me right in the middle of work and expects me to drop what I'm doing and chat, and all she wants to talk about is the dog, or her idiot neighbor who bugs her. Then the next day she calls again and talks about the same things! I love her, but please, she just doesn't get it! I'm way too busy for this.*

First, you can connect to your perspective using Observations, Feelings, and Needs, which helps you step out of being reactive:

+ **Observations**: "Mother calls me when I'm working. She talks about things I don't want to talk about. She repeats the same things when she calls."

+ **Feelings**: Irritation, frustration, and maybe some sadness

+ **Needs**: Respect for you and your time, efficiency, and wanting to have a more meaningful connection while talking about things that *you* care about

Now move into the chair representing your mother's perspective. Put yourself in her shoes, and see what comes up for you. What do you (playing her role) say about the situation? Perhaps something like, "I love my daughter and I've devoted my whole life to my family, and she can barely give me the time of day. When I call her to talk, she rushes me off the phone as fast as she can, and I barely get anything in! I thought I taught the kids respect for their elders, but I guess not. I'm just some irritating old biddy to her and she can't be bothered to pay me any attention."

Again, use Observations, Feelings, and Needs to connect to your mother's perspective:

+ **Observations**: "My daughter doesn't call me. When I call her, within a few minutes she tells me, 'I really have to go, Mom.' I notice that I'm interpreting impatience and irritation in her tone and thinking that she doesn't have room for me in her life."

+ **Feelings**: Sadness, anger, hurt

+ **Needs**: Connection, respect, and acknowledgement for all that I've given to the family (contribution, love)

Now imagine that you move fully into the mediator chair. From this place, you can see both your own perspective and your mother's. Can you hold them both at once? Can you see what is prompting all the judgments, how those judgments are driving each person's actions, and how the feelings and needs are playing out in the pattern of the relationship?

PRACTICE PAUSE

Do the above exercise with a real conflict you are experiencing. "Sit" in each of the chairs—first yours, then the other person's—using Observations, Feelings, and Needs to connect to that perspective. Then sit in the mediator chair and hold both perspectives at once. What do you notice? How does the conflict feel different to you now?

In our trainings, we have people rotate chairs in exactly this way, so that even with a single scenario, each person has the experience of taking each perspective. When you bring a conflict you are experiencing to this exercise and take each of the three perspectives, including that of the person you are in conflict with, it is a particularly powerful way to gain new understanding and insight into the conflict, and then to take the new approach of embodying "mediator mind."

HOW TO BE YOUR OWN MEDIATOR

If you are in conflict with another person, it can be helpful to have someone who can sit with the two of you; even a friend who can help you both hear each other can be a contribution. In most cases, however, you probably don't have that third person. Instead, you can apply this template of three chairs, and in particular the idea of the inner mediator's chair, or "mediator mind," to help you shift how you are in a conflict so that you can facilitate getting to a resolution you're comfortable with. Let's take a closer look at how the mediator mind can help you in difficult conversations.

Imagine you have just been on the phone with a friend who said something you found hurtful. Search for a specific example if you can and actually close your eyes for a moment, remembering that time in the past, such as when a friend of yours said something painful, perhaps sounding like they were putting you down in some way. You'll notice your version of the stress response gets triggered immediately. What happens for you? How does your body feel? What thoughts are running through your mind? What actions do you immediately want to take? Do you want to call them back and yell at them? Are you imagining that the next time you see them you'll make a snide comment? Or do you just write them off completely and decide you won't see them again?

Again, we encourage you to make this real for yourself, noticing in particular what is happening in your body as the scenario plays out in your imagination. After you experience the emotions of the exercise, jot down what you notice in your body and mind.

Now imagine a different scenario, thinking about a time when you felt joyful and expansive and how that feels in your body. Perhaps you are on vacation in your favorite place, or have just indulged in something—a spa day, a playful outing with a close friend, or even curling up in front of a fire with a favorite book. You feel centered and grounded, connected with yourself and the world, and open. Notice how your body feels and what is happening in your mind. Close your eyes and do this now, then write down some notes on your sensations and mental state.

Now, in that expanded state, consider how you might respond to the situation you imagined with your friend.

What would it be like to have *centered, grounded, expansive you* available to you, even in the midst of *reactive you*? To be able to make choices from *grounded you* that compassionately respond both to what's going on in *reactive you* and also to what the other person is doing? To have choices that help you emerge from the fight or flight response, bit by bit, that allow you—even while still in some reaction—to respond in a way that helps you act from your values instead of your stress-response chemistry?

Would that be helpful to you?

If so, then this book is for you. We will teach you how, in the midst of a conflict between yourself and another, to be able to embody the perspective of the mediator. We will show you how to step into a part of yourself that can clearly see your own needs and those of the other person, as if all the needs are piled up together in the space between the two disputant chairs. We will teach you how to be your own mediator.

> **mediator mind** *n.*
>
> the ability to access multiple perspectives and make connecting choices even while in the midst of a difficult conversation

When you internalize mediator mind, you:

✦ are able to resolve conflicts even when you are convinced they're impossible to resolve

✦ more easily see your position and strategy instead of being owned and controlled by them

✦ can get unstuck from holding onto your viewpoint and being against the other person's

✦ can clearly see the needs of both perspectives

✦ free yourself from the polarizing me-versus-them mentality

✦ will have a powerful set of choices that will help you facilitate a resolution you can feel good about

✦ can facilitate a conversation between you and the person you are in conflict with that helps you hear each other— and be heard—in a way that you can become connected, allowing new possibilities to emerge for your relationship

Throughout this book, we will help you be both in your own chair and the mediator's in the midst of a conflict; that is, to sit in your perspective and in that of someone able to hold all perspectives. Learning to internalize mediator mind—as you will in this volume—gives you access to your grounded, expansive self, even when you are in the midst of a difficult or stressful conversation. From this expanded self, you can escape from the *power over/power under* way of being and access a *power with* mindset.

As you recall your reaction to the imagined scenario on page 33 or to actual conflicts you experience in your life currently, you might think this is a tall order, doubting whether you can learn to embody mediator mind. By the end of this book, however, you will have the tools, skills, and knowledge to be able to begin internalizing your own mediator mind, with all the additional skill, perspective, and capacity that it promises.

You *can* learn to be your own mediator.

THE POWER OF "POWER WITH"

If you practice and use what is in this book, what is the potential? What's truly possible when you can embody mediator mind? Let's revisit the scenarios from earlier and explore the promise of these tools for living a more connected and enjoyable life.

SCENARIO 1 (NEGATIVE OUTCOME)

Your partner asks you to go to the company event. You've had a busy week and long to curl up with a cup of tea and a book in front of the fireplace and have a quiet evening. You suck it up and go anyway, telling yourself that your partner's position is important, and because it's the work that's paying most of the bills, you ought to be supportive. The event feels like it goes on forever, and you strain to keep a smile on your face and be pleasant to your partner's colleagues.

Have you noticed that when you are in a conflict with someone close to you, you tend to worry about the other person overwhelming you, that you are going to have to give something up, or that they are going to extract an agreement against your will? People often give in even when these fears arise from the unconscious. When you become connected, all of those thoughts and feelings tend to fade away; it's like they were never there, and you may even have trouble remembering that you experienced such discomfort. You've stepped into a reality that's on the other side of turmoil.

Here's another way this scenario might proceed if you are in touch with your needs and willing and able to communicate them to your partner.

SCENARIO 1 (POSITIVE OUTCOME)

Your partner asks you to go to the company event. You've had a busy week and long to curl up with a cup of tea and a book in front of the fireplace for a quiet evening. You talk to your partner, expressing your needs for rest, quiet, and care. Your partner says it would really meet his needs for companionship and support if you came to the event. As you both continue to talk about it, staying focused on your own and each other's needs, you begin to feel yourself shift into a little more willingness. You also notice your partner relaxing and expressing some desire to stay at home too, while also expressing a concern that not going to the event would reflect poorly on him in his boss's eyes. It slowly becomes clear to both of you to go for at least a short time to the event, checking in regularly with each other, and agreeing that either one of you can decide that it's time to leave. You feel good about this decision and gladly accompany your partner. You find you enjoy the event more than you expected, and after coming home you both relish some time relaxing with each other.

When you can act out of an awareness of meeting your own needs and wanting other people's needs met as well, you can bypass any sense of being anxious or combative. Being connected to your needs means you have awareness that before there can be an agreement, you have to say yes. The agreement has to meet your needs too. Even if your partner had a demand about going to the event, you can still connect with both of your needs, and continue to discuss it until you will both be satisfied.

If you "know" what is right and what should happen in a situation, rather than giving in, you might try to get what you want through a variety of means, including manipulation and threats.

SCENARIO 2 (NEGATIVE OUTCOME)

Glancing into your daughter's room, you notice she is playing a game on her computer instead of doing her home-work. You feel angry as you walk into the room, ordering her to stop playing games and get to work. Her sullen look says it all as she slowly finishes the level she's on and stops the game.

When you go into a conversation with the outcome already decided in your mind, you are in a *power over* type of mindset; you are entering the conversation with a demand and not open to hearing the other person's needs and taking those into account. It is easy to go into a conflict with some image of what the outcome should be. If the final goal is to have your daughter do her home-work, you might meet that goal with the above approach, but at what cost? The willingness to be fully in the conversation and in connection with the other person is very powerful.

SCENARIO 2 (POSITIVE OUTCOME)

Glancing into your daughter's room, you notice she is playing a game on her computer instead of doing her homework. You feel angry as you walk into the room, then remember mediator mind. Instead of yelling at her to do her homework, you take a breath and say you are concerned that if she continues to play on her computer, she may not complete her homework. You express some needs she might be meeting by playing her computer game, to which she sighs and says she just wants to be able to decide for herself when she does what. As the two of you talk, she reveals that she is having trouble in one of her classes and doesn't want to do the homework because she doesn't understand it. Upon hearing her embarrassment and fear about this class, the two of you begin to come up with strategies to help her. She volunteers that she does want to complete her homework and do well in her classes, and you work out an agreement that satisfies both of you—your desire for her well-being as well as her need to make her own choices.

In this situation, being open to connection instead of forcing an outcome allowed more information to come forward about what was going on for the daughter.

It's a powerful experience to be in a place where you are clear and connected to your own inner experience and what's true for you, such that you are open to the outcome. When you haven't made a final decision yet, you are open to hearing the other person, because you want to make sure that whatever happens is in the best interest of both of you. You care, not just about meeting your own needs, but about meeting the other person's too. There's great power in this mindset, yet it is not *power over*; there's no sense that you are going to make someone align with your decision or that you're going to resist someone else's. You are open.

It's important to note here that being open to the outcome does *not* mean you are open to an outcome you aren't satisfied with; rather, it means being open to an outcome you *cannot necessarily conceive of* before entering the conversation. A possible strategy may arise during the conversation—which is more likely since the needs of the other person will be on the table as well—that you would not think of beforehand. As a result you can assert yourself, not in a veto-type manner, but out of the abiding confidence that if you can figure out how you and the other person can have your needs met, you will both like that outcome better. Yes, it takes trust. If you can stick with it long enough to where everyone is satisfied, you will come to favor that unexpected strategy—and with trust you can be open to not knowing ahead of time what the outcome will be.

Having a *power with* mindset going into a conversation does not necessarily mean that your needs are going to be met, or that they are going to matter to the other person; if you go in with this expectation, you would have a demand. But the *power with* mindset gives a kind of freedom to sincerely work toward having all needs met—yours *and* the other person's. Knowing you are not going to give something up, and that you might end up being willing to shift during the conversation when you hear the other person, creates a certain attitude that allows you to be present in the conversation in a new way. Though, as we said, it does not guarantee that your needs will be met, it does increase the likelihood that they will. It can be almost magical how things suddenly turn around once you connect with each other, and how new possibilities emerge that no one had thought of a few moments earlier.

In sum, instead of assuming one person holds the power in a relationship, realize it is possible to be in a disagreement with the understanding that both people have power—the power to be clear about their own needs and to be present and connected with themselves and each other. Being able to be in a *power with* relationship is key to getting from argument to agreement. If you learn, practice, and apply the skills and knowledge we present in this volume, you will consistently increase your capacity to be in a difficult conversation while staying connected to yourself, willing to hear the other person, and open to working toward a possibly unfathomable yet utterly satisfying connection and resolution.

—*m*—

"Ok, kids, have a great day at school," James says as he pulls up to the curb. "Mags, I'll pick you up this afternoon to take you to soccer. Corey, you're taking the bus back later, right?"

Maggie bounces on the back seat as she leans forward and gives James a quick hug from behind. "Ok, Daddy. See you later, alligator." Corey merely nods as he gets out of the car, waving his hand behind him.

James pulls away and drives to his office, still feeling all the heaviness from the morning's conversation with Sally. Before heading in to start his day, he calls his buddy Shawn. Alicia and Shawn are close friends of his and Sally's, and both are far more experienced in embodying the Mediate Your Life skills.

James fills Shawn in on the conversation with Sally that morning. "I know I shouldn't have said that maybe she'd eventually come to her senses, but I was just so upset. I don't know how we're going to do this with her working. I can't see a way."

Shawn says, "So you were feeling hopeless about making this work, and now you regret what you said to her?"

James sighs. "Yeah. But there's so much going on at work right now. I've got a new guy starting today on my team, and we have so much pressure on us right now with all the healthcare changes ... I can't be missing work all the time for family stuff."

"It sounds like you're concerned about being able to do your job and being seen there as committed."

"Exactly. And we still have to rely on my job to pay for things because Sally's still in the process of getting clients."

"Hmm," Shawn says. "It sounds like you have a concern about sustainability in your family, with you being the primary breadwinner. What do you think is going on for Sally?"

"I know how important it is to her to go back to work. I think she was pretty antsy as a stay-at-home mom," James says ruefully. "I remember times Sally said she felt unfulfilled and I'd tell her what she was doing was important, but I think mostly I was afraid of exactly what's happening between us right now. I bet Sally thought I was brushing off her concerns."

Shawn says quietly, "That might be something to check with her. If she did feel that way, do you think that impacted your conversation this morning?"

James sighs. "Maybe. I just keep coming back to not being able to see any way to work this out, though." James rubs his face. "I know I should be able to come up with a solution here, but I'm kind of at a loss."

"That's putting a lot of pressure on yourself," Shawn says. "You're not the only one in this; the two of you are in it together. Maybe it's less about you coming up with a solution and more about the two of you being in conversation about it and letting the solution come out of that dialogue. What do you think?"

James pauses for a moment, thinking. "That makes sense. I guess it's hard to remember that when we're so alienated."

Shawn and James continue to talk for a few more minutes about James getting connected with himself and then with Sally. The weight James felt earlier begins to lift, and before heading into the office, he dials Sally's number to leave a message, knowing she will be in her meeting by then.

"Hey, hon, I just wanted to say that I regret what I said this morning ... and I want you to know how proud I am of you. I know we need to talk more about how to make this work, but for now, I just wanted to say how much I love you, and I hope your meeting goes well. Talk soon!"

2 | STARTING WITHIN
CONNECTING WITH YOURSELF

You can't change what's going on around you until you
start changing what's going on within you.
—UNKNOWN

JAMES SHUTS THE DOOR TO HIS OFFICE A LITTLE TOO hard. The first team meeting with Aaron present had not gone well at all. Irritated with Aaron's behavior, James has to keep himself from throwing a stapler across the room.

Who does he think he is? he says to himself. *He's brand new on the team, and he's completely disrespectful. Downright insolent, really. I can't believe Scott authorized moving him over to my team. What was he thinking? He should have given me more say in this. There's no way I can work with someone who's so clueless.*

James paces his office. "I should call Scott right now," he says out loud. "Aaron comes in and just because he's been in the company a long time, he thinks he was brought in to run the whole show. So arrogant."

Continuing to pace, James reflects on the difficulties they are all facing. With healthcare changing all the time, every week brings another set of policies his team needs to disseminate to the clinics the company manages. James feels the pressure from Scott (his boss) and the rest of higher management to get the changes out quickly and effectively, because non-compliance can have serious consequences.

I need team players who are on board with playing nice and getting the work done, he thinks. *I don't need someone who waits to speak up until we've practically decided on a strategy and then says why it won't work. I never thought Aaron would be this way.* James had known Aaron for a number of years, crossing paths at company events. Though cordial, their respective work had never put them close enough to know each other well. James had recently lost a team member, and restructuring in the company had caused Aaron to be reassigned. Scott had informed James of the assignment without consulting him first or allowing him to interview Aaron.

"Amazing," James says. "You can know someone for years and have no clue how insolent and disrespectful they can be." He realizes at that moment that he isn't sure whether he means Aaron or Scott with that statement ... or both.

Think about the last time you were in the midst of a sticky disagreement with someone. Did you want to hear their side of the story?

If you're like most people, you probably had less interest in listening to them than in being heard yourself. This urge to be heard regardless of the consequences often leads to further hurt and disconnection; yet, as we said in Chapter 1, being able to listen to the other person, as well as express your own viewpoint in a connecting manner, opens up the possibility of resolution.

So how can you shift from wanting to be heard to wanting to hear? How do you step out of not caring about what's going on for the other person to being open to considering their experience, or, at best, to feeling a genuine concern for their well-being?

In the next three chapters, we lay out the tools and maps that will help you do just that. Starting in this chapter, we'll look at how to connect to yourself regardless of what's happening around you; in Chapter 3, we outline an exercise that supports you in escaping the fight-flight-freeze response and becoming less trigger-able; then, in Chapter 4, we introduce a map that will assist you in reducing the power of judgmental thoughts, whether they are about yourself or the other person.

The maps and tools in these three chapters are all internally focused. While it may seem strange to spend so much time on *internal* maps in a book on *interpersonal* conflict, starting within is the key to successfully navigating conflict with other people. As you will see, if you are not connected to yourself, if you are unable to be aware of and reduce the impact of your stress response or be free of judgment, it is more difficult—if not impossible—to connect to others. If you use these tools, however, you will get to a point where you are sincerely curious about what the other person experiences, feels, and needs.

INNER WORK

Being open to hearing another person starts with doing your inner work. When you tend well to yourself, you can listen with interest, hear the other person, and understand what is going on for them.

Working through a conflict with someone else starts with connecting to yourself.

If you are in a conflict with someone or even thinking about a disagreement, you will know you're not connected to yourself yet if you:

+ don't want to know where they are coming from

+ have intense emotions like anger or fear that are running your behavior

+ are not sure what it is you might want as a resolution

+ don't ask for what you want because you figure you won't get it anyway

+ are not willing to hear anything other than yes to any request you make

+ are coming from *power over* or *power under*

In the story that begins the chapter, James reacted to his perception of Aaron's behavior, and his thoughts and feelings indicate that he is neither connected to himself nor to anyone else; he is instead caught in his habitual reactions. Being run by emotion, he has no interest in what is going on for either Aaron or Scott, and in part because of his position as team lead, he is stuck in a *power over* outlook.

Doing inner work is essential to staying connected with yourself and the other person, and that inner work starts with being able to notice and respond to the stress you experience when in conflict.

PRACTICE PAUSE

What are your best indicators that you are not connected to yourself? See if you can come up with a short list of mental, physical, and behavioral signs of disconnection.

FIGHT-FLIGHT-FREEZE IN CONFLICT

The fight-flight-freeze response is the physiological reaction to stress that the evolutionary past on the savannah instilled in the human race. When faced with a danger, the body is designed to automatically gear up in an attempt to survive, either through fighting, fleeing, freezing, or fainting. When this happens, a certain class of hormones called catecholamines are released, which create a whole set of physiological reactions, including accelerated heart rate; paling, flushing, or alternating between them; slowing of digestion; constriction of blood vessels in some parts of the body; and dilated pupils. This is the evolutionary reaction we need when we face dangers in the form of a charging rhinoceros or a hungry mother lion. The purpose of the physiological response is to prepare the body for the violent muscular action needed to get us out of danger.

While this stress response still serves people well when in true physical danger, most people are rarely challenged by the same types of situations in the modern world. The problem is that this response operates at the same level whenever you merely *perceive danger*. As such, your body goes into the same physiological response when you are triggered by your partner, get into a conflict with a coworker, or feel threatened by your boss.

For most people, conflict with others triggers a stress response similar to seeing a car crash in front of them, except that it lasts much longer—days, weeks, or even months and years. Disputes with those close to you can be particularly powerful triggers, setting in motion a chain reaction that hijacks your ability to make conscious choices.

Your version of the stress response in conflict will be based on your own personal history and personality. Even growing up with a similar situation, two people may develop different fight or flight patterns of response. Let's look at two examples.

EXAMPLE 1: BRIAN

Brian, the middle child of three, grew up with an angry father who used *power over* to dominate him, his mother, and his siblings. Brian felt afraid of his father and used to hide when he knew his father was in a temper. Now that he is an adult, when Brian gets into conflict (or even thinks he might get into one), he tends to freeze or flee. As such, he is highly conflict avoidant, to the point where his relationships have become stuck. Rather than continuing to grow, he sidesteps any issue where he might come into disagreement.

EXAMPLE 2: SARAH

Sarah was also the middle child of three who grew up with a highly critical and temperamental father. As a child she became angry when her father used his rage and criticism to control the rest of the family. She learned early on that it wasn't smart to show that anger to him, but she learned from his example that anger and criticism were an acceptable way to get what she wanted. Now that Sarah is an adult, she has a tendency to fight when she gets into conflict, using the same *power over* tactics she saw modeled as a child. She can come across as almost looking for a fight, and is certainly always ready for one, even expecting it any time the slightest disagreement may arise. Using anger, she tries to force her strategies on other people—with any situational power she has, along with the strength of her personality—damaging the health and growth of her relationships.

PRACTICE PAUSE

Do you recognize yourself in either of these examples? What is your predominant fight-flight-freeze response to conflict?

When faced with conflict, instead of responding in a calm, rational manner, you probably react the way you learned as a child to keep yourself safe and to help you survive in the world. This response became a habit, a pattern that now limits your choices when you're in conflict with others.

As demonstrated in the last chapter, Sally tends to fight when in a conflict with James. Her stress response is indicated in her racing heart, the thoughts whirling in her mind, and the tension she feels in her body as she leaves the house. James has a stronger tendency to flee, which in a disagreement can look like giving up and giving in, as he does when he agrees to take Maggie. With his son Corey, however, James is more likely to fight, as depicted in *Choosing Peace*. He uses his *power over* as a parent, just as his father did with him. Corey tends initially to freeze, which looks to James like he's being sullen and uncooperative, but if James continues to push, Corey explodes and fights back.

These patterns cause conflicts in their household to unfold in typical ways: Sally makes her demands, James gives in, and both are angry and upset. James gets angry with Corey and yells, Corey freezes, and then if James continues to push, Corey fights. Regardless of the situation, the pattern repeats and no one—Sally, James, or Corey—feels heard or understood about what is really important to them.

As we see with James, it's possible to have a different stress response depending on the situation or person you are in conflict with. James responds in two specific ways with Sally and Corey, while his response to Aaron is somewhere in between. His anger and thoughts indicate a fight response, and yet he doesn't confront Aaron directly in the meeting, instead fleeing to his office to react. This in-between response may be situational; it may also come as a result of the work James has already done to understand his typical stress response, and to learn new ways to work with it that are more effective than his habitual pattern.

Understanding your own typical fight or flight response to conflict helps you be more alert to it and able to intervene using the tools in this and the coming chapters. Intervening can help you escape from your habitual responses that keep you from truly connecting with others.

PRACTICE PAUSE

Your typical fight-flight-freeze reaction may change based on certain people or circumstances.
Think of three people in relationships with you: perhaps a parent or child, partner, boss, or friend.
How is your fight or flight reaction the same or different when in a disagreement with each person?

When caught in a stress response, your choices tend to be limited and driven by the biochemical response in your body: you lash out in anger, freeze in fear, or simply hide. So how do you expand the range of choices?

First, you have to be conscious of being in a stress reaction. Often, people are not aware until sometime after the fact that they were triggered and responded in a way they didn't like. That's natural; as long as you use the maps in this and other books of this series (and don't go into blame, shame, and punishment), you will be able to shorten the time it takes to be cognizant of the moment that the fight-flight-freeze reaction is triggered in you.

Once you are aware, you can come back to presence, to a centered and grounded state. Once present, you have more capacity to see the range of options available to you, and to choose one that matches what you want to create in the world.

This simple (but not always easy) formula underlies every map we offer:

1. Become aware

2. Return to presence

3. Make a choice

This formula is directly related to the three-chair model and mediator mind we introduced in Chapter 1. These three steps represent moving into the third chair of the mediator, either literally or metaphorically, shifting into mediator mind. In that third chair you are aware of yourself as separate from the perspectives in conflict. You are present and can make choices to create connection.

Your connection with another person is an extension of your connection with yourself.

self-connection *n.*

the ability to be aware of and present with what is
happening within you—physiologically,
emotionally, and mentally

The central aspect of making better choices is being able to be
present, so how do you become present? There are numerous ways;
in fact, you likely already have a few you use. In this book we offer
a map we call the Self-Connection Process, and it's a way to practice shifting into mediator mind. We ask you to try this and then
decide for yourself which approach you favor.

SELF-CONNECTION PROCESS (SCP)

Getting out of the stress response and your habitual reaction to
conflict gives you more space in which to see your options and
decide how to respond. While there are many ways to become
present when in a stress response, the map we use is the Self-
Connection Process (SCP). The three steps of this map are:

1. Breath
2. Body
3. Needs

One of the most effective ways to intervene when in a stress
response is to start on a physical level. This first, nonverbal part of
the practice is inspired by similar customs from spiritual traditions
worldwide. Spiritual and meditative traditions were where we
started to see the value of incorporating practices with the breath
and body that can have an immediate effect on countering the fight-
flight-freeze response. From this nonverbal, physiological interven-

tion, you will move into the verbal part of the practice, using feelings and needs to name what is going on. The combination of these elements—the physiological and the verbal—provides a powerful method of reconnecting to yourself when you are triggered into a fight or flight response.

SELF-CONNECTION PROCESS (SCP)

1. BREATH

   Focus on your breathing. Deepen the inhale as you breathe in, and extend the exhale longer than the inhale. Do this several times while being aware of your breath.

2. BODY

   Focus on what you are feeling. Feel the sensations and emotions, the aliveness and energy, by being *in* your body and experiencing that fully. At this stage you are solely being present with and experiencing sensations, scanning your body and noticing what you are feeling and where. You then shift to talking to yourself about what you're experiencing, using whatever language you are comfortable with to describe it. Finally, name the feelings you are experiencing (use the list in Appendix A to help).

3. NEEDS

   Connect with the needs that are met or not met in your current situation. Now that you're aware of your feelings from Step 2, look into what is prompting you to feel that way. A way to do this is to ask yourself, "If I'm feeling this way, what need is the unconscious part of me interpreting as met or not met?" Connecting to needs within yourself in this way can greatly help you be present when the fight or flight reaction is triggered in you (refer to Appendix B for a list of needs).

mediateyourlife.com/self-connection-process-video/

James soon slows down enough to realize he is triggered. He has enough experience to recognize that it's not a good idea to try to talk to Scott or Aaron when he's like this, that he needs to become more connected with himself first and think through things a little more clearly. Not sure how much he can change in only a few minutes, he decides to try the Self-Connection Process.

James begins focusing on his breath. He notices how shallow it is, mostly in the upper chest. For a few breaths he pays attention to it, then slightly deepens it on the exhale. This helps him move the breath lower into his belly. He can feel the tension in the muscles in his neck and shoulders, and he notices how stiff his back feels. Starting with small movements, he rolls his neck and shoulders, stretching slightly to ease the tension. James can still feel a lot of energy in his body, which he attributes to anger. Though it is difficult to simply be with that feeling, he focuses on allowing it to be there without having to do something with it.

The anger prompts James to consider what needs aren't met. The first one that comes to mind is respect. *I would really like respect for my role as the leader of this team and the way I go about my job*, he thinks. *It isn't just respect, though. I feel he was actively undermining me. That's not about respect, that's more about ...* James stops, contemplating what is motivating the thought that Aaron was undermining him.

I think it's that I'd really like support and cooperation, he imagines. *I want a sense that our team is all working together toward a common goal. And there's something I reacted to that was more than wanting support.* James is stumped for a moment, then realizes that by saying Aaron was undermining him, something inside him wants competence and effectiveness, or possibly recognition for the expertise he brings to the table. He supposes being seen and recognized by the team would give him the satisfaction of knowing he's contributing and making a difference, and that he is trusting his abilities to do so.

James spends another minute "deepening into" the needs that are not met from the morning meeting, imagining and feeling on a visceral level what it would be like to have those needs met completely in his life. As he does this, he notices that his breathing feels a little easier and the anger has diminished slightly.

—*w*—

PRACTICING SCP

The Self-Connection Process is a map to use when you are triggered "in the wild"—when something has happened and you are in the stress response. Being able to do this in the moment, however, requires practice. If you have not practiced in a non-stressful situation what you want to do when you realize you're in fight or flight mode, it's unlikely you'll be able to spontaneously perform the steps of the map while in the intensity of your physiological reaction. For this reason, we suggest two ways to practice so that the Self-Connection Process is available to you when you most need it.

First, we suggest practicing SCP during a set time in your routine. Perhaps you have a morning practice of some kind that includes meditation, prayer, yoga, ritual, or other body movement disciplines. Take a few minutes at the start to connect to yourself using the steps above, and then continue with your morning practice. If you don't have a regular meditation or similar practice, set aside a predictable daily time to run through the technique. It doesn't have to be long; even five minutes can suffice. The idea is to work on the process outside of a stimulating environment so that you begin to create a habit out of it, building up the neural pathways so that you can count on them when you need to.

The second way to practice is to use habits you already have as a cue. For example, you do several simple things every day that can be used as reminders to connect with yourself—walking down a hall at work or home, going through a doorway, brushing your teeth, washing your hands, waiting in line, booting up your computer, being on hold on the phone, taking a shower, or going to the bathroom. All can serve as times to remind yourself to practice. A similar reminder may be deciding to practice every time you switch from one activity to another. This can be a wonderful way to re-center before you change tasks, and it will likely remind you to be present through more of your day.

Using either cues or a daily meditation allows you to connect with yourself as a way to strengthen your awareness, presence, and choice when you're *not* in the midst of a reaction. Use these feelings to help you identify what it is you like or don't like about what's happening in a given moment. Ask yourself, "What's going on that is prompting me to feel this way?" or "What do I really need right now?" See if you can answer in a way that is not tied to a particular person, place, time, or thing. The idea is to identify what it is you are or are not getting in this situation, in a global, universal sense. The more you build the body memory of a self-connected state, the more easily you can notice, remember, and come back to it when you lose it.

When you practice connection with your feelings and needs several times a day, you will probably begin to notice patterns in the needs that arise in you. This self-examination fosters self-knowledge and personal growth, and it results in expanded capacity to use your developing skills in new situations.

PRACTICE PAUSE

Make a list of at least three things you do throughout the day that you can use as cues to remind yourself to practice SCP.
When you do remember to practice, make sure you celebrate that you did it!

SCP ENHANCEMENTS

The three steps of breath, body, and needs we've outlined comprise the basic process we recommend you use, both when triggered and also as part of a daily practice. However, there are a couple of alternative ways to go about connecting to breath, body, and needs that we like to mention as well. Practicing these options can help you deepen your connection to yourself.

When focused on the breath in Step 1, one option is to breathe into particular parts of the body. Throughout history, various systems of thought have recognized three focal points in the body —the belly, the heart, and the head. As you put attention on your breath, first breathe into your belly for a few breaths; then do the same with your heart area; then focus on the head. You might imagine your breath coming into or going out of any of these areas, or you may simply keep your attention on the area while breathing. Focusing your breath on these areas of the body helps you naturally flow into Step 2, Body.

If you find it's difficult to focus on your body in Step 2, you might begin with a few relaxation techniques. Relax your abdominal muscles by letting your belly drop forward. Let your tongue lie on the bottom of your mouth with its tip lightly touching the back of your lower teeth. Relax your jaw by opening your mouth slightly so you can exhale through it while inhaling through your nose. Let your shoulders drop and take the full weight of your arms. Feel any tension draining out through your feet into the earth. Using these types of relaxation techniques can help you get more in touch with the sensations in your body.

When you then begin to inquire about your needs, a particularly powerful enhancement when performing the SCP as a daily meditation is to focus on three core needs—well-being, connection, and self-expression. As you say these needs to yourself, continue to be aware of your breath and feel the sensations in your body. You can also associate these needs with the three body centers—belly, heart, and head.

For example, as you say "well-being" to yourself, put your attention in your belly and focus your breathing there. Then move to the need for connection, focusing your attention and breathing into the heart. Finally, focus on the need for self-expression and turn your attention and breathing to your head region (throat, forehead, and top of head).

It can also help to have a visual image (such as a happy childhood memory, a favorite place in nature, or loved ones). You can associate the vision with each need and body center to help you connect with the feelings—such as peace, love, and joy—that arise when those needs are met for you. In this way, you can experience the feeling of your needs being met internally, even if they're not currently met by what's happening externally. It is likewise a way to experience peace and joy independent of the external situation. Through this practice, you will find that you have great power in every moment to focus your attention on meeting needs within yourself.

If you are working with a situation in which you were triggered into the fight or flight response, you might connect with the needs not met first, and then deepen your self-connection by focusing on the three core needs. Play around with different options and see what helps you return to a calm and centered state. Whichever version of the SCP works for you, make sure that you don't simply focus on breath and body, but also get to a place where you are deeply connected to your needs—either those that are or are not met at that time—or those of well-being, connection, and self-expression.

Feeling more space open up in him after connecting to his needs for respect, cooperation, and competence, James focuses on his belly and the need for well-being. He brings to mind his image for well-being, which is a scene from a place he vacationed frequently as a boy. The cabin had a dock on the lake, and in the early evening, after a busy day spent playing, fishing, and swimming, the peaceful fading light on the lake coalesced all the fulfillment of the day into a single image that James has always carried with him. As he breathes into his belly and senses what it's like to have total well-being, his body feels infused with that feeling.

He then moves to his heart area and the need for connection, and in that moment creates a new image. He sees and feels his team operating seamlessly, with understanding and care between them as they work toward a common goal. He allows that image to permeate his heart area.

He then focuses on his head and self-expression. For James, work is a critical component of self-expression, giving him meaning and contribution to a greater whole. As he taps into an image of his role in people being truly cared for in the healthcare system, he feels the joy of knowing he is fulfilling an important purpose.

SELF-CONNECTION IN MOMENTS OF STRESS

The process we described above is what we suggest to practice connecting to yourself, but what do you do in the heat of the moment when you get triggered into the fight-flight-freeze response?

First, it's important to recognize that until you have practiced enough, there will be times you may not remember in the moment that you *want* to do something else, much less *do* it. You may be so caught in the emotions and habitual reactions that it is only later, as when James is pacing his office, you realize you know a process to help yourself emerge from the stress response.

When you do come back to awareness, see if you can acknowledge yourself for it. Often people tend to go into blame, saying, "I know this process; why couldn't I remember it when I needed it? How stupid am I?" Staying in blame keeps you disconnected from yourself and doesn't help you remember more quickly the next time. If you find you're judging yourself harshly, go ahead and do the full Self-Connection Process to find some centeredness, searching for what needs the judging part of you is seeking to meet. Then, honor yourself for becoming aware. When you can give yourself a pat on the back for becoming aware *whenever that occurs,* even if it's a week later, that acknowledgement along with practicing the process will help you remember sooner the next time. Before you know it, you'll become mindful that you have new options in the moment of stress.

If you're in the midst of a situation with someone else that is triggering your habitual reactions, and you know you want to make a different choice but feel unable to access it, you can take a break from the situation to go through the Self-Connection Process on your own. Or, as in the example with James at the beginning of the chapter, you may have a natural break soon after being stimulated into fight-flight-freeze when you can take a few minutes to go through the SCP. When you once again feel connected to yourself, you can return to the conversation with more presence and choice.

Once you're able to become aware in the midst of a situation, you may find it's not feasible to do the full version of the SCP in that moment as laid out above. As we've said, in doing the practice while you are not triggered, you are creating a body memory of being self-connected. In the moment you are triggered, the idea is to remember to access that body memory of calm peacefulness that you experience in the full practice so that you can shift quickly into a self-connected state.

We find it most helpful in moments when we're triggered to access body memory by focusing on the breath. Changing your breathing not only has a clear physiological effect of calming the nervous system, it also has a cognitive effect. Shifting attention to breathing uncouples you from the thoughts that are driving the fight or flight response, giving a little more space to make different choices. At that point, you may be able to connect quickly to one or two needs and shift yourself completely out of being triggered. Experiment with what works for you.

Meditative traditions similarly talk about using a longer practice to lock in a body memory. When you practice breathing into your belly and heart and focusing on something you love or feel good about on a regular basis, it becomes a part of you, allowing you to go straight to the breath and access the feeling. It happens in a split second, but only after you have practiced a longer version on a regular basis. Regular practice leads to your having immediate access to the feeling in your body, such that you can swiftly shift back into a state of coherence. This is the effect you want: to integrate the practice to such an extent that in the moment you need it—when you are triggered and in a physiological state of fight or flight—you have enough access to the body memory to regain some foothold on awareness, presence, and choice.

Another way to talk about this is that in performing these practices daily, you are developing neural pathways. Once you have that foundation in place, you can learn other ways to stimulate those neural pathways without going through the entire cognitive process of the practice. For example, you may use body cues, or remember the way you felt before and stimulate the state of presence. Then, in the face of becoming aware that you are in fight-flight-freeze mode, you can choose to do something about it, dropping into body memory in your own particular way.

Just as you can practice the longer Self-Connection Process regularly, shifting quickly into self-connection is also something you can practice, even when you aren't triggered. At any point in the day, see if you can remember to self-connect, shift focus to your breath, and access the body memory of that state. As you practice your rapid return to self-connection, you may find your own version of a shortcut that will help you reconnect in the moment.

We offer these practices in case you don't already have the body memory and cues in place, but you may also have your own way of creating, identifying, or remembering the body cues that bring you back to a centered state. If so, we encourage you to keep using those; perhaps through exercise, yoga, or prayer you access a calm and peaceful state where you feel connected to yourself and the world. Find the best ways for you to remember that state and bring it forward when you need it.

YOU'RE CONNECTED TO YOURSELF—NOW WHAT?

The Self-Connection Process is a fundamental one in our work because any connection with others begins with self-connection. We always recommend to begin here, and many, if not most, of our maps to navigate conflict either include it as an initial step, or prescribe some version of self-empathy that serves the same purpose.

Just as it is important to know the signs that you are disconnected from yourself, it's also crucial to know when you are connected and ready to make a choice about what to do next. These signs can act as a benchmark for you when using the SCP in your daily life. As you become adept at practicing self-connection, notice the experience in your body and mind, as well as how you're feeling or thinking about the situation once you are in a centered state.

For example, you may notice that your body feels lighter and more open and expansive when you are connected. Perhaps your breathing feels freer and you have less tension overall. You may likewise experience a sense of tenderness and care toward yourself, where thoughts are less intrusive and more balanced and spacious.

As you reflect on the situation that prompted your stress response, you may notice a shift toward the other person—from harboring a lot of judgment to becoming naturally curious. What is going on for them? Where are they coming from?

In Chapter 4, we'll discuss what to do when you notice this curiosity arising, but for now, take note when you become curious and feel more expansive, knowing that these states indicate you are connected to yourself. In this calm and centered place, you have more freedom to choose what to do next. While what you choose will depend on the situation, we will give you multiple tools and maps in the rest of this book that will help you continue to navigate any challenging interpersonal situation.

———◦∿∿◦———

James continues to deepen into his needs for well-being, connection, and self-expression, as well as the needs of respect, support, and competence triggered by the meeting with Aaron. As he taps into his body, he notices greater spaciousness and ease. His breath comes more freely and deeply, and the tension and stiffness has lifted from his shoulders and neck.

In this openness, it occurs to James that maybe Aaron wasn't trying to undermine him. As he ponders Aaron's behavior during the meeting and his own interpretation of that behavior, he realizes he assumed Aaron was insolent, yet when he recalls what Aaron actually did, it springs to James's mind that Aaron might have merely been nervous. He was quiet while James presented an issue and the group discussed it, then when he put a proposal out for agreement, Aaron suddenly blurted out how the proposal wouldn't work. Without holding eye contact, he simply glanced around at everyone.

James realizes he thought that Aaron was trying to get others to see his viewpoint over James's, and was therefore being disrespectful. While that may be true, James can now see that it also might not. *Maybe he was just nervous about being the new guy,* James reflects, *so when he had something to say, it came out a bit strong. I can remember times I've been nervous and it got mixed into what I was trying to say, so I didn't communicate the way I would have otherwise.*

James shakes his head, remembering one particularly painful experience in which he had spoken out of nerves and nearly lost a job because of it.

As he recognizes himself in Aaron's frustrating behavior, he concedes it may be worth talking to Aaron to see what was going on. Even though Aaron might have simply been nervous, however, James still resents Scott for forcing him to take someone onto his team. He suddenly feels a bit of irritation rising in him, then quickly reconnects to his body memory of self-connection through his breath, body, and needs.

So what would I really like here? he asks himself. *I want to be included, to have some say in the decision process when it affects my team.* James then imagines what it would feel like to be included, tying it in with all three body centers as he takes a breath into each one. In the expansiveness he now experiences, he begins to wonder what was really happening with both Aaron and Scott, and he determines he will take steps to find out.

—◌—

NEXT UP

Knowing how to connect to yourself is a powerful tool, and you will likely run into situations where it feels impossible to actually do it. When someone pushes your buttons, self-connection can feel like a distant memory as the stress response lays claim over you and your behavior. In the next chapter, you'll learn an exercise you can do in those moments to increase your ability to access self-connection.

3 | STAYING POWER

RETURNING TO PRESENCE IN THE FACE OF CONFLICT

Freedom is the capacity to pause between
stimulus and response.
—ROLLO MAY

L EAVING THE BUILDING AFTER HER MEETING WITH potential clients, Sally feels drained. While the people were all pleasant and seemed to have good relationships, Sally isn't confident that they are savvy in business. More than once in the meeting, she'd felt doubt, first about whether it was a good idea to accept this gig if it was offered, and then about her ability to step into her new work as a consultant.

Sally turns her phone back on and notices that James has left a message. Her heart sinks, wondering what he said. She clicks on the voicemail and listens: "Hey, hon, I just wanted to say that I regret what I said this morning ... and I want you to know how proud I am of you. I know we need to talk more about how to make this work, but for now, I just wanted to say how much I love you, and I hope your meeting goes well. Talk soon!"

By the end of the message, Sally's anger from that morning comes simmering back to the surface. She jabs at the screen to delete the message and misses. *How dare he!* Seething, she remembers the morning conversation and imagines calling him back, relishing the thought of saying, "Which part exactly do you regret? When you said you couldn't leave work for the kids, but that I should be able to? When you said you had to turn into Mr. Mom? Wait a minute, I know, it was when you suggested the only work that counts is yours. Or maybe when you implied that I'm out of my mind and it's my fault that everything is screwed up."

Sally shakes her head, wondering how to begin to unwind her hurt and anger toward James, as well as her own doubt and uncertainty about her new direction and its impact on her family.

—⁓—

Do you know your own triggers? Are there certain people in your life who say or do something in just the right way to set you off? The stress response takes over and your heart pounds, you feel hot, your vision tunnels, and you find your jaw and hands clenched.

In her argument with James, Sally felt this way when she heard her husband say he had to turn into Mr. Mom; she also felt it when she interpreted that he discounted her work. James, on the other hand, felt it when Sally said that he had to take off work to drive Maggie to her tryouts; he also feels it regularly with Corey when he doesn't respond to things James tells him. Both James and Sally feel it when Maggie resists doing something they've asked her to do.

We've already seen how difficult the stress response can make it to act in a centered manner in the heat of the moment. When you are feeling calm, you might have the best intentions about acting in a way you desire; if you're aware that a certain situation often leads you to act out of your habitual stress response, you may think, *Okay, next time I'm not going to react. I'm going to stay calm and in control. I'm going to be kind, compassionate, and understanding.*

But how do you actually do those things? It's easy to say, "I'm going to be kind and understanding next time I see my mother," but then when she's standing in front of you criticizing the way you look—again—those intentions fly out the window in the face of your hurt. You may well decide that the next time your child is grabbing everything in the store, you will take three deep breaths before responding, but in the moment, with grocery disaster looming and other shoppers throwing glances your way, it's difficult to remember those three deep breaths, much less take them.

> ## PRACTICE PAUSE
>
> When do your buttons get pushed?
> Name at least one specific, recurring situation in
> which your stress response is activated and you act
> in ways you later regret.

GETTING TRIGGERED

We talked in the last chapter about the Self-Connection Process as a map to choose when you are triggered into the fight-flight-freeze response in your daily life. Practiced regularly when you're not triggered, SCP helps you anchor into body memory the capacity to quickly return to self-connection. But even with awareness and the practicing of the Self-Connection Process, you may find that this body memory is not readily available to you when one of the people in your life pushes your buttons.

Do not feel disheartened when this happens! If you intended to not react, and then still became triggered and acted in ways that led to further hurt and disconnection, it doesn't mean you are a bad person, your willpower is lacking, or you are doomed forever. In these cases, you simply need a combination of desensitization and a specific practice that puts all the following pieces together:

+ the trigger

+ your particular stress response

+ awareness

+ returning to a centered state (presence)

+ being able to respond from that state (choice)

In this chapter, you'll learn the Intensity Exercise, a powerful practice that will allow you to not only become reconnected to yourself and respond in those sticky triggered moments, but it will also help you become *less* triggerable. The Intensity Exercise is a way of setting up a situation where you know you get upset, and then consciously practicing the SCP in order to experience the internal shift of re-centering. When practiced regularly, the Intensity Exercise will increase your capacity to handle moments when you are provoked; as a result, you will find you are more immune to becoming triggered.

THE RELATIONSHIP SIMULATOR

Have you ever regretted how you behaved with someone and later thought, *Can I rewind the clock? I really wish I could have a do-over!* The power of the Intensity Exercise and other activities we offer is that they give you a chance to try again (and again). These exercises mimic what happens in the real world, and you get to practice, in safety, what you want to do in those situations. They are like a flight simulator for interpersonal relationships.

Pilots learning to fly a jet practice in a replicated setting of real-life conditions to learn the skills they need, before their own and other people's lives depend on it. Training in simulated situations has now also become cutting edge in other fields where people need to operate effectively while experiencing the stress response, such as first responders, emergency room personnel, and military Special Forces.

Though conflicts and difficult conversations may not normally be life-or-death situations, being able to act as you wish has far-reaching impact on your well-being and relationships. In a relationship simulator, for example, you can create artificial situations that model real life so you can have a do-over—in other words, you can screw up and then go back and practice again and again until you're able to respond the way you desire in the critical moments of your life.

As flight simulators also have the ability to dial the difficulty up and down based on your skill level, so too do the simulators we propose. The point is not to see how many times you can crash and burn or how much you can take, but rather to learn new skills and ways of being in intense situations. This type of learning is incremental; as such, the Intensity Exercise is designed to present some similarities to real life—adrenaline, your body getting amped up, being under stress—so that you can practice what you would like to do in those moments. The only way to learn is to keep some control over how much stress you experience so that you are safe and in your optimal learning zone.

THE CAPACITY TO BE IN CONFLICT

In the Intensity Exercise, you intentionally allow yourself to become triggered in a safe space, and then practice coming back to a state of self-connection and centeredness using the Self-Connection Process. Three benefits come from this exercise:

1. You become highly sensitized to your physiological reactions in the fight-flight-freeze state.
2. You learn to embody mediator mind.
3. You desensitize yourself to the trigger.

The initial part of the exercise asks you to notice the first hint of a stress response and stop the exercise there. These two steps create awareness physiologically of finer distinctions in your individual response. For example, you may initially be aware that your heart starts beating faster, but as you repeat the exercise, you may notice that before your heart speeds up, you feel a wave of energy through-out your body, or you sense a brief shock in your system. These finer distinctions allow you to become conscious of becoming triggered earlier in the process so that you can intervene more effectively.

The Intensity Exercise also utilizes the three-chair model of mediation that helps you begin to embody the mediator mind. Even though it is just you and your partner, we recommend you set up three chairs, one for each of you and one for the mediator. As you go through the exercise, when you are the one being triggered, you will physically move into the mediator's chair to do certain parts of the exercise.

When you practice by actually setting up different chairs and physically moving to the mediator's chair, it helps in the learning process to distinguish these two different parts of you—the reactive part that holds strongly to your point of view in a conflict, and the mediator part who can remember a process and make choices that come from a more centered and grounded place.

Moving from one chair to the other helps you shift out of the continuous flow of your reactive thinking and reduces the internal experience of the conflict. You will shift, at least a tiny bit, the fight-flight-freeze reaction, while accessing a part of yourself that can make choices based on your values instead of on your stress-response chemistry.

Once you have practiced moving between chairs to embody each role enough times, you will no longer need to move to a separate chair. Why? Because you will have internalized the chairs, such that part of your brain is now associated with the mediator role. As a result, you will have access to this part of yourself in real-life situations and step into it to make choices about what to do. In short, you will be able to embody mediator mind.

While practicing becoming triggered and then reconnecting, you are likely to find that the trigger you're working with begins to diminish; that is, it doesn't trigger you at all, or to a much lesser extent. This seems to happen from learning to respond to the low-level exposure to the trigger.

Think of it like an allergy you have developed to a particular stimulus. When you encounter that stimulus—be it a look from your partner, a phrase said in a certain way by your boss, or even words you say to yourself—your brain and body respond immediately to the danger you interpret. In this exercise, you train your nervous system to quickly return to a calm, relaxed state in the face of the verbal or nonverbal cues, and in doing so increase your tolerance for it. Your brain and body therefore learn that the danger does not exist, or is at least not as bad as you believed. With practice, this tolerance extends to real-world encounters, where instead of becoming provoked and acting in ways you later regret, you are able to stay connected to yourself and choose the kind, compassionate, understanding response you intended.

Taken together, these three benefits—becoming sensitized to your physiological stress response, embodying mediator mind, and achieving desensitization of the trigger—make the Intensity Exercise the most effective way we've found to increase people's capacity to be in stressful situations and act as they would like. As a capacity-building exercise, it helps you increase your emotional ability to engage with interpersonal conflicts in a way that is healthier than your habitual stress response. Using it on a regular basis holds the promise of increasing your ability to be in conflict situations in a way that is satisfying and brings you the results you desire.

> ## PRACTICE PAUSE
>
> Think of the recurring situation in which you become triggered. How might your life improve if you were able to stay calm and centered in those times and choose a response that matches your values?

—⁓⁓—

Sally drives back to her office. She had planned to use the time before her next phone meeting to prepare, but now she feels like her preparation ought to include how upset she is over the morning conversation with James. Re-triggered through hearing his phone message, she dials her friend Alicia, knowing she needs some help.

Sally fills Alicia in on her morning, tears starting as she recounts James's words. Alicia empathizes with her, asking her if she's feeling hurt when she thinks James discounts her work.

Sally's voice breaks as she replies, "Yeah, but I'm also frustrated. I mean, we've talked about what it means for me to go back to work, but when it comes down to it, he can't just step up and do it."

"So are you also frustrated because you're not seeing agreement between what he says when you talk and what he does in the moment?"

Sally shrugs. "I guess so."

"Hmm," Alicia continues, "it seems like this is a recurring thing. I think I've heard you say before how angry you get when you hear James say some of these same things. Does that seem true for you?"

Sally sighs. "Yes, I know I've been angry, spitting mad even, when James has said similar things. Like I remember when he called my work 'casual,' implying that his job was serious and mine wasn't."

"Can I make a suggestion?" Alicia asks. "Do you think it would help you to not be as angry when you hear words like that or interpret that James is diminishing your work? What I mean is, if you could be centered and calm, maybe you could find a way to respond that would help you both."

"I'm not sure it's possible, but yeah, I think it would be nice to not react so badly, and maybe find a better response than leaving the room." Sally remembers her feelings that morning. "I mean, leaving was probably the best response I could have made at that point, otherwise we would be in even more of a mess, but it doesn't help us get through this, that's for sure."

"It sounds like you believe you were doing the best you could, and it gives you some relief to have that understanding for yourself. And I'm hearing how impossible it feels to you to have done anything different, but it sounds like you'd like to find another way, is that right?"

"Yeah, I *would* like to find another way."

"Is there something you want to work on that would help you right now?" Alicia asks.

"Maybe. Didn't I do the Intensity Exercise with you when I was upset with Maggie for something? I can't even remember now what it was she did, but I do remember how surprised I was when the next time it happened it didn't even faze me. Maybe that will help me with James. Would you be willing to go through it with me?"

Alicia agrees, and Sally feels a little more energy as she anticipates finding a way to change her reaction.

SETTING UP THE INTENSITY EXERCISE

In this exercise, you can work with anything you would consider intense in an interaction with another person or in your own mind. If your boss interrupts you in a meeting or if your daughter rolls her eyes when you say something, you can bring that into the Intensity Exercise. If you find you're saying something to yourself that upsets you, perhaps telling yourself that you're stupid, you can externalize that and work on it as well.

The idea is to choose something that when it is delivered to you, it stimulates the cascade of hormones typical of the fight or flight response. In this way, you actually experience those feelings sitting in the chair across from your partner. Sometimes the stimulus is less in the words and more in the body language or tone of voice, and we take that into account in the practice.

Enlist someone in your life to be your practice partner who is also interested in changing their relationship to the stress response. If you would like to find a practice partner in the Mediate Your Life community, you can go to the book page at mediateyourlife.com/from-conflict-to-connection/ and find instructions there.

> ## PRACTICE PAUSE
>
> Who in your life can you make a request to practice with? What specific trigger would you like to be able to defuse in the Intensity Exercise?

Divide your practice time in half so that each of you can experience being the partner receiving the trigger and the one delivering it. At the beginning of your practice time, set aside three chairs, two for yourself and your partner, and one representing the mediator. The receiving partner—the person becoming triggered and practicing returning to presence—will use that chair to physically embody moving into the mediator mind, as reflected in the steps of each part of the practice. (In Appendix J, we have included a cheat sheet of steps for the setup and debrief of the practice.)

At the beginning, the receiver gives the delivery partner one observation of the trigger they want to work with. This is not a long story about the whole situation or the history of the relationship; it's merely a statement such as:

"My partner says, 'why can't you just do it?' while raising his voice, and he leans toward me while he's saying it."

Another example might be:

"My daughter says, 'Geez, Mom, do you have to be so embarrassing?' in a dismissive tone while she's rolling her eyes."

While we encourage you to use the actual words someone says, if you don't remember exactly, or if it feels more triggering to use what you hear (in other words, what you interpret the other person to be saying), then use that as your triggering statement.

Also discuss some agreements with your partner, including the signal you will make to stop delivery of the trigger, and anything else that will help the practice feel safe for you.

Though most effective done in person, you can also do this exercise with a long-distance partner. If you're on the phone, the nonverbal cues will be missing, but the practice still works. You can also use online conferencing to create an experience similar to being in person. Either way, both of you can set out an extra chair to move into during those steps of the process.

Because this is an exercise, we suggest you do *not* attempt to practice with the person who initially delivered the trigger to you. Also, it's best to choose someone who can be in your experience without judging it or trying to educate you as to how you should have acted in the first instance—or in the future.

The Intensity Exercise

When beginning this exercise, we recommend breaking it up into segments. These build on one another until you are performing the full practice. The segments are:

1A.   Practicing without content

1B.   Practicing with content

2.   Responding to a first trigger

3.   Responding to a second trigger

We list the steps and some notes for each level on the following pages, but you can also see Appendix D for a list of the steps for each level, or visit our website mediateyourlife.com/from-conflict-to-connection to print out the steps and refer to them when you are practicing.

LEVEL 1A: PRACTICING WITHOUT CONTENT

The first step to being able to intervene when you are triggered is to recognize your physiological patterns of fight-flight-freeze, and to separate the *experience* of being triggered from the trigger itself. In order to differentiate the two, we ask you to first practice without verbal content. In this way, you can learn the feeling experience of being triggered that is not about what's being said, only the intensity of it: the tone, the volume, the body language—or what triggers you on a nonverbal level. Since people tend to add meaning to others' body language and tone of voice as much as to what they say, this first level separates content from nonverbal cues. In doing so, you find out what exactly is triggering you and what it feels like when that happens.

Here are the steps to this level of practice:

1.   The receiving partner performs the Self-Connection Process, then asks the delivery partner to present the trigger.

2.   The deliverer says a neutral phrase, such as "Water is wet" or "Snow is white" in a conversational tone, pauses, then

repeats it, gradually increasing the volume, intensity, and aggression level of the words, amping it up slowly.

3. *As soon as* the receiver notices their body reacting to the intensity level, they raise their hand as a nonverbal way to ask their partner to stop delivering the trigger.

4. The receiver then physically moves into the mediator chair and performs the Self-Connection Process out loud until they feel calm, physically relaxed, and no longer in a fight-flight-freeze reaction mode.

5. The receiver moves back into the receiving chair and asks the delivery partner to begin again.

6. The deliverer starts by saying the same words as before at a lower intensity level than what triggered their partner, and again incrementally amps it up in intensity.

7. Repeat steps 3–6 until the receiver has practiced to the degree they desire or notices not being triggered anymore, no matter how intense the delivery.

8. Share with each other what came up for you (see feedback section beginning on page 89).

mediateyourlife.com/intensity-exercise-video/

You might develop your own version of self-connection, but at the beginning, we recommend people do the following when they raise their hand to stop the delivery and reconnect with themselves.

First, perform a nonverbal component, as we described in the Self-Connection Process in Chapter 2. Focus on your breathing, maybe through the heart. Then, begin to empathize with yourself out loud, naming what you're thinking and feeling, then what needs are not met, and then anything you desire in that moment. Your request might be for your partner to support you in some way, perhaps by reflecting back what they heard. We ask you to do it out loud so your partner will be included in your experience, and so that she or he can support you in completing all the steps, including identifying your needs that aren't met.

Again, the idea here is to return to the body memory you develop in the Self-Connection Process, learning to tap into that body memory more and more quickly in the face of being triggered.

As you perform the self-connection part of the process, we find it is crucial to make sure you pinpoint your needs. Skipping over this step or doing it on a surface level will make it unlikely that you'll be able to defuse the trigger. When you name your need, get in touch with it and with how it would feel to have it met. Needs are the key piece to shifting the intensity level at which you become triggered.

When you feel a calmness and non-reactivity in your body, ask your partner to start off again at a low level of intensity and raise it up until you experience the trigger again. Usually, you can take more intensity the next time before feeling triggered. Repeat the process until you feel comfortable doing it.

The intention here is not for the receiving partner to prove they can "take it" or to withstand as much intensity as possible. The goal is to start at a level so low that it's not triggering at all, and for the person being triggered to notice the *first flicker* of when they get stimulated. This helps train the receiving partner to become more sensitive to noticing when they begin to react so they can intervene more effectively.

It is much easier to come back to center from a low level of stimulation than it is from a higher one. If you can achieve this, you will defuse the trigger, before flooding your system with stress response hormones, by incrementally noticing, coming back to center, receiving more intensity and noticing the reaction, and again reconnecting with yourself.

LEVEL 1B: PRACTICING WITH CONTENT

In the next level, the exercise is the same except that instead of a meaningless phrase, you now practice with words that are hard for you to hear or tend to trigger a reaction. They could be words you say to yourself, such as ways you judge yourself harshly, or that someone else says to you that cause a reaction. For example, if you know you sometimes tell yourself, "That was really stupid" or "You totally screwed that up" or "What the hell is wrong with you?" you could choose one of those as the content statement you give your partner. Or, if you find that you react to your spouse saying, "You're so insensitive and absorbed in yourself all the time," you can work with that sentence in your practice. Continue to include the body language and nonverbal cues from previous levels that tend to trigger you, such as certain facial expressions, tone of voice, and gestures.

We ask you to do the Self-Connection Process at the beginning to set a baseline of connection to yourself. Why? Because it's a common experience that merely thinking about the situation, or about telling your delivery partner what words to say and how to say them, will trigger you into the stress response. If this happens, you can take that as the delivery of the first trigger, and proceed to Step 4 on the next page.

Here are the steps to this level of practice:

1. The receiver tells their partner what words they want to use for the practice, giving instruction on how to weave them together with specific tone, volume, or body language. For example, if the words are from another person and often

come with a particular gesture and tone of voice, the delivery partner can incorporate that gesture and tone along with saying the words.

2. The receiver performs the Self-Connection Process, then asks the delivery partner to begin.

3. The deliverer begins presenting the trigger at a low level of intensity, gradually increasing.

4. *As soon as* the receiver notices their body reacting, they raise their hand as a nonverbal way to ask their partner to stop delivering the trigger.

5. The receiver physically moves into the mediator chair and performs the Self-Connection Process until they feel calm, physically relaxed, and no longer in a fight-flight-freeze reaction mode. When they feel they have choice about how to respond, they are ready to continue.

6. The receiver moves back into the receiving chair and asks the delivery partner to begin again.

7. The deliverer presents the same trigger as before, starting at a lower intensity level than what triggered their partner, and again incrementally amps it up in intensity.

8. Repeat steps 4–7 until the receiver has practiced to the degree they desire or notices not being triggered anymore, no matter how intense the delivery.

9. Share with each other what came up for you (see feedback section beginning on page 89).

To recap, the partner begins delivering the trigger with no intention of causing a negative reaction. In doing so, the receiving partner can feel the distinct difference between not being triggered and being triggered. As in Level 1A, the receiving partner practices reconnecting with themselves and then re-enters the practice for another round.

LEVEL 2: RESPONDING TO A FIRST TRIGGER

Level 2 adds the layer of how you want to respond to the person delivering the trigger after you have practiced self-connection. Let's walk through the steps so you can use them to practice with a partner.

1. The receiver tells their partner what words they want to use for the practice, giving instruction on how to weave them together with specific tone, volume, or body language.

2. The receiver performs the Self-Connection Process, then asks the delivery partner to begin.

3. The deliverer begins presenting the trigger at a low level of intensity, gradually increasing.

4. *As soon as* the receiver notices their body reacting, they raise their hand as a nonverbal way to ask their partner to stop delivering the trigger.

5. The receiver physically moves into the mediator chair and performs the Self-Connection Process until they feel calm, physically relaxed, and no longer in a fight-flight-freeze reaction mode. When they feel they have choice about how to respond, they are ready to continue.

6. The receiver says out loud (still sitting in the mediator chair) how they want to respond to this person now, choosing between empathy or self-expression.

7. The receiver moves back into the receiving chair, responds accordingly, and asks the delivery partner to begin again.

8. The deliverer then presents the same trigger as before, starting at a lower intensity level than what triggered their partner, and again incrementally amps it up in intensity.

9. Repeat steps 4–8 until the receiver has practiced to the degree they desire or notices not being triggered anymore, no matter how intense the delivery.

10. Share with each other what came up for you (see feedback section beginning on page 89).

mediateyourlife.com/intensity-exercise-video/

If you choose empathy as your response, you will respond to what you hear from the delivery partner by translating what *they've said* into feelings and needs. If you choose expression, you will respond by relating *your own* needs and wants.

While we suggest saying your choice out loud and then returning to the practice and performing it as a learning step, it's not important at this point exactly how you carry out your choice. The primary point here is to consciously choose what you want to do and then do it.

In short, either focus attention on the other person and empathize, or strive to express yourself in relation to your needs. Don't worry too much about the technique or if you're executing your empathy or expression "correctly." This exercise is about developing your capacity to return to presence in the midst of being triggered and to consciously choose what you want to do next. Later we will provide exercises that focus on *how* to execute your choice.

LEVEL 3: RESPONDING TO A SECOND TRIGGER

With Level 3, we introduce a second trigger, the one that occurs as the delivery partner reacts to the empathy or expression of the receiver. Psychologist David Burns and others in cognitive therapy call this the "feared fantasy," or that which you are most afraid will happen.

As the receiver, you may want to tell your partner ahead of time what kind of response would be most difficult for you to hear; otherwise, that person can merely share a spontaneous response. The practice of coming back into self-connection upon experiencing the feared fantasy, and then responding accordingly, makes it less scary.

Here are the steps to follow:

1. The receiver tells their partner what words they want to use for the practice, giving instruction on how to weave them together with specific tone, volume, or body language.

2. The receiver performs the Self-Connection Process, then asks the delivery partner to begin.

3. The deliverer presents the trigger at a low level of intensity, gradually increasing.

4. *As soon as* the receiver notices their body reacting, they raise their hand as a nonverbal way to ask their partner to stop delivering the trigger.

5. The receiver physically moves into the mediator chair and performs the Self-Connection Process until they feel calm, physically relaxed, and no longer in a fight-flight-freeze

reaction mode. When they feel they have choice about how to respond, they are ready to continue.

6. The receiver says out loud (still sitting in the mediator chair) how they want to respond to this person, choosing between empathy or self-expression.

7. The receiver moves back into the receiving chair and responds accordingly.

8. The deliverer presents another trigger by reacting to the choice, saying something that would be hard for the receiving partner to hear.

9. The receiver physically moves again into the mediator chair and performs the Self-Connection Process until they feel calm, physically relaxed, and no longer in a fight-flight-freeze reaction mode. When they feel they have choice about how to respond, they are ready to continue.

10. The receiver says out loud (still sitting in the mediator chair) how they want to respond to this person now, choosing between empathy or self-expression.

11. The receiver moves back into the receiving chair, responds accordingly, and asks the delivery partner to begin again.

12. The deliverer presents the same trigger as before, starting at a lower intensity than what triggered their partner, and incrementally amps it up.

13. Repeat steps 4–12 until the receiver has practiced to the degree they desire or notices not being triggered anymore, no matter how intense the delivery.

14. Share with each other what came up for you (see feedback section beginning on page 89).

mediateyourlife.com/intensity-exercise-video/

THE ROLE OF THE DELIVERY PARTNER

In the instructions above, it might seem like there is little for the delivery partner to do; however, we have found there is also significant learning for the person in this role. When the receiver gets triggered, the deliverer shifts from presenting the trigger to supporting the person in reconnecting. It is a considerable skill to know how to support someone in distress, in a way they perceive as helpful. As such, the person in the delivery role has an opportunity to increase their skill in supporting another person.

In tandem with this, when the receiver is performing the Self-Connection Process, we suggest they request ahead of time (if possible) whether they would like verbal or silent support. The deliverer can then be thoughtful about what type of support their partner wants, paying close attention to the cues their partner gives.

For example, the deliverer can ask:

"Would you like me to reflect back what I'm hearing you say or would you prefer that I be silent?"

The deliverer can also be spontaneous in their response, using body language and other cues to guide them on whether or not the receiving partner wants empathy, and how. For instance, if they want to stay internal for the moment, the deliverer can take the opportunity to practice presence and silent empathy, or to guess the partner's feelings and needs based on an interpretation of their body language and what they say. As a result, the person in the delivery role is learning a life skill of being present with and supporting someone who is triggered.

GIVING AND RECEIVING FEEDBACK

Feedback is a vital factor to enhance learning. Consequently, you don't want to take the last step—sharing with each other what came up for you—as an add-on that can be skipped. Learning is dependent on receiving feedback as quickly as possible after the exercise. When you do, you learn faster, can talk about what you might do differently, and are able to try out new approaches right then and there.

In day-to-day life, you may be able to use other people's demeanor as a form of feedback, but how often do you get the opportunity to discuss with someone how your communication choices created connection or disconnection? This part of the practice is a precious opportunity to find out.

Let's be clear that when we talk about feedback, we do not mean evaluation, judgment, or analyses. People often interpret feedback as equating to judgment because of the way it's often given in other contexts, but we're talking about something quite different. We liken it to *biofeedback*, in that the feedback we encourage people to give to each other is *their physical reaction* to what their partner did at various points in the exercise. This might sound like:

+ "My heart opened when you empathized and said to me, 'So is it that you really want some respect?'"

+ "I felt my heart close when you ...."

+ "I pulled back and felt irritation when you asked me what I needed."

✦ "After the second trigger when you said, 'I'm feeling scared because I'd like to know that you care about me,' I felt this sense of relief and was more open after that."

When providing feedback, it's important to stay specific in the observations (what the other person said and did) as much as possible, focusing on feelings, as well as if you felt more or less connected to your partner.

This type of feedback is measuring the *quality of connection* with the other person. The Mediate Your Life work rests on the idea that when you are present, you can make choices that create connection. In the Intensity Exercise, you get to measure both parts of that equation. First, you learn to measure for yourself if you're present, reconnecting through the Self-Connection Process when you notice you are triggered. Second, you get feedback from the other person about whether your choices support creating connection with them.

The simplest way to enter the feedback stage is simply to ask each other, "How was it for you?" The receiving partner can share what it was like to go through the process of hearing the trigger, becoming reconnected, and striving to make a new choice. The delivery partner can likewise share their experience of delivering the trigger and being there for support. After sharing at that level, you can go into more specific feedback—or biofeedback—such as how the choices to empathize or express felt for the delivery partner, or how support choices made by the deliverer felt to the receiver.

Though we lay out the steps for the exercise in a linear way and encourage you to use them for practice, we hope you take the opportunity to hear feedback from your partner at the end of the steps, then go back into the exercise to try a different option, receiving immediate feedback again. This will allow the exercise to become more fluid.

We want to add two final, and critical, recommendations for giving feedback.

First, never assume your partner wants feedback of any kind. Even if you have the most life-changing response that you're certain will contribute to your partner, ask if they want it first. In order for learning to take place, people need to be open to it. You might think your feedback is fabulous, but if your partner is still trying to process their own experience, they may not be able to take it in; even if it's positive, it may be triggering. We recommend that you ask, "Would you like some feedback?" or something equivalent that asks if it's welcome, and if so, what it might sound like.

Second, we recommend focusing on positive feedback first, and sometimes exclusively. Though many tend to think that feedback about what doesn't work leads to greater learning, we don't find this to be true. Knowing what *does* work allows you to grow, and those successes give confidence to keep increasing your skill. Positive feedback is also easier to hear as people feel less resistance to it, so let your partner know what worked and what choices they made that were connecting for you. Often this feedback is all that's needed, especially early in the learning process.

Once you've gained some experience and built a level of trust with your practice partner, you will likely find that you crave more information about what didn't work. Feel free to ask for it! Trust depends on knowing your partner is not judging or evaluating how "good" you were. When you're both engaged in exploration and testing, willing to try something and then hear from your partner what physically happened for them, the best learning takes place. Likewise, when you both give and hear feedback, the exercise becomes a communication laboratory, with both of you discovering and integrating new possibilities to create connection.

Let's be honest: just because your partner responds in a particular way to what you say or do doesn't mean that other people will do the same. But in terms of learning, it really doesn't matter. It's a gift to receive this kind of feedback, and it allows you to try multiple options and build a repertoire of choices to draw from in your daily life. Though you will generally rely on body language for feedback outside of practice, when you've increased your own capacity to be present in any intensity and have multiplied your possible responses, you'll find that you can take those skills into everyday situations.

People starting a new skill often want a formula that will work every time, but in communication there are no sure formulas. Though that may sound discouraging, it's actually very freeing! Why? Because if you make a guess that doesn't create connection in the way you hoped, instead of wasting time and energy being distressed about not getting it "right," you simply use the most recent reaction as valuable information to make another, hopefully more informed, choice. This allows you to be at ease making your best guess, as you are present and responding to what is happening at that moment.

Experiencing Intensity "In the Wild"

As you go about your daily life, you will find times when you are triggered into the fight-flight-freeze response. When you name it and relate to it from your experience of having practiced the Intensity Exercise, it makes your stress response in the moment less threatening. You can remember intentionally becoming triggered in your "flight simulator," experiencing intensity, and then doing something about it through the Self-Connection Process and making a new choice.

When you are "in the wild" and are triggered, framing it as the Intensity Exercise takes the charge away and makes it a little less scary. It becomes more like a game, putting your experience in the perspective of something you have done, survived, and maybe even enjoyed. You can then bring the same sense of curiosity and adventure to your real-world experience of being triggered.

While we've laid out the previous exercise with a partner, when you find yourself triggered in your daily life, you can also practice it—and receive benefit through doing so—on your own. By visualizing what the person said that you found challenging, you can take yourself through the Intensity Exercise in your mind. While it's particularly powerful to have another person who can deliver the trigger to you, that may not always be practical; imagining going through the process still allows you to come back to self-connection and the mediator mind, thus defusing the trigger.

CLIMBING THE INTENSITY MOUNTAIN

The point of the Intensity Exercise is to eventually (perhaps not in one sitting but over time) not become triggered by the same conduct or words. If you feel like this isn't possible for you, we encourage you to simply try it out. As we've said, the practice tends to build on itself—each time you're triggered and then reconnect with yourself, you're able to handle a higher level of intensity before becoming re-triggered. Practiced enough, you can come to a point where you stay grounded and centered, regardless of how intense the words, tone, and body language are.

We want to stress that we offer this exercise as a way for you to return to choice in any situation. We're not suggesting that if someone acts toward you in a way you perceive as disrespectful that your best option is to learn to passively accept that behavior. The purpose in our work is to always have choice. If you react to another person's behavior out of the stress response, you are at the mercy of their conduct. When you practice with the Intensity Exercise, you can get to the point where you are no longer at the mercy of their behavior. In short, this exercise is not about being a doormat—it's about empowering you to be present and choose your response, which helps you be more effective at creating the change you desire.

⸺ɔ୰ɕ⸺

After Sally puts another chair nearby and makes some agreements with Alicia, including that she will say "stop" when she begins to feel triggered, Alicia asks, "So what would you like me to say?"

"Well, the last thing James said was basically that I was crazy. I think maybe that got to me the most."

Alicia tries to clarify the observation. "Are those the actual words he said: 'You're crazy?'"

Sally thinks back. "No ... not exactly. It was something like 'after we lose everything, maybe you'll come to your senses.' And he said it with anger, but he was also kind of dismissive. He went right back to the paper, like that was the final word on the subject."

"Would it work for you if I say, 'maybe you'll come to your senses,' and I'll work with the tone you just used?" Alicia asks.

"Sure. Let's try it."

Alicia starts off delivering the trigger to Sally in a conversational tone, barely putting any emotion into her delivery before Sally feels her body begin to tense, like a hard shell is forming over her, and asks Alicia to stop. Sally moves to the mediator chair to perform the Self-Connection Process. After focusing on her breath first, and then how her body feels, she says, "I'm noticing the tension in my body and I'm feeling anger, but also fear. I'm angry because I think he's saying what I want doesn't matter, so I'd like to know that I matter, that there's some respect for my desires. And then I'm also afraid he's right, that this is all just crazy, so I guess I'd like some confidence and to trust that I know what's right for me and for our family." After a few more breaths and tapping into those needs, Sally feels her body relax and a sense of peace come over her. She then considers how she wants to respond.

"I think I'd actually like to express," she says, moving back to the other chair.

"James, when I hear you say 'maybe you'll come to your senses,' I feel angry and scared because I'd really like to know that my needs matter. I'd like to feel trust that I'm making the right decision, even if it's difficult for us to make the transition."

Sally takes a deep breath and asks Alicia to start again. As each round passes and it takes longer for Sally to feel herself becoming tense, her excitement grows. In exploring how to respond with both empathy and expression, she plays with different options and soon asks Alicia to give another trigger after she responds to the first one.

By the end of their time, Sally is able to reflect to Alicia, "I feel so much better! I don't know what will happen the next time this comes up with James, but I feel more confident that I can be present with it all and not just walk out angry. I think this will also really help me bring up with him that we need to talk about it."

After thanking Alicia and hanging up the phone, Sally remembers the phone message from James. She listens to it again, this time hearing only the care behind his words. Smiling, she begins to prepare for her next meeting.

—⁓—

Since people often think it is impossible for them to get to the point where they won't feel triggered by a situation, we like to use the metaphor of climbing a mountain to understand what this exercise is accomplishing. This metaphor comes from the April 1996 issue of *National Geographic* about a group of climbers who scaled a sheer vertical face of rock in Pakistan called Trango Tower. Led by Todd Skinner, the climbers trained by finding the most difficult 20–40 foot stretches of rock in the United States and elsewhere, the theory being that if they could climb those pitches, they could stack one difficult pitch on top of another until they had reached the top of the 9,000-foot face of Trango Tower.

While it may seem like an extreme example, it's actually similar to what you are doing in the Intensity Exercise. In starting with that first twenty feet—the lowest level of stimulus—and working on reconnecting with yourself from that level, you master it and move on to the next twenty feet, with a slightly higher level of intensity. As you keep working in this way, with each step making the next possible, eventually you will have climbed 9,000 feet. At that point, you are able to stay connected with yourself in intense situations that you would have previously never believed possible.

NEXT UP

Even after you are able to defuse the most difficult triggers from people close to you, you may still find that you have judgments of them that create disconnection. In the next chapter, you'll learn a process that will help you transform your judgments so that you can relate to others with spaciousness, presence, and care.

4 | FREEDOM FROM JUDGMENT
TRANSFORMING ENEMY IMAGES

*As I walked out the door toward the gate that would lead
to my freedom, I knew if I didn't leave my bitterness and
hatred behind, I'd still be in prison.*
—NELSON MANDELA

⸺◊⸺

JAMES STARES AT HIS COMPUTER SCREEN, THE WORDS
of the report he's trying to write floating on the page. He
glances at the clock in his office and sighs. *Not even noon yet.*
Though he feels better after doing the Self-Connection
Process, the lack of resolution—both at home with Sally and at
work with Aaron and Scott—is disrupting his concentration.
He leans back in his chair, pondering his phone call to Sally
before the meeting and how to talk to her about his concerns of
taking time away from work. "Then again," he says, "I'm not
helping matters by not being able to focus while I'm at work."

Shaking his head, he returns his attention to his computer just as the phone rings.

Hoping it's Sally, he picks up the receiver. "James here."

The rough, gravelly voice of his father, Dan, comes across the line. "Hey, Jimmy!" he says, as James grips the edge of the desk. "Just calling to see about dates for your visit. Your mother's chompin' at the bit to see you and her grandkids."

"Yeah, Dad," James says, trying not to sound annoyed. "I told you we'd get back to you. We've got to figure out when both of us can take time off and it works with the kids' schedules."

"Hm. Guess that's what happens when you let your wife go to work," Dan says. "You know, when you were a kid, *I* decided when we took a trip. There was none of this 'does it work with everyone's schedule' thing."

James grips the phone harder as a few retorts flit through his mind. Holding back, he simply says, "Different times, Dad."

"Yeah, guess so." Dan pauses. "How's Corey doing? His grades up?"

James thinks, *Ah, now we get to the real reason for the call.* He hesitates, reflecting on his conversation with Corey about his grades and school. His pause is just a moment too long.

"I knew it," Dan sighs, "he's not shaping up, is he?"

James feels the energy drain out of him as he anticipates what is coming and tries to head it off. "Dad, we've had this conversation before and I really need to get back to—"

"No, you listen," Dan interrupts. "Clearly what you're doin' with him isn't working. Kids need boundaries and rules—they need to know who's boss and how to act ... and they need strong consequences if they don't. They need to know God's watching them and He doesn't suffer fools or lazy bums. Mark my words, if you don't nip this in the bud now, he's just goin' to get worse. Next thing you know it'll be drugs and stealing. You listen to me, boy, I know what I'm talking about. I raised you and your brother, remember?"

Throughout this speech James feels his blood beginning to boil, tension increasing in his body until he is close to exploding. Hearing his father call him "boy" finally pushes him over the edge.

"Yeah, and remember how that turned out? You pushed both of us until neither of us wanted anything to do with you. I left and didn't speak to you for years, remember? And all your rules and consequences and 'God is watching you' didn't keep Nathan on the right side of the law. When was the last time you talked to him, anyway? No thanks, Dad. Now if you'll excuse me, I need to get back to work."

James hears only silence on the other end as he hangs up the phone, his hands shaking.

Have you ever monitored your thoughts to notice when you are judging yourself or someone else? Walking down a street, you might see someone and think, *That person needs to clean themselves up.* Or, after talking with your friend's partner at a party, you reflect on the conversation with, *She's a bit rude; my friend could do better.* Or, as a coworker talks to you, you notice the thought, *Wow, she sure is getting bossy after her promotion. I should have gotten that position. I guess I wasn't good enough.*

Judgments are a part of life. Most people unknowingly go through their lives judging themselves and those around them—if not constantly, then certainly a significant amount of the time. Many of these thoughts are fleeting and seem inconsequential, while others take over your mind and undermine your well-being

and relationships. At worst, judgments lie at the core of interpersonal conflicts, creating misunderstandings and prolonging
disagreements.

When you consistently interact with others, such as family,
colleagues, and friends, you might have a good understanding of
them, but your judgments can also become more insistent and
ingrained in your thinking. For example, when your partner forgets
to buy an item at the store, the thought runs through your mind,
Not again. Why can't he just read the list? It's right there! With your
family, judgments not only become ingrained, but often carry
substantial "evidence" from years of experience to back them up.
Both James and his father are caught in a web of judgments from a
lifetime of interaction with each other.

Judgmental thoughts, whether they are regarding someone
you've never met or those closest to you, are what we call "enemy
images." When we talk about enemy images, we are not referring
to a hated adversary as in a literal war; the term is far more general.
You form an enemy image any time you have a thought or cluster
of thoughts that create a barrier, preventing you from seeing the
other person as they are. This barrier disconnects you from yourself
and the other person, and it blocks you from feeling connection
with and compassion for that person.

> ### enemy image *n.*
> any image, thought, or judgment that disconnects
> you from yourself and others, creating a barrier that
> prevents you from seeing clearly

As this definition implies, anytime you feel disconnected from
someone, you may have some image of them—perhaps a story you

are telling yourself, judgments, analyses, or diagnoses—that are getting in the way of connection.

PRACTICE PAUSE

Think of one person in your life you notice judgmental thoughts about. What are your enemy images of that person?

THE COST OF ENEMY IMAGES

Judgments are such an overlooked part of everyday thinking that many people discount the cost of them. *They're just thoughts*, you may think. *What impact could they possibly have?* But holding enemy images actually creates significant impact, both within you and between you and other people.

Think of someone from your past or current life for whom you have judgments. Notice what goes on in your body while thinking about that person. Do you feel open and expansive? Trusting and caring? Or are you closed off, shut down, tense, or tight?

Since body and mind are connected, the state of your mind reflects that of your body. You may have noticed that when you have strong judgments, your mind goes on autopilot; the same thoughts run around and around like hamsters on a wheel. Perhaps you replay the situation over and over, always coming to the same conclusion about how you are correct in your analysis of what happened and how the other person acted. If you're aware you are judging and want to shift, then perhaps you try to talk yourself out of your thoughts or ignore them. While this approach can sometimes shift your attention, it does nothing to reconnect you to yourself or to the person you are judging.

Your physiology and thoughts then affect how you act. You might think, *As long as I don't tell him he's a jerk to his face, it doesn't matter how much I think it. He'll never know.* The problem is, whenever you hold an enemy image, you indeed act out of it, whether you realize it or not. Even if you don't say your judgment out loud, your nonverbal body language communicates what is going on within you. Your thoughts and the feelings they prompt in you leak out through your facial expressions, tone of voice, and gestures, and others pick up on these subtle cues unconsciously.

While talking to his father, for example, James feels tension and anger, and his voice comes out tight and clipped. If Dan were there in person, he would undoubtedly pick up on physical cues that showed James was upset in the way he held his shoulders, his stance, and his facial expression. In addition, internal judgments can often lead to overt actions—as when James "boils over" and talks back to his father—that further the conflict.

When you are holding an enemy image, it obscures the shared humanity between you and the other person. It's difficult, if not impossible, to feel care, compassion, and kindness for someone you judge—it's like putting them in a box labeled "other" and shutting the lid. It then becomes much easier to act in ways that are experienced as hurtful.

Metaphorically, enemy images are like a weight you are carrying. Your sense of health, well-being, peace, and happiness in the world suffer to the degree that you are carrying disconnecting images. How can you work with these images and lay down that weight, or even dissolve it entirely? In this chapter, we cover the Enemy Image Process, which is specifically designed to help us come out from under the weight of our judgments.

The term "enemy image," as well as how Nonviolent Communication skills can shift enemy images, come directly out of

Marshall Rosenberg's work. Based on that, we have created a framework and map—the Enemy Image Process (EIP)—to apply the skills and transform these disconnecting images.

> ## PRACTICE PAUSE
>
> What is the cost of holding the enemy image of the person you thought of in the previous Practice Pause? Think both in terms of your own well-being and in your relationship to the other person.

—⁓—

James's first impulse upon cutting off the phone call with Dan is to call Sally and share his irritation and disbelief at the gall of his father—but he catches himself. With things unsettled between them, he doesn't want to add something new. Instead, he lets his thoughts go back to the call. *How dare he try to tell me how to raise my kids. He's such a meddling busybody. He doesn't have enough going on now that he's retired from preaching, so he has to stick his nose in other people's business. He's totally out of touch with the realities of raising kids today, not to mention that bringing his Bible-pounding preacher job to being a father didn't work anyway. Yet he still insists it's the only correct way to raise kids. He can't admit he's wrong, so he uses any hint of imperfection in my kids to push his viewpoint. He's an old fart who couldn't get it right the first time around, and now he thinks he can tell me what to do.*

James continues to rant internally for a few minutes before he runs out of steam. In a brief moment of mental quiet, he recognizes how good it feels to be right about the situation, yet also the futility of it. Not only is it disrupting his day even further, he can feel the tension and unease throughout his body and mind, the whole tirade being all too familiar. He has been over it before; rehashing the conversation and bringing up old hurt from his boyhood will change nothing. Though he longs to change his dad, he knows he has no control over him. Instead, he needs to focus his attention on what he can control, shifting his own thoughts, feelings, and actions.

THE ENEMY IMAGE PROCESS (EIP)

Everything is a strategy to meet a need, even judgmental thoughts. When you stay at the level of thinking judgmentally, you are unaware of *why* you are judging, and the motivation behind those thoughts—one or more fundamental needs that weren't met—remains unidentified. Simply telling yourself not to judge or to think differently, you turn down the opportunity to uncover the needs you are seeking to meet. When you can connect to those needs, you reconnect to yourself.

Similarly, the actions or words of the person you're judging are also strategies to meet needs. When you connect to the needs the other person may be seeking to meet, you can dissolve the enemy image, even when the person isn't physically with you. You are then free to consider what to do next in relation to them, unencumbered by your judgments.

Therefore, the process to get from being in judgment and disconnect to connection and freedom has three steps: empathy for self, empathy for other, and new possibilities. The steps for the Enemy Image Process can be laid out in brief as follows:

ENEMY IMAGE PROCESS (EIP)

1. EMPATHY FOR SELF

   a. Notice your thoughts that are judgmental or diagnostic about yourself or someone else.

   b. Experience your feelings and name them.

   c. Ask what universal human needs those thoughts are trying to meet, and linger with the experience of having identified those needs.

2. EMPATHY FOR OTHER

   a. Consider what the other person said or did that you are judging.

   b. Consider what they might be feeling.

   c. Ask what universal human needs they are seeking to meet through their actions and deepen into those needs.

3. NEW POSSIBILITIES

   a. Learn: What have you learned from your awareness of the needs you uncovered?

   b. Plan: What would you like to do as a result of what you have learned? This may include a request of yourself or someone else. The quality of self-connection that comes from showing empathy helps you see new possibilities for ways of thinking and of taking action that are more likely to be effective.

   c. Practice: If your request of yourself includes taking some action or changing a behavior, you may want to practice it so you are more likely to be able to access it when you need to.

mediateyourlife.com/enemy-image-process-video/

When first learning the EIP, it helps to go through the process on the previous page in detail, using the first three of the four components of NVC—observations, feelings, and needs—in the two empathy steps. In doing so, you continue to practice the distinctions related to these components (if you need a refresher on these distinctions, see *Choosing Peace*). As you become more experienced and at ease using the EIP, you will be able to do it more on the fly by focusing primarily on needs—yours and those of the other.

In order to perform the EIP, you must first notice that you have a judgment. This may take some practice as you observe your thoughts, the way you feel (agitated, uncomfortable, angry, frustrated), or interactions with people or situations in your environment. One of these is likely a common entry point for you, tipping you off to look within for an image of yourself or another person that is creating disconnection.

Now let's walk through the steps of the EIP in greater detail, illustrating each one using the example of judging co-workers who leave the kitchen area in your office a mess. You'll also follow each step with James working through his judgments about his dad.

EMPATHY FOR SELF

In the first part of the EIP, you focus on yourself. When you notice a judgment of someone else, take a look internally. What is your observation? This could either be about your thoughts or about the other person, but be careful to keep judgments out of your observation, otherwise your efforts are less likely to lead to transforming your enemy image.

For example, the observation related to your coworkers would not be, "They are such slobs" or "These people are so clueless about cleanliness"; it would be more along the lines of, "I saw dirty dishes left in the sink four times this week and the counter had crumbs and spilled coffee." Notice the difference between the *judgment* and the *observation*—the *observation* relates what you saw without adding your intrepretation. Your observation could also start with your own thoughts, which might sound like, *I'm having the thought that people are waiting for their mom to come along and clean up after them.* Though a judgment ("people are waiting for their mom to come along ...") may be inherent in your thought, when phrased this way ("I'm having the thought that people are waiting for their mom to come along and clean up after them."), it becomes an observation. This is when you may see that having that thought could be the stimulus of your current feeling state.

After clarifying your observation, check in with how you feel. First, simply experience the feeling in your body, and then name it. If you need help naming it, refer to the feelings list in Appendix A. As you stand in the kitchen, for example, perhaps you feel uncomfortable, angry, disappointed, or maybe disgusted.

Next, connect with why you feel that way. What need of yours is not being met? If you need some help, you can refer to the needs list in Appendix B. In the example with your coworkers, you may need consideration, kindness, respect, cleanliness, or order. When you name your needs, consider what it would feel like for them to be met.

At this point, you may begin to feel a shift within yourself. Perhaps you feel a little more relaxed, less agitated, or more in touch with what is motivating you. If so, move on to empathizing with the other person. If not, determine if there is more empathy you desire—are there more feelings and needs you can connect with?

James recognizes little will get done until he deals with his turmoil and decides to take his lunch break early. While eating, he pulls out a notebook to help him go through the Enemy Image Process. He writes "Observations," "Feelings," and "Needs" across the top of a page. As he looks at the empty Observations column, he considers all his judgments of his dad. Eventually he comes up with this list:

- I'm thinking Dad's sticking his nose where it doesn't belong, telling me how to raise my kids.
- I'm thinking he couldn't get it right the first time and is still trying to prove he's right.
- I'm thinking he's saying I'm a failure as a father.
- I'm thinking he's still pushing religion on me.

James turns attention to his feelings, and the first ones that come to mind are anger and irritation. As he inquires further, he finds fear is there too—the fear he feels when a part of him agrees that he actually is a failure as a father. He also touches on his sadness at feeling disconnected from Corey but also from his own father. James recalls when he was young how he'd looked up to Dan, but that had given way long ago, replaced by fear and then followed by rebellion and anger. Though he has taken steps in recent years to re-establish some relationship with Dan, he is not sure whether real connection is possible.

This train of thought leads James to focus on needs, and in that column he writes:

- I'd like to be understood and accepted by Dad.
- I'd like to be treated as an adult (I'd like to be called James, not Jimmy and "boy").

- I'd like acknowledgment for what I'm doing with Corey and how much I care.

- I'd like a sense of competence in my role as a father.

As James looks over this list, he questions whether "to be treated as an adult" is a need. As he taps into what he means by that, he realizes it is about being seen and respected as someone who makes his own choices and takes responsibility for them, and having a sense of equality with his father. He refines the list to focus on his genuine needs:

- Understanding, acceptance

- Respect and equality

- Acknowledgment and appreciation

- Competence

As he reflects, he feels a bit hopeless about having these needs met. But wanting to find a way, he adds "empowerment" to the list.

―――

EMPATHY FOR OTHER

When you turn your attention to empathizing with the other person, you will utilize the same process.

First, note your observation, but this time be more specific about what the other person did. If the scene had been videotaped, what would the recording show? As you think back to the scene in the office kitchen, perhaps you've noticed that people leaving dishes in the sink are moving quickly, or that they're talking to one another as they pour their coffee.

When you turn to feelings, imagine what your coworkers may be feeling. Perhaps someone is feeling distracted, rushed, indifferent, or even eager. Connect with those feelings within yourself—how do you feel when you are rushed or distracted?

Then turn to inquiring into what *their* needs might be. Perhaps one person is meeting a need for efficiency, another for connection in talking with colleagues, and another, anxious to fulfill work commitments, is meeting a need for productivity.

As you consider all possible needs that come to mind, remember to not be concerned about whether your guesses are accurate or not—they're not for the other person; they are for you to be able to shift your own internal experience and transform the judgments you are holding. Since the other person's needs are inevitably ones you share (otherwise you are not in touch with universal needs), when you put attention on them, it helps you feel more peaceful and compassionate and less triggered and reactive.

If you would like a further challenge, ask yourself in the second step, "What needs of *theirs* are not met by what *I* am doing in this situation?" If you find this question brings up blame or shame in you, return to Step 1 before continuing. The point here is not to make yourself wrong; it's to connect you to what may be going on for the other person. This question won't be relevant in all situations in which you have a disconnecting image, but it can be particularly powerful if you're in a current conflict with someone close to you. Your insights here will lead to a deeper level of compassion and understanding for their reaction to your role in the conflict.

—w—

James feels calmer after empathizing with himself and labels another sheet for his father with the same three columns. He thinks about the call and under "Observations" writes:

- Dad called me "Jimmy" and "boy."
- He said what I'm doing with Corey is wrong.
- He said I let Sally go to work and that he used to decide our vacations. I'm thinking he was implying that I should be in control of my family but I'm not.

As James writes these, he feels triggered again and has to offer himself more empathy before continuing to think about where Dan is coming from. When he can continue with Step 2, he has more space to actually wonder what Dan is feeling. The first thing that comes to mind is that Dan might actually miss them and want to see them. *He did call about the trip,* James remembers, *and though he said it was Mom chomping at the bit, I wonder if he is too.*

James reflects on the other observations and wonders if his dad feels sad or embarrassed about his relationship with both of his sons. *Maybe he wants to protect me from the same thing happening to me with Corey.* James realizes that protection is a need and writes it down.

Suddenly, a new thought strikes him. *Are these all ways he's trying to show he cares?* James experiences his world turn upside-down with that insight, and at the same time, he wonders why it hadn't occurred to him before. Though James doesn't like how his dad tries to show it, he suddenly sees Dan acting out of care for him and Corey. With this new reflection, James adds "care" and then "connection" under the needs column, considering that maybe Dan uses this type of conversation as a way to connect with him so that he can pass on to his son what he learned as a father.

James returns again to Step 1 as he feels the hurt from his father's parenting, as well as his intense desire to parent Corey differently. When he looks at his father's needs now, he adds to the list "contribution" and "meaning." James knows that religion has always been Dan's North Star; as a preacher, it was how he contributed to people, and he still sees it as a way he can help others. Reviewing the list of Dan's possible needs, he now sees protection, care, connection, contribution, and meaning.

After empathizing with yourself and with the other person, check in to see how you are feeling now. If there has not been a significant shift in your enemy image, go back to empathizing with yourself and the other person before moving into the final stage. Most likely, in connecting with your own feelings and needs, and in imagining the feelings and needs of the other person, you will be much more open, maybe even feeling some compassion for both of you.

After identifying one or more needs, we encourage you not to skip immediately over to figuring out what to do. Stay with the needs for a moment, going back and forth between the needs you want met as well as those the other person wants met, and see if you can hold them all together until you feel the enemy image dissolve. If it doesn't, you may not have empathized with yourself or the other person as fully as you could. If you find yourself struggling to do so, enlist the help of someone else. An empathy buddy can sometimes help you deepen into empathy when you're caught in an enemy image you're unable to transform on your own.

NEW POSSIBILITIES: LEARN, PLAN, PRACTICE

Once you go through the steps of self-empathy and empathy, what happens is not only quite complex, but also a bit magical. People often find that there's a sense of "getting to the other side" when they deeply connect with their own and the other person's needs. You begin to see them as a human being just like yourself. People tend to say things like:

+ "Oh, I see it differently now!"

+ "So that's what was going on!"

+ "You know, at the time it seemed like I didn't have any choices, or the choices were unacceptable, but now I see others I can make."

You can often tell when you're ready to shift out of the first two steps and into the last when you feel these new possibilities begin to emerge. That moment, when you see the world in a different way, is the "a-ha" moment of learning.

Out of that a-ha moment can come some idea of what you want to do next. The world looks different; possibilities exist that were not available to you before. You may have thought of those possibilities earlier but dismissed them immediately as impossible, or you may not have even conceived of them. Now, however, they seem completely possible. When you are connected to needs, there is more creative space for newly emerging ideas. These become the basis for your request.

After going through the first two steps, think about what you have learned. What new insights do you have about yourself or the other person? What is your a-ha? Consider whether these insights naturally lead you to some new choices about what you would like to do.

Think for a moment about the example we've been using of your coworkers, and consider how you might act without performing the EIP. Perhaps you post a sign in the kitchen that screams at people to clean up after themselves. When you happen to cross paths with them, still holding that enemy image, you might complain about people leaving dishes lying around, hoping they get the hint. Even if you don't say anything, your body language will communicate your thoughts—your actions might be more abrupt, with your facial expression showing displeasure as you wipe the countertop.

When you go through the EIP, however, you will see new choices, and the action you take will be very different. Out of a connection to needs, you may decide to go ahead and clean up the kitchen, which you may have done anyway, but *how* you do it will be significantly different. How? By acting out of a connection to needs rather than a connection to an enemy image.

Another choice may be making a request of the people in the office. Requests are an important part of this process; they are how you take the new possibility you've chosen and turn it into reality. That request is most often to yourself, but even if you decide to make a request of another person, you have first made a request of yourself to take the action necessary.

Once you decide what you want to do, you may find planning and practicing helpful. These two steps keep you focused on how to carry out your request while staying in alignment with your values. If you decide to make a request of others, you might plan what you want to say and practice it with a friend or willing coworker.

When you are in an ongoing relationship, it's likely that one request will be to have a conversation with the person. When you know you're going to have a further interaction, you might first plan how that meeting will take place. This could include making requests of yourself, such as arranging a time to talk with the other person, and making requests of others, such as planning a session with a support team to get additional help, if necessary.

If you decide a future conversation is important to you, you will want to practice how you wish to be in that conversation. This could mean playing out scripts in your mind until you find one that helps you feel a kind of open presence or satisfaction with how it feels. Or, your practice could include role-playing the conversation with someone who is willing to support you. In role-playing, you can actually practice what you want to say and how you want to say it, as well as practice how to respond to various comments the person might make.

The idea behind practicing is not to use the exact words when you speak to that person that you used in practice; rather, it's to build up a lexicon of ways you would like to communicate in certain situations, and to familiarize yourself with the possibilities of how you could respond to each other. What you may find, then, is that these bits and pieces will pop into your mind while in a real conversation, because you have primed yourself through creating that mental situation and practicing it.

As you consider the expanded possibilities for how you can act, it's likely that multiple options will arise out of the first two steps of the EIP. Take each choice and weigh it against the needs you identified during the process. As you do this, allow your final decision to be a visceral one, rather than an intellectual one. Go with the choice that feels right in the moment—the one that has the most life or energy to it. When we are connected to needs, we find that we can implicitly trust our intuition.

James sits back in his chair and stretches, feeling more in touch with his father. He reflects on how he sees the situation now, thinking Dan might actually be coming from wanting to show his care and concern and to connect with him as an adult, despite the fact that pushing his views on his son is the only way he knows how to do it. *I guess even the way he tried to raise me and Nathan was his way of showing he cared*, James thinks. Feeling sadness as he contemplates how Dan's attempt to show care had tragically resulted in the opposite—disconnection and estrangement—James sees that neither he nor his brother had a hint that care might have been at the root of Dan's actions. James also mourns that it has taken him so long to come to this realization; at the same time, he experiences relief, as the insight gives him renewed hope about moving forward. "I'd really like to find a way to interact with him outside of what he thinks shows care," he says out loud.

James knows he will be talking to Dan again soon—he will have to clean up the mess he made—and ponders how to prepare for it, wondering who he can ask to role-play the conversation. As he considers what Dan may say that he will react to, he realizes he can use the Intensity Exercise to defuse the trigger of Dan calling him "boy." He decides to ask Shawn if he will role-play the conversation, and ask Sally to do the Intensity Exercise with him.

EIP IN PRACTICE

One of the best ways to practice the EIP is with judgments you have of people you don't know. It's common to walk down the street and see someone who automatically triggers a judgment because of the way they are dressed or what they are doing, or to judge the teller in the bank who was "rude," the cashier in the store who took too long, or the other driver who was too slow or too fast. You can carry these enemy images with you even after leaving the situation, and using the EIP with strangers is often easier than with someone you know and will interact with again later.

It's one thing to lay out the basic structure of this process, and another to actually experience it. As such, we always recommend setting aside time to practice when you're first learning a map, closely following the steps and noticing how it shifts your experience. As you do this, you become familiar with the linear steps; however, using the map with a real enemy image is often not as linear. In the next segment, we attempt to give a more experiential view of going through the process and how it might unfold.

Here's the EIP map again for reference:

1. SELF-EMPATHY
    a. Notice your thoughts that are judgmental or diagnostic about yourself or someone else.
    b. Experience your feelings and name them.
    c. Ask what universal human needs those thoughts are trying to meet, and linger with the experience of having identified those needs.

2. EMPATHY FOR OTHER
    a. Consider what the other person said or did that you are judging.
    b. Consider what they might be feeling.
    c. Ask what universal human needs they are seeking to meet through their actions and deepen into those needs.

3. NEW POSSIBILITIES

    a. Learn: What have you learned from your awareness of the needs you uncovered?

    b. Plan: What would you like to do as a result of what you have learned? This may include a request of yourself or someone else. The quality of self-connection that comes from showing empathy helps you see new possibilities for ways of thinking and of taking action that are more likely to be effective.

    c. Practice: If your request of yourself includes taking some action or changing a behavior, you may want to practice it so you are more likely to be able to access it when you need to.

In the first part of the EIP (self-empathy), use the components of NVC—observations, feelings, and needs—to deepen into self-connection. Observe your thoughts, keeping some distance from them so you are not completely identified with believing you are right and the other person is wrong. When you step back and witness your thinking, it helps you begin to shift.

Then, drop into your body, solely experiencing the sensations of feeling and emotion that occur when you're present with your body. The thoughts you observe and the feelings you have are telling you about your needs. This is when you'll determine the needs that aren't being met. Your goal here is to get a sense of needs that exist apart from this particular person or strategy, focusing on the need itself.

For example, let's say in the situation you're reflecting on that another person is nagging you. Once you notice you have the enemy image of "he's a nag" or "he's pushy," you look for the observation of what he does that you're calling "nagging"—perhaps he's reminded you three times this week to schedule the gardener to come clean up the yard. You also consider how you feel when you think of him as pushy or nagging, or when he reminds you to take care of this chore. Maybe you're frustrated or irritated. Either the observation or the feeling (or both) can be the doorway to your underlying need that is not met—such as the need to be self-sufficient and to make your own choices.

As you go through this process, more thoughts may come up to observe and more feelings to experience. That's normal. Afterward, when you return to needs, you may notice new ones that have surfaced, or that you refocus on those you were already aware of. Eventually, you will find your reactive thinking subsides a bit.

Now, as you enter the second part of the EIP, try to empathize with the other person's observations, feelings, and needs. Sometimes, simply shifting to consider their point of view can trigger you again and raise more judgments. If so, return to observing your thoughts, experiencing your feelings, and then inquiring into needs. In this way, you can advance to connecting with what might be going on for the other person (Step 2). Moving into Step 3 and considering requests can also trigger more reactions, in which case you'll want to return again to Steps 1 and 2.

The EIP is an iterative process—you'll often alternate in your mind between you and the other person as you try to stay connected to your needs, and as you then try to imagine the needs of the other person. Imagine loosening a boulder with a crowbar using movement, rocking back and forth until enough momentum is built up to topple it. The Enemy Image Process has this same sense of movement to it—a sense of rocking back and forth between connecting to your own needs and the other person's until the enemy image topples over.

POSITIVE "ENEMY" IMAGES

So far we've used examples of enemy images that are negative, and this is the most common use for the EIP. Nonetheless, it's worth noting that judgments can also be positive.

But wait a minute, you may be thinking, *what would be the problem of thinking that my boss is incredible or a local celebrity is a beautiful person?* Acknowledging the gift and contribution of people in your life is, of course, a wonderful way to meet both yours and their needs. Where it can become a problem, however, is when it *disconnects you from them or from yourself.*

Let's take a look at how that might happen, using the examples of the incredible boss and the local celebrity.

Here are two different ways a person might think about his boss:

"Charles is amazing—he's the perfect boss! I can't imagine ever being able to do what he does. He's so nice to everyone, and he always seems to have time for us while still getting things done. I'm just in awe watching him. I wish I could be like that."

Or

"I have so much respect for Charles. He seems to really listen to all of us, taking into account what we need when he makes decisions. I enjoy working with him, and I feel acknowledged and respected for my contribution at work. I learn a lot from watching how he is with people."

While both of these statements express a positive view of the the boss, notice which one feels to you like the speaker is more connected to themselves and to Charles. In the first statement, the speaker has Charles on a pedestal, expressing a subtle, negative view of himself in saying he can't be similar. Here, the speaker is likely to feel disconnected from both Charles and himself.

In the second statement, the speaker states his feelings and the needs that are met, while still acknowledging the positive things he notices Charles does. He hasn't placed Charles so high above him that he is disconnected from Charles, but instead sees how he can learn from Charles's example.

Meeting a celebrity can also bring up positive images that put people in a box that diminishes their shared humanity:

"Oh my gosh, I just love your work. I feel so tongue-tied right now. I think you're amazing. You must have such an awesome life, being able to travel around the world, working and partying with all those other rich and famous people."

Or

"It's so nice to meet you! I have long been an admirer of your work. I was really moved by your portrait of _____ in the movie _____. It helped me understand in a new way how I relate to the world. Would you be willing to tell me what prompted you to take on that role?"

People often idolize and worship celebrities, projecting onto them their own dreams about what it would be like to be rich or famous—or how it would solve all their problems. If you do this, the contrast between how you view the celebrity in your idealized picture and how you see yourself causes you to disconnect from yourself and from them. You make the celebrity superior to you, instead of recognizing that they're merely a human being who shares the same needs. While you may not realize you're doing it, you disconnect from compassion for their humanity as well as your own.

The second statement still acknowledges admiration but ties it to a specific observation (the role and movie) and need (understanding). The speaker is self-connected, expressing themselves in a way that is more likely to foster connection with the celebrity.

If you notice positive "enemy" images that disconnect you from yourself and the other person, you can use the EIP in the same way you would with a negative judgment. Transforming positive images will lead you to a deeper level of connection and compassion for yourself and the other person, and allow you to interact from that connection.

PRACTICE PAUSE

Who do you have a positive image of that in some way disconnects you from yourself or from them? Use the EIP to shift your judgments of yourself and the other person.

EIP AS BLUEPRINT

In our view, the EIP provides nature's blueprint for how human beings move from conflict to connection. To explain, we'll use two metaphors: Russian nesting dolls and holons. A holon, as defined by Ken Wilber, is a whole that is part of a larger whole. The entire universe is made up of holons: atoms to molecules to cells to organs to creatures; letters to words to sentences to paragraphs to books. At each level, there is a greater wholeness, a new level of organization that transcends what came before, and in which more is synthesized.

When you use the EIP, you can re-enact this movement from one whole to a larger, more complex level of organization, within your own mind. You start from a sense of otherness, split internally with some part of yourself being "other" and the person you are judging as "other." Here, you are the smallest of the Russian nesting dolls, or the lowest level of a holon.

In the first part of the EIP, you practice self-empathy, which can heal the split within so you are no longer in judgment. When you become whole within yourself, you're able to move to the next larger Russian doll, yet you still feel completely separate from the other person. They are still the "enemy" in some sense, in opposition or against you in some way.

In performing the second part of the EIP and empathizing with the other person, you again sense that you are still individuals but part of a greater whole. This is when you transcend to the next level of the holon, where your sense of self now includes the other. When you work to find a strategy at this point, new possibilities are available to you because you are no longer separate. Your needs include the other person's.

FREEDOM TO ACT, FREEDOM TO SHIFT

So far, we've covered three internally focused processes. The Self-Connection Process in Chapter 2 allows you to reconnect with yourself quickly when you are triggered into the fight or flight response; the Intensity Exercise in Chapter 3 helps you defuse strong triggers and practice reconnecting quickly and making new choices; and the Enemy Image Process in this chapter allows you to relieve yourself of the burden of judgment you have been carrying.

All of these inner-work processes cause you to feel more compassionate and peaceful in thinking about the situation or person. This in and of itself is a powerful incentive to use these processes in your life, but it's not the only benefit, as the way you feel inevitably affects the way you act.

A consequential benefit of doing your inner work and feeling better is acting in the world in a way that is more in alignment with your values—one you are less likely to regret later on. Getting to the other side of empathy shifts you to an internal guidance system. Though people tend to think that using internal guidance to direct actions will lead people to always act in selfish ways, we do not agree. In fact, people are more likely to act in ways that are selfish when they are *disassociated* from themselves, trying to act from an alignment with some absolute "truth," not when they are actually connected with their inner selves in an ongoing process. Doing the inner work of Chapters 2–4 increases the likelihood of using skillful means.

How do you know when the inner work is "done" and you are ready to engage again with the other person? Well, in one sense inner work is never finished. Living and interacting with others commands an ongoing process of becoming disconnected and reconnected over and over again. Nonetheless, we have found a few indicators that let you know when you have connected with yourself and are more likely to be able to connect with others.

THEY ARE NO LONGER THE "ENEMY"

A crucial indicator that you are self-connected is when you can be with another person and not see them as your enemy. If you still have a lot of judgmental thoughts, analyses, and diagnoses of them, you may find that these will leak out in your words or actions unless you do more internal work first. In this case, you'll return to the Enemy Image Process, either on your own or with the help of a supporter, and shift those judgments.

BEING HEARD IS LESS URGENT

Another indicator that you are connected is you will not feel urgent about your need to be heard. Often when people have difficulties with someone else, they mostly want to be heard instead of being willing to listen. Have you noticed when you are in conflict how imperative it feels to let the other person know how *you* see the situation and how it's affecting *you*? With enough empathy and connection to yourself, feeling hurt and the urgency to be heard dissipate. You experience more spaciousness and can more easily live out of wanting to understand before being understood.

As Marshall Rosenberg said on a *Peace Talks* radio show:

> When somebody says something, especially if what they're saying is something we don't believe or agree with, we want to jump in and correct them, or, we want to defend ourselves, all of which is not the best way to connect with that person. We show, as hard as it is, how to take a deep breath and, if you're not able to do this right away, at least see what's going on inside you. Give yourself enough empathy to see what is triggered in you. Learn how to do that to yourself, so that you can, then, put your full attention on the other person.

To listen to the full show, visit:
goodradioshows.org/peaceTalksL36.html

BEING HEARD IS A REQUEST

Even if you really do want to be heard—maybe even first—if you've done your inner work, you will less likely hold it as a demand. You can hear the other person, then move into expression of what you want to say, all while staying present, fluidly moving between listening to and reflecting what the other person says and expressing yourself.

You might find that when you have this kind of spaciousness inside you and can sincerely hear the other person, you may not have a lot to be "heard about." Even if you do, if you can intently listen to the other person, it tends to make them much more receptive to hearing what you have to say, allowing a shift and opening up a space where you can talk. In doing this, you are much more likely to be satisfied with what happens between you than simply pushing to be heard without hearing the other person.

HOLDING PERSPECTIVES LIGHTLY

When you use these inner processes over time, there is a subtle shift that takes place in holding a point of view. You obtain more clarity of perspective and are willing to take responsibility for it, but also to change it. Hearing and truly striving to understand other people's points of view brings an openness to shifting your own perspective. You become not only willing to change your point of view, but to seek out the possibility that it *can* be changed, that you can broaden it and see in new ways.

When you learn over and over again that your own view is not the only one, you begin to assume that if there is disconnection, it likely comes from not perceiving something the way the other person does. If you want to get back to connection, you must open up to expanding your own perspective through considering the other person's, knowing that understanding one another does not necessarily mean agreeing with each other. Understanding another's perspective can be deeply enriching even if you continue to see things differently. There is then space and appreciation for diversity and uniqueness, as well as underlying commonality and connection in the experience of being human.

Your *intention* when entering into conversations with others where there is disagreement or conflict affects the manner in which you engage with them. If your intention is truly to reach resolution, this means being open to hearing another person's perspective. You cannot assume that others have the same skills you do; in fact, it is best to assume they don't and take the responsibility.

This is why we highly suggest using the internal skills, especially EIP, before going into a difficult conversation. If you have an ongoing relationship and find yourself in conflict with the person, doing the EIP before any interaction with them, and certainly before a conversation regarding the issue you have a dispute over, can drastically affect how you proceed in the conversation. With any conversation you think might be difficult, try to prepare fully for it by getting your own need for empathy met, guessing what the other person's needs are, and then planning and practicing how you would like to interact with them.

It is when you enter into an interaction with someone that you see the difference in your behavior—that which results from your intention and connection with yourself. If you have truly done your inner work, you can be with the other person in a totally new way. Your body language will be different—you will hold your body in a softer, more open way; if the conversation happens over the phone, the way you speak and the words you choose will be different. The other person will pick up on these cues, even if unconsciously, and your conversation is more likely to flow toward connection and resolution.

—◦◦◦—

James looks at the clock and notices he still has time for a walk before getting back to work. His step buoyant, he leaves the building to walk through the park next to the office, the sun and breeze mirroring his lighter mood. Feeling his body respond to being outdoors with a surge of energy, he contemplates how he has shifted in only about thirty minutes of the Enemy Image Process. His feeling of hopelessness is even gone, and he actually looks forward to putting his plan in place and seeing where it might lead. He wonders whether his guesses about what is going on with his father are accurate, and he anticipates a conversation in which he might be able to ask, or at least be able to hear what Dan says through the lens of needs, instead of merely reacting from pain and hurt.

—◦◦◦—

Next Up

Now that you are connected with yourself and have transformed any enemy images you have of the person you're in conflict with, you are ready to have that difficult conversation. Going into that conversation with a process—the Interpersonal Mediation map—will help you fulfill your intentions to connect with them and resolve the issue. In the next chapter, you'll learn this map and the skills that will help you navigate difficult conversations with ease.

5 | ROADMAP TO RESOLUTION

BEING IN A DIFFICULT CONVERSATION

Whenever you're in conflict with someone, there is one factor that can make the difference between damaging your relationship and deepening it. That factor is attitude.
—WILLIAM JAMES

———

JAMES TIDIES HIS DESK, PREFERRING TO LEAVE EVERY-thing cleared off and put away at the end of the day. The clock shows 7 p.m.—later than he'd like, but since he left work to take Maggie to her tryouts this afternoon, he has stayed late to finish things up for the day.

He smiles, remembering seeing Maggie on the soccer field. It had been fun to see her doing her thing again. Watching her games always brings back memories and reawakens his competitive spirit from his own soccer-playing days. It hadn't been that bad to leave work, especially since Sally's sister, Peg, was willing to pick Maggie up from tryouts. He wasn't gone long, he was able to enjoy seeing Maggie nab a spot on the team she wanted, and Maggie got to spend a little time with her aunt and grandmother afterward. All in all, it worked out.

As James heads out of the building, he crosses paths with his boss, Scott.

"So, must be nice to have Aaron on your team now!" Scott says, giving James a friendly slap on the shoulder.

James feels a little taken aback. "Actually," he says, "I wanted to talk to you about that. It didn't go that well today."

Scott looks surprised. "Really? That's odd. Seems to me he's perfect. He already knows the company and you don't need to bring someone totally new up to speed. What could possibly be the problem?"

James goes cold. His tongue feels like it's tied in knots. He tries to clear his throat, which is suddenly constricted. "Ah, well, he just seemed, I don't know, maybe not okay with the move to my team."

Scott shrugs. "Well, James, it's your job to bring your team together. That's what management is about. See you tomorrow!"

James feels his face flush as he watches Scott walk away. All the way home he alternates between feeling anger at Scott, wanting to hide, and harboring irritation with himself.

———※———

Navigating a difficult conversation can feel like being in the rapids in a raft. You feel out of control, rocks suddenly appear in your path, the raft spins, and you end up disoriented. At best, you manage somehow to stay afloat and make it down the river, battered and exhausted; at worst you capsize along the way. Your ability to navigate successfully depends on the sturdiness of your raft and your own skills and capacity to stay present in the face of conflict. This chapter provides the tools to build that strong raft, giving you the adeptness to carry you successfully through a difficult conversation.

This work is not for the faint of heart; the willingness to stand in the fire of conflict requires courage and determination. You need courage to be open to another's point of view, to be present with your fight or flight reaction and choose a new response, and to say what's true for you. You need determination to maintain your intention to be in conflict in a new way when it's easier to go with your habitual response, and to learn from whatever happens during the conversation, taking it back into practice so that your skills and capacity continue to grow.

If this sounds more difficult than it's worth, let us assure you that it's not. Numerous rewards follow when you can be present in a conversation and ensure that you and the other person are heard. We hear touching stories all the time from people in our trainings about long-standing conflicts resolved, reconciliations between estranged family members, and people enjoying a deep level of connection and communion between themselves and those closest to them. But don't take our word for it. Try it for yourself.

Using the maps and exercises in the preceding three chapters— the Self-Connection Process, the Intensity Exercise, and the Enemy Image Process—you have what you need to prepare to be in a difficult conversation. This chapter will outline the primary challenges you tend to face in a conflict and how to get through them, then give you the roadmap to being in the conversation, along with some helpful skills. Later in the chapter, we discuss using this map "in the wild" and how to practice so that it's available to you when you need it.

WHAT IS A DIFFICULT CONVERSATION?

Some difficult conversations are obvious. You want to talk to your boss about giving a key opportunity to someone else. Your mother said something you found hurtful and you want to let her know how you feel. Your partner says he wants to talk to you about moving to a new city to pursue a job opportunity, and you love where you live. At times, it's clear you have a tricky conversation coming up; when that happens, you can easily use the skills and maps in this book.

Some situations, however, are not so clear. Think about the example we used in the last chapter of your coworker leaving dishes in the sink. If you decided after performing the EIP to make a request of the person to clean their dishes, you might not see that as a challenging conversation, yet still feel nervous about talking to them.

For clarity's sake, a difficult conversation is any conversation that feels difficult *for you*. The topic may be weighty and life changing or merely a small matter that would make a difference in your world. You may know you will be talking to the person ahead of time, or someone else may come to you with a request or a demand, throwing you headlong into the rapids unexpectedly.

But whether it's a planned conversation or one that happens in the moment, you can only use the tools in this chapter when you recognize the situation as one in which to use them. How can you help yourself know this?

Think back to a few recent difficult conversations of which you've been a part. No conversation is too small to be included in your list; what's important is your thoughts and feelings about the person and the talk you had. What did you feel both beforehand and while in the conversation? What were you thinking? Your thoughts and feelings can provide landmarks in the future, alerting you that you are now navigating the territory of a challenging exchange.

For example, before speaking with someone about a problematic topic, you might feel trepidation or anxiety. You might ruminate about what to say or what happened in the past that you want to discuss. The stress response you've become more aware of through the past few chapters is also likely to arise, letting you know that some part of you perceives danger. Identify and name the specific physical, emotional, and mental reactions you have in a difficult conversation so that you can notice when they occur, prompting you to apply the maps and skills while you're in the midst of it.

PRACTICE PAUSE

What will alert you that you are in (or will be in) a difficult conversation? Identify at least one "landmark" in each of these areas: your physical sensations, your emotions, and your thoughts.

CHALLENGES

The primary challenges of a difficult conversation—the rocks, if you will—are as follows:

+ Disorientation and not knowing how to get where you want to go

+ Managing your stress response

+ Believing "I'm right!" and being unwilling to hear another's perspective

+ Fear that hearing another's perspective is "death" or giving up

+ Fear of the other person's reaction if you speak your truth

+ Focusing on problems, strategies, and solutions without first establishing connection

Let's look at each of these difficulties and how to overcome them so you can bring ease to a difficult conversation.

DISORIENTATION

Some conflicts come on suddenly, triggered by current or past hurts, and you are thrown into the stress response and embroiled in an argument. All your own perceptions and interpretations vie for your attention with your sense of what's going on with the other person and how they are responding, leaving you feeling inundated and overwhelmed. Disorientation can come through confusion about what direction the conversation is going, not remembering why you are agitated, or not sure how the whole thing started, much less how to resolve it in a way you feel good about.

It helps immensely to manage disorientation if you have a framework that orients you and a set of steps that guide you in the choices you make during the conversation. Mediator mind and the Interpersonal Mediation (IPM) map in this chapter give you this framework and these steps. The IPM map, as with our other maps, is a particular sequence of skills that can be used in a checklist fashion; it is the roadmap to use when you're in the heat of a difficult conversation, making it more likely you'll end up at the destination you desire. When you feel confident about being able to create what you want in the conversation, you can keep the disorientation at bay. Having the map allows you to achieve this by giving you a limited set of choices at each point in the conversation that are likely to lead to connection. With connection, you and the other person will be more likely to create a mutually satisfying outcome.

MANAGING YOUR STRESS RESPONSE

We have already talked quite a bit about the stress response. Your habitual triggers may have gotten you into the conflict in the first place, and if you are in an ongoing relationship with the person, it's likely that during your conversation you will become triggered, probably multiple times. Expect this, and guard against assigning meaning to it when it happens. When you are triggered, it is simply "what is" in that current moment, and you have various tools you can choose from to manage it.

Doing the inner work of the previous three chapters before a conversation (if possible) will go a long way toward helping you be more centered throughout the conversation. It will also continue to solidify the body memory of self-connection and your ability to come back quickly to presence and make a choice. The IPM map also includes a step to help you remember to tap into your body memory of self-connection. If you discover that your fight or flight reaction keeps you from being able to continue in the process the way you wish, you can always request a time-out so that you can do more inner work, then return to the conversation.

BELIEVING "I'M RIGHT!" AND UNWILLINGNESS TO HEAR ANOTHER PERSPECTIVE

When you are in a conflict, do you think you're right and the other person is simply not seeing the way things are, that they aren't getting it? If so, you're not alone, but when you believe you're right, by implication the other person is wrong. Fixed in this viewpoint and desperately wanting your reality to be heard and understood by the other person, you have no space to hear the other person's reality. This is the paradox of conflict: both parties have their own realities they want the other person to not only understand, but also to agree with. It's no wonder conflicts often become entrenched!

Mediator mind and the three-chair model are key to stepping out of being right and becoming willing to hear the other person. You'll recall that when you frame an interpersonal conflict in terms of mediation, you are playing two roles. Since you don't have someone to act in the role of a mediator to help you resolve the dispute, you are your own mediator—you are playing the role of yourself in conflict with the other person, as well as the role of the mediator trying to facilitate empathic connection and collaborative resolution.

This is where the three-chair model applies. Because you are playing two roles, you can imagine there's a third chair present and you are moving between two of them. At times you are in the "self" chair across from the other person—the place where you have your thoughts, perspective, and emotions about the conflict, including becoming triggered into judgments, emotional reactions, and conflict patterns. When you move to the inner mediator's chair, you access mediator mind, use the mediation skills, track where in the process you are, and make choices about what to do next. From the mediator's chair you move back into the "self" chair to carry out the choices you made, empathize with the other person, and express your own point of view. The more you have practiced the SCP, Intensity Exercise, and EIP, the more comfortable you will be bringing mediator mind back to the "self" chair and interacting with the other person from that expanded perspective.

When you can keep the three-chair model and the role of the mediator in mind, it reminds you that the other person is probably thinking exactly the same thing as you: they know *they're* right and *you're* just not getting it! The physicality of moving between chairs during practice helps you to embody the perspective of the mediator, which is a view that understands the importance of you both being heard. It helps you step out of your own "rightness" to be able to support the two of you becoming connected and resolving the issue at hand.

PRACTICE PAUSE

Are you willing to step out of your rigidly held beliefs enough to be able to at least attempt to understand and see the perspective of the other person? Do you trust in yourself to learn to do that?

FEAR THAT HEARING A DIFFERENT PERSPECTIVE IS GIVING UP OR DEATH

Think of a recent conflict you were in, and name the viewpoint that was at the core of the conflict. For example, perhaps you and your partner were at odds over a decision affecting one of your children, or you differed with a coworker about the best way to proceed on a project. If nothing comes to mind, think instead about a strong viewpoint you hold, perhaps a political or ethical idea. Tap into your perspective and really stand in it. Now, what happens for you when you imagine being open to sincerely hearing the other person in the conflict, or someone who has a very different political/ethical viewpoint from yours? What happens in your body? Is there any sense of gripping, a kind of hitch in you, or resistance even to the idea?

One of the reasons it's difficult to be willing to hear another person's viewpoint is that most people have a deep fear of having to give something up if they are open to another perspective. When you really listen and try to see the world as another person sees it, you have to let go of your own perspective a little bit, holding your beliefs about what's true and the way the world is a bit more lightly in order to step into their world.

Identity and perspective are intimately intertwined. Your views and beliefs form a large part of your identity, and loosening your hold on them, or perhaps their hold on you, can feel like a threat to your very identity. When you confront expanding your perspective, it can easily feel like you might lose yourself and disappear. In short, it can feel like a death.

In his book, *On Becoming a Person: A Therapist's View of Psychotherapy*, psychologist Carl Rogers talks about how frightening it can be for people to empathize with someone with whom they disagree because they may be changed in some way. They'll have to let go of something they've been holding onto, which can threaten an inner sense of safety and security. In discussing why empathic understanding is not more widely used, Rogers said:

> In the first place it takes courage ... If you really understand another person in this way, if you are willing to enter his private world and see the way life appears to him, without any attempt to make evaluative judgments, you run the risk of being changed yourself. You might see it his way; you might find yourself influenced in your attitudes or your personality. This risk of being changed is one of the most frightening prospects most of us can face.

It takes courage and trust to know that if you are willing to see from another's perspective, your existence is not going to terminate. Being able to develop the mediator mind creates a space of willingness and curiosity, a desire to understand the other person without its being a violation of your existence or truth. Reading this section will probably not convince you of this, but the truth is, you will not be obliterated if you hear their perspective. The fear of losing identity is so deeply ingrained in most people that it takes experience to develop the courage and trust that hearing another person's truth is not a threat to your own truth and identity.

If you notice the reaction you experienced in the prior exercise coming up during a conversation, you can remind yourself that this is a fear of having to give something up to hear the other person.

Tell yourself that just because you are listening doesn't mean you've conceded or let go of your truth—you are simply listening. If you stay present, pay attention, and use the tools, you can find your way forward.

If it comes up before a conversation, this fear can be a significant form of resistance that is often helpful to work on ahead of time. The Enemy Image Process is one tool you can use; in doing so, you may find this fear arising when you start to empathize with the other person. If this happens, go back to the first step of EIP and empathize more with yourself. Through experience and practice, you will build the capacity to stay present with your own reactions without acting them out, and to accept the other person for where they are. Even when you don't agree with their strategies, you can accept what's true for them without losing yourself in the process.

FEAR OF SPEAKING YOUR TRUTH

We want to stress that even though a lot of focus in mediating conflict conversations goes to empathizing with the other person, *you also need to be able to speak your truth.* Many people find honesty difficult in a conflict; it may be scary to say some things because of fear about how the other person will react, especially if they become upset or angry. You may even be afraid of physical or verbal violence being directed at you if you speak your truth. We want to acknowledge that these fears might well be real.

Having your needs met, however, requires your honesty. It requires the courage to speak what's true for you even though, no matter how you say it, the other person could still hear it in a way that triggers a reaction. Despite that risk, creating connection demands having the courage to speak. If the other person reacts in a negative way, you can empathize with their truth, strive to hear how reality looks to them, and understand their feelings and needs. At the same time, you can stay connected to yourself and your own truth. Connection is equally about being able to empathize and be honest.

It's important here to note that we're not talking about the courage to blurt out your judgments about the other person. All too often, people perceive speaking their "truth" as letting out all the mean, spiteful, or judgmental thoughts they've been holding back. Hurling these at the other person causes a kind of cathartic release, which is a fleeting satisfaction. It may feel good in the moment to speak freely and tell someone what you think about them, but it generally doesn't create what you want in the relationship, in your life, or in the world. In fact, it usually creates exactly the opposite of what you truly want and value.

The courage to be honest we are referring to requires building both skills and capacity: skill to be honest in a way that does not make you right and the other person wrong; capacity to hear and respond to the other person—regardless of what they do in reaction to your honesty—with understanding.

PRACTICE PAUSE

Think of a specific situation in which you find expressing your truth scary or difficult. Give yourself empathy by naming your feelings and needs.

FOCUSING ON PROBLEMS, STRATEGIES, AND SOLUTIONS

"Well, of course I want to focus on the solution!" you say. "I want out of the conflict!" This common approach to conflict comes from the belief that if you can adequately define the problem and find the strategy or solution through it, all will be well. You and the other person can each happily ride off into the sunset because you have the answer to the problem.

This may work in the sense that you get to some kind of solution; however, we don't find focusing on the solution to be the most effective way through a conflict, nor to be the most likely to result in healing or lead to the best solutions. Why?

First, because your definition of the problem may be quite different from the other person's, hence your answer to it will also be different. For example, James sees the problem as Scott not respecting his role as team lead or considering his view on whether a particular person will work well on the team. Scott may not see any problem at all, or he may see a different problem, such as that James is only considering his work and not the whole of the company. Without understanding how each person sees the conflict, it is likely to stay entrenched.

Second, reconciliation does not necessarily occur out of a good solution. If the underlying disconnect is not addressed, the conflict may not actually be over. The solution is merely a temporary fix, and you'll find that the conflict erupts again later. When you focus on connection first, reconciliation has a greater chance to occur and the solution that you arrive at more likely to stick.

Third, when people arrive at solutions through the typical means in a conflict—compromise—they may not have reached the ideal solution. Why? Because compromise means that each person has to give something up and give in. When that's how people approach a resolution, the level of investment in making it work may not be very high. But when people are connected, they *collaborate* toward a solution, motivated to contribute to each other's needs in a way that optimizes what's possible for everyone.

Connection lends to reaching solutions that people feel pleased about, and therefore more invested in following through. Plus, the solutions people come up with when working together tend to be better, meaning they are more creative and usually meet people's needs more effectively. Collaborating toward a solution is a completely different framework from everyone having to give something up.

A primary difference between mediation based on the tools of Nonviolent Communication and other forms of conflict resolution is this: the place to focus when in conflict is on *connection*, not resolution. When you focus on connection first and foremost, a strategy will emerge. To be clear, strategies and solutions are not eliminated when you seek connection; it's merely a different path to achieve the desired outcome. This shift to connection serves two purposes—it repairs relationships, and it tends to create better solutions because people collaborate rather than compromise.

Ultimately, this works because when the focus is on needs—the underlying motivations behind different perspectives—there is no separation. Each point of view rests on a foundation of what is fulfilling and life-enhancing for all of us, and can exist without being criticized because each is valid for someone. The connection phase is intended to take you to this level of understanding and commonality.

When that goal is reached and opposing perspectives connect with each other, the solution typically appears quite readily. We see again and again that within the chaos of conflict, there's a natural kind of emergent order—the strategies and solutions arise and synthesize once you create connection.

—∿∿—

Sally comes downstairs and curls up next to James on the couch, smiling with relief. "Finished the story and Maggie's asleep."

"And I said good night to Corey," James says. "He was still reading but said he'd turn off the light in a few minutes." James reaches for Sally's hand. "I'm really glad we talked earlier about this morning, at least a little bit. I know we need to have a longer conversation about it, and I really want to tell you about this conversation with my dad today, but would you be willing right now to help me with this situation I have at work?"

"Sure. What's going on?"

James fills Sally in on his meeting with Aaron and the team, and his anger at Scott's assigning Aaron without letting James have a say in the decision. Then he tells her about his brief conversation with Scott before leaving.

"I got clammed up. I realized I'd started all wrong in the first place, and then he said Aaron was perfect for the team, and it was like I had no right then to have another opinion." James shakes his head. "Now I'm just stuck."

Sally nods as she shifts her position toward James. "It sounds like you were confused about what to say, especially since his words didn't match your experience of the situation. Is that right?"

James stands up and starts pacing. "Yeah, I mean he's my boss, so I'm torn. I want to stand up for myself—he's wrong to do something like that without considering the effect on me and the rest of the team. But now if I talk about it, I think he's going to see it as I can't manage my team. I already feel like he's not respecting me, and that will just add to it."

"So is it respect that you're really wanting?" Sally asks.

James nods. "It is, and that came up too when I was thinking about Aaron. But also just, I don't know, consideration? That Scott would have the decency to know that adding a new person to the team is going to shift things ... talking to me about it before making the decision would have been nice. Is that too much to ask?"

"So you would have liked him to ask you, is that right?" Sally says.

"Yeah, exactly!" James exclaims.

"And for you, being asked is really about consideration for your role and respect for your position as the team lead?" Sally asks, clarifying what she's heard.

"Yes, I'd like to know that he understands the impact and is supporting me."

Sally nods. "Are you afraid when you think of talking to him about this?"

"I guess so. I'd like to be able to stand firm in what's going on for me, to talk to him about it and trust that he'll hear me."

James sits back on the couch. Connecting with his needs, he feels a little more grounded. He then asks Sally to use the Enemy Image Process with him to help him empathize with Scott. In doing this, James guesses that Scott wants things to go well in his department and that he'd appreciate the support of the people who work for him. He also thinks that perhaps Scott would like to be trusted for his decisions and the wisdom of his experience.

In the third stage of the EIP, James reflects on how he feels about the situation after empathizing, and then he asks Sally to role-play a conversation with Scott. By the time they are finished, James knows he has a good plan for how to approach his boss.

—∿∿—

MEDIATING YOUR OWN CONFLICT

With the many challenges we've outlined for being in a difficult conversation, how do you learn to navigate one with any sense of ease or success? We suggest focusing on three primary tools:

+ a **framework** to orient yourself in the conversation

+ a **map** to follow

+ a set of mediation **skills**

The framework that will help you orient yourself is the *mediator mind.* We've discussed it already in each of the previous chapters— it is the place of awareness within yourself where you can step out of your perspective enough to see both viewpoints and mediate between them, even when you are part of the conflict. It helps you shift out of being in a face-off with the other person—me against you—and into that broader perspective in which you can be present, step outside your habitual reactions, and be in the world in the way you desire. In short, it orients you to what you can do and the choices you have available.

The map we provide is the *Interpersonal Mediation map*, which is a set of five steps we will detail shortly to navigate the conversation.

There are two *mediation skills* integral to using the IPM map, and seven additional skills that, once you are familiar with the map, can help you choose from all possible options in mediating a conflict between yourself and another person. Though we will outline all the skills in this chapter, we encourage you to focus first on learning the two skills that are included in the steps of the map.

You already know from the mediator mind orienting framework that the basic premise in mediating a conflict is that there are at least two perspectives—or two conflicting points of view—and the mediation process reconciles those points of view. Reconciliation

happens by uncovering the needs that the points of view represent;
once the needs of each perspective are known and understood, they
are connected through shared needs and a strategy can be found to
reconcile the points of view. Another way to regard this is through
the thesis/antithesis/synthesis model. The two points of view—
thesis and antithesis—resolve into a synthesis when the perspectives reach understanding and connection.

Though this may sound like a complex set of steps, you'll soon
see that the process is quite simple and follows a natural progression. Once you're familiar with it, you'll inherently fall into the
prescribed pattern, becoming a master at diffusing and resolving
conflict. All it takes is awareness and practice.

There are two phases involved in mediating a conflict: Connection and Resolution. In the connection phase, you surface and
understand the needs of each perspective. In the resolution stage,
you reach a synthesis, a strategy that will meet the needs of each
point of view. In the table that follows, you can see how the phases
of connection and resolution are linked to the process and steps of
the Interpersonal Mediation map and the nine mediation skills.

INTERPERSONAL MEDIATION (IPM) MAP

1. PERFORM THE SELF-CONNECTION PROCESS (move into
   mediator mind)

2. ASK YOURSELF, "CAN I HEAR THE MESSAGE AS A
   'PLEASE'?"

3. EMPATHIZE WITH THE OTHER, IF YOU CAN

4. SELF-EXPRESS

5. MAKE SOLUTION REQUESTS AND AGREEMENTS

	CONNECTION		RESOLUTION
Mediating Between Yourself and Another	**A's Needs**	**B's Needs**	**Synthesis/ Strategy to meet all Needs**
Process	Empathize with other person: surface other person's needs through guessing and reflection	Connect with yourself, express your own needs, ask other person to reflect your needs	Engage in dialogue regarding how both of you can get needs met. What do you want to give to them? What do they want to give to you?
IPM Steps	1. Perform the Self-Connection Process 2. Ask Yourself, "Can I hear the message as a 'please'?" 3. Empathize with the Other, if you can 4. Self-Express		5. Make Solution Requests and Agreements
Nine Mediation Skills	1. Empathy 2. Connection Requests 3. Pulling by the Ears 4. Emergency Empathy 5. Tracking 6. Interrupting 7. Self-Empathy 8. Self-Expression		9. Solution Requests

mediateyourlife.com/interpersonal-mediation-map-video/

To put the following steps into a context for you, we've created a scenario that will progress through each one. The setup is as follows:

> Janet and Donna have been close friends for fifteen years, frequently reaching out to each other to share positive news and to seek support in difficult times. Lunching together one day, Janet brings up a challenge she's having with her teenage daughter Rae. "Every time I try to talk to her, she just gives a 'humph' back and stays buried in her cell phone or iPad, texting or who knows what with her friends. It's really driving me up the wall."
>
> Donna replies, "Oh, well, she's a teenager. She probably just thinks you're going to complain about something or tell her what to do. Leave her be."
>
> Janet notices her body become tense on hearing Donna's response. All the signs of her stress response show up: her neck and spine feel rigid, her breath is shallow, and her shoulders creep up toward her ears. Realizing her strong desire to leave or change the subject indicates that she has interpreted Donna's words as judgmental, flippant, and discounting her concerns, Janet immediately recognizes that she is in a difficult conversation and begins to use the IPM map.

STEP 1:
PERFORM THE SELF-CONNECTION PROCESS

The first step of the Interpersonal Mediation (IPM) map is to perform the Self-Connection Process we discussed in Chapter 2.

SCP is first because people often find they are easily triggered when in conflict with others. Even if you are going into a difficult conversation having prepared ahead of time and feeling centered, a difficult conversation can easily throw you off.

Performing SCP has two main purposes:

1. It helps to connect you to yourself in the present moment by anchoring you in your body and with your needs.

2. It reminds you of the mediator mind perspective.

We mentioned in Chapter 2 that SCP is a way to step into mediator mind, and in practicing it as part of the Intensity Exercise, you'll recall that we ask you to move into the mediator chair. By actually switching chairs, you learn to associate the SCP with being in mediator mind, sitting at a ninety-degree angle to the conflict. The mediator perspective reminds you that you and the other person have different perspectives; it also reminds you that you are more likely to be satistied with the outcome if you include the other person's needs, not just yours, in the resolution you seek.

From Chapter 2, you'll recall that the steps of the SCP are:

1. BREATH
   Focus on your breath, increasing the length of the exhale to be longer than than your inhale.

2. BODY
   Focus on feeling your body sensations, then name what you're feeling.

3. NEEDS
   Identify one or more needs.

Janet performs the Self-Connection Process by first taking a deep breath. She feels the sensations in her body and identifies emotions of anger and sadness. Reminding herself of the feeling of being centered, she quickly finds it, having practiced SCP daily. *What needs are not met here?* she asks herself, and notices she'd like care and understanding.

STEP 2:
ASK YOURSELF: "CAN I HEAR THE MESSAGE
AS A 'PLEASE'?"

The second step of the IPM map is to ask yourself, "Can I hear the other person saying 'please'?" This comes from the idea that when someone is speaking, they are either asking "please" or saying "thank you." When you can listen underneath the person's words to hear whether they are asking for unmet needs to be met or expressing gratitude for needs that are being met, you can respond by connecting with them at a deeper level than when you stay with the surface thoughts they are expressing.

For instance, a father says in exasperation to his teenager, "If you don't learn this lesson now, it's going to get in your way for the rest of your life!" Can you hear that he is asking for his son to *please* learn the lesson? Or, when a motorist yells out his window, "You crazy fool, watch where you're going!" can you hear the driver saying, "Please drive more carefully. I was frightened by the wreck you nearly caused."

In a conflict, expressions of appreciation are unlikely. If the person you are in conflict with is expressing their frustration or telling you what they think is wrong with you, you might be inclined to take what they say personally and react defensively, either submitting or counter-attacking. Asking yourself if you can hear a "please" prompts you to shift perspective and step into mediator mind for a moment. It serves to remind you that something is going on in that person that they are saying "please" about —in other words, they have some needs they desire to have met, and what they are saying is an attempt to meet those needs.

Similar to the first step, this one is also entirely internal. You don't ask the other person out loud if they are saying "please," but rather infer it to be able to hear them with less reactivity, and to look for the needs they might be trying to meet.

Choice is key in the IPM map—these first two steps are designed to raise your awareness if you are in any way triggered by what's going on. If so, you will be able to be present with yourself and choose a response that is in harmony with your values, instead of one stemming from feelings and habitual reactions.

Reminding herself of the second step, Janet thinks, *Can I hear what Donna has said as a "please"? Is there something she wants from our conversation or from me?*

STEP 3:
EMPATHIZE WITH THE OTHER, IF YOU CAN

As a mediator, one of the primary choices to make is where you want to focus the empathy—toward yourself or the other person. When the attention is focused away from you, you are using the skill of empathy to help the other person be heard in the way they desire. This is the step in which you are being courageous about releasing any fixation on your own beliefs and being willing to hear the other person's perspective. As such, we suggest you choose to empathize with the other person, if you are able to. If you are in too much pain to do so, move ahead to Step 4.

We identify four elements of empathy:

+ Presence

+ Silent Empathy

+ Understanding

+ Need Language

PRESENCE

The first element of empathy is to be able to be present with someone. To do this, simply bring your attention to that person, focusing on your perceptions of their tone, body language, facial expressions, and all the information that's coming from them, verbal or nonverbal. Presence is about taking all of this in without thinking about it or trying to understand it, but simply being with them in a holistic way. Another way to say this is that presence is about directly connecting to what is "alive" in the other person, listening from the heart rather than the head.

SILENT EMPATHY

In the second element, you shift into thinking about what this person is trying to say—what's going on in them, what's important to them, what they are thinking, wanting, or needing—but doing it all silently. You might choose this option when you don't predict that saying something to the other person will help or is what they want, so you silently connect with their feelings and needs as they are speaking.

UNDERSTANDING

In the first two elements of empathy, you are with the person silently, either only in your presence or in connecting with their feelings and needs. In the third element of understanding, you respond verbally to what you are hearing from them. The intention of understanding is to let the person know you are hearing them the way they want to be heard. To do this, you repeat their words— guessing what's deeper or inserting your own interpretation—by simply reflecting the essence of what you've heard, either using some of their words or paraphrasing with your own, or both.

NEED LANGUAGE

In the fourth element of empathy, you use the language of needs to reflect what you're hearing the person say. You can reflect observations, feelings, needs, or what the person wants, but the most helpful component to focus on is needs. Needs not only help connect you to what is alive in the person, but they also help the other person clarify their deeper motivations. Strive to hear the needs behind their thoughts, feelings, desires—and even their enemy images of you.

When you reflect any of the other components of observations, feelings, or requests, you can also tie it back to needs, making the relationship between them clear. In other words, instead of simply reflecting that someone is upset, you might say, "Are you upset because you would like to be cared about?" Or rather than only reflecting a strategy, you can tie that to a need by saying, "It sounds like you really want Jane to apologize because that would give you a sense that you matter."

NEEDS

Observation/ Evaluation	Feelings/ Thoughts	Strategies	Requests/ Demands

When you use the elements of empathy, you might start in the sequential order we offer, from presence to silent empathy to understanding to need language. Once you are more used to each element, you can sense moment to moment which one you predict is going to be most connecting. There is not a right or wrong choice; it's simply about making a choice and seeing what happens, and then possibly making another choice, always learning from whatever is happening.

The element of presence is first because it is largely the foundation from which the others emerge. If you can always be in presence, choosing one of the other three becomes easier; in presence there's no anxiety to choose correctly or have the right answer, and no being stuck or muted by fear that you don't have the answer. You are simply present at every point in time with the other person as you choose one of the other three elements, being in tune with what happens from there. How does that work? When you are present, you can trust and rely on your intention, and there's a level of intuition that emerges that lets you know what to try next. When you have the calmness that comes with presence, you can listen for the next choice that would contribute to what you want to create.

Why do we recommend beginning with empathy for the other person? Marshall Rosenberg used to say, "Empathy before education." Before you try to educate the other person about what you would like them to hear from you about the situation, first hear their perspective and strive to discern their needs. In this way, you help them meet their need for empathy.

For example, James would like Scott to hear his point of view about adding someone to the team without consulting him. If James simply tries to tell Scott his perspective, Scott may not be able to hear it since he has a different point of view. James can increase the chance that Scott will hear him by first understanding where Scott is coming from, and *letting Scott know that he understands*. When Scott knows that James has heard what matters to him—when his need for empathy is met—he will be open to hearing what matters to James.

While you don't have to take this approach, we have found that it's more likely to lead to *your* being heard for what you desire, and more quickly. As Steven Covey's maxim states: "Seek first to understand, then to be understood." Yes, it can be difficult to listen and empathize when you want to express your perspective. Yet, if you can hear the other person to the point where *they are satisfied* that you have understood them, it opens up a whole set of possibilities for moving forward in the conversation.

In times when you don't feel you have the capacity to empathize first, because it's difficult to be willing or able to hear the other person or to guess their feelings and needs, move ahead to Step 4. If you can speak your truth in a way that provides you some empathy, it can also sometimes help the other person hear you in a new way.

> Though she doesn't have an immediate answer, just asking herself the questions, *Can I hear what Donna has said as a "please"?* and *Is there something she wants from our conversation or from me?* makes Janet curious. Though still feeling a bit hurt, she has enough space to wonder what is going on for Donna and decides to empathize. Feeling like it's a stab in the dark, she says, "Did you tell me to leave her be, hoping it would help me?"
>
> Donna shrugs. "Yeah, you two have been at odds for a long time. Maybe you could lay off a little."

STEP 4: SELF-EXPRESS

In the fourth step, you shift the spotlight back to yourself. You may have empathized with the other person for awhile, and they may be feeling more heard, but *you* still need to be heard. And you still need empathy for what's going on in *you*.

Courage resides within Step 4 in speaking your truth, even if it's hard for the other person to hear, as well as expressing yourself in a way that does not blame or make yourself right and the other person wrong. In short, you simply say how you see things (observations), what you are feeling, what your needs are, and what you would like as a result.

Since you are facilitating your own conversation, at times it can be difficult to discern when to move from empathizing to expressing yourself. As such, you can always ask yourself the question, "What do I predict will create connection between us right now?"

One way you might know the other person is ready to hear you is through their body language and tone of voice. They may be more relaxed than they were initially, with softer facial muscles and shoulders dropped, and their voice lower and quieter.

Another way to tell that they are ready to hear you is when they start asking you questions. They may say, "Why did you do that?" or "What's going on with you?" or "What do you have to say about that?" When you make the choice to move into expression, you remain in the mediator perspective but shift the focus to yourself, essentially asking the other person to listen and empathize with you. You're expressing your own truth and honesty.

To begin, ask yourself if there is anything you now want the other person to hear. What observations, feelings, needs, and requests are you aware of at this moment? Which of those do you want to reveal to meet your needs in the conversation?

Here are some possibilities for how you might express yourself:

+ Tell the other person how you feel having heard what they just said, tying it to your needs, such as "When I hear you say that, I feel sad because I care about you and would like to contribute to your well-being."

✦ Connect first with the needs you want met in the situation with this person, and then express by letting what you say to them flow naturally from your attention on those needs. Do your best to own your perceptions and thoughts, and to connect your thoughts, feelings, and what you'd like from this person to meet your needs.

✦ You might use the "training wheel" sentence, which incorporates all four of the components, or focus in on only one or two, such as feelings and needs. As you may recall from *Choosing Peace*, the basic format of the training wheel sentence is: "When I see/hear ... [Observation], I feel ... [Feeling], because I need ... [Need]. Would you be willing to ... [Request]? Note: Generally, letting them know your needs will be the most connecting.

Reacting anew to Donna's words, Janet does SCP again, taking a deeper breath, feeling her anguish, and connecting to her needs for respect, consideration for all she's done with her daughter, and understanding for how difficult it's been. She then does Step 2 again, asking herself, *Can I hear a "please" in what Donna is saying?* Though she does get that Donna cares, Janet feels stirred up by the whole situation and frustrated about not getting the support she wants. She doesn't feel like she has the capacity to empathize, so she decides instead to express what she does want.

"Donna, I really get that you're trying to help, and I do want help, but what you're saying to me isn't helping right now. I'm frustrated ... I've put so much into trying to support my daughter and be in a good relationship with her. Can you just, for right now, tell me what you're hearing me say? I want to make sure I'm being understood."

Donna looks surprised. "Well, I hear that you're frustrated about what's happening with Rae. I guess with Roy I'm just more hands-off." Donna pauses, sighing. "Maybe I already gave up because I haven't felt like I can get through to him."

CONNECTION AS AN ITERATIVE PROCESS

These first four steps form the connection phase of the IPM map. During this phase, mediator mind and the IPM map give you something to hold onto in the disorienting rapids: What are your needs? What are the other's needs? and Are you hearing each other's needs?

Remember that while the five steps of the IPM map are intended to give you a navigation aid in the turbulent waters of a difficult conversation, *it is always your choice what to do at each point in the conversation.* We have found these steps to be simple enough to remember in those times we have the least capacity to do so, and to keep us on track with our goal: to act out of our values instead of our conflict habits, creating connection with the other person to find a mutually satisfying resolution.

Connection most often emerges out of alternating between empathizing with the other person and expressing yourself. The steps of the IPM map are an attempt to give some guidelines about when to choose either one, and to help you remember to stay connected to yourself on the way to connection with the other person.

The Connection phase is rarely a simple process whereby you empathize with the other person, express yourself, and you're finished. Instead, think of it as a progression through these steps multiple times on the way to connection with the other person. Here's a short outline of how the process unfolds:

+ Perform Steps 1 and 2 internally, grounding yourself and becoming curious about the other.

+ Go to Step 3 and empathize if you can.

  · If you can empathize with the other person, do so.

  · If you can't empathize, go to Step 4 and express
    yourself.

+ Listen for the other person's response to your empathy or
  expression.

+ Begin again at Steps 1 and 2, grounding yourself and
  asking if you can hear a "please."

Each time the person responds, it's like a reset point where you connect again to what's going on in you, remind yourself to look for the "please" in what the other person has said, and then move to Step 3.

At some point, if you've been able to empathize, you may become aware that the other person's need for empathy has been met, and you may choose then to express yourself instead of empathizing further. Though the focus is often on empathy to create connection, telling the other person what's going on for you can also achieve that result.

In other words, becoming connected is an iterative process, one that requires repetition. When starting out, it's helpful to create a guideline for yourself going into the conversation, such as deciding you will always at least make one empathic guess when the other person says something, no matter how much you want to respond immediately.

Equally important in the connection phase, of course, is staying connected with *yourself*. Being able to express yourself in a way that is more likely to lead to connection is dependent on your self-connection. Having said that, however, it is also a good idea to give yourself a break. When first learning, you may find that staying connected with your own feelings and needs while in a difficult conversation is impossible. If so, you may want to practice taking breaks or time-outs from the conversation, reconnecting to yourself, then coming back to it. As you practice more and more on your own to get reconnected with your feelings and needs, you will be able to find your own shortcuts that will help you stay connected within a conversation.

As a conflict conversation evolves, the needs often change; as much as possible, strive to stay connected with yourself and your needs *at each moment*. Knowing your needs, you can then express them to help the other person better connect with you. At the same time, you want to stay in touch with what the other person's needs are, since they are also likely to shift throughout the conversation.

Let's see how Janet and Donna's needs continue to shift in their conversation.

Janet quickly connects to herself again using SCP, noticing that she still doesn't quite feel heard. When she considers whether she can hear a "please," she realizes that Donna may want empathy for her relationship with her teenage son, which is the same thing that Janet would really like from Donna. Choosing to empathize, she says, "Oh, so you're feeling hopeless about improving your relationship with Roy and are trying a more hands-off approach? And when you heard me express my frustration, did you want to show your care by offering that as a possible way forward?"

Donna looks thoughtful. "Yeah, I guess so, I've been thinking it's impossible to change things with Roy. But then I feel bad about that when I see how much you still try with Rae. I know how much you care for her and I've seen you go the extra mile so many times. I guess I just spoke out of my hopelessness when you started talking about Rae. I don't feel good about what I'm doing either."

Janet's needs start out as care and understanding, and quickly shift to respect and consideration after Donna responds to Janet's empathy. Janet's guesses of Donna's needs also shift, from a desire to help to wanting empathy for her relationship to her son.

Most interpersonal conflict situations are complex to a degree; as such, when there is any intensity in the conversation, the process of becoming connected will be extended. You can still use the basic model as a guide, but be aware that the connection phase will likely be significantly longer, with a lot of back and forth, striving to hear the other person and to be heard and understood yourself. It's normal to be triggered multiple times and to have to stop to give some self-empathy, or to get angry and judge the other person, then catch it and go back to empathy and expressing needs. In the actual doing, the process is rarely elegant! Nonetheless, by using these steps and sticking with it, you can both become connected and understand what is going on for each other. When that is achieved, it's then time to move into the resolution phase and talk about requests and agreements.

RESOLUTION PHASE

In the connection stage, the focus is on striving to understand and connect with each other; when you move into the fifth and final step of the IPM map—the resolution stage—you shift to focus on the concrete actions, solutions, agreements, and strategies that will resolve the issue between you and the other person. The goal is to come to a resolution that emerges out of being connected, and that is about contributing to one another's well-being. This goal arises out of the practical insight that in order to arrive at a resolution by mutual agreement, both of you must be sufficiently satisfied to say "yes." For this to happen, at least one of you must understand that in order for your needs to be met, so must the other's.

In those interpersonal conflicts where there has been a misunderstanding, all that's commonly needed is the connection phase. The misunderstanding is cleared up, the conflict peters out, both of you move on, and neither one of you has any requests of the other.

In many cases, however, you or the other person may have some requests, and the resolution phase is where you work together to reach a strategy that will meet the needs of both of you. The transition between the connection and resolution phases is often quite fluid; both you and the other person feel heard and naturally move into resolution. If, however, either of you needs to be heard again, you may move back into the connection phase before returning again to requests.

STEP 5:
MAKE SOLUTION REQUESTS AND AGREEMENTS

The fifth step of the IPM map is also one of the mediation skills: making solution requests and agreements. From the mediator mind perspective, in this step you are taking all the needs that you and the other person have surfaced, and facilitating the process of making requests that will meet those needs.

There are three aspects of making solution requests, each of which supports the intention to create resolution that meets everyone's needs.

First is the nuts and bolts, meaning that when we talk about requests, we signify they are present, positive, and in action language.

- ✦ **Present** means you are clear that you're asking for a present-time agreement; even if you are making an agreement about something in the future, you're clear that you're simply asking for the person's present intention to do something in the future.

+ **Positive** means you ask for what you want instead of what you don't want.

+ **Action language** indicates something doable, specific, and concrete.

A second aspect of solution requests is to make a *request* and not a *demand*. If your true intention is to request, you are open to hearing a "no" from the other person; in fact, you want to hear a "no" if that is the truth. You are also willing to empathize with anything less than a full "yes," sincere in your desire for the other person to do what you ask *only* if they can do it with true willingness, and preferably from the eagerness and enjoyment of contributing to your well-being. Another element of this skill is to hear a request from the other person, even if the way they say it sounds more like they're making a demand. (See *Choosing Peace* for more details on the elements of a request.)

The third aspect of solution requests is to come from a sense of interdependence. This means that your focus is not just on having needs met for yourself; rather, it's on trying to meet the other person's needs as well as yours, and asking them to do the same. Interdependence comes from an understanding that you are not likely to have a satisfying result unless everyone's needs are met. You can view interdependence as both a value to hold, and a highly practical and effective way to meet your own needs.

Once a request is on the table that both of you can agree to—meaning that both of you think it might meet your needs—you can reach an agreement. We will cover what types of agreements to make in detail in the next chapter.

As Janet connects with herself and listens for the "please" in Donna's words, she notices that her own need for empathy was met just in hearing that Donna shares her feelings. She wonders whether they might find a way to support each other more directly with their teenage children.

Deciding to make a request, she says, "Would it help you if we were able to talk about when something happens with our kids and brainstorm different things we might try? I know how easy it is to go into hopelessness when you try something and it doesn't work, but maybe we can help each other by talking about it and coming up with strategies. What do you think?"

Donna nods. "Yeah, I don't want to give up on my relationship with Roy. And I'd love to see you and Rae more like you used to be when you were so close. Maybe we could see this as a fresh start with them. Would you like to set a time each week to talk about this?"

Janet smiles. "Yes, we generally talk anyway, but I think it would be great to know that we're going to connect at a particular time about what's going on with our kids and what we're doing."

If you are in an ongoing relationship with the other person in the conflict, the request phase is often about working on agreements for dealing with similar situations in the future. Janet and Donna, for example, might make additional agreements about how to respond when one of the them states a concern, or how much to listen versus give advice when they have discussions about their kids.

mediateyourlife.com/interpersonal-mediation-map-video/

> ## PRACTICE PAUSE
>
> Think of a recent request you've made or one you would like to make. Write it down and consider it in light of the three aspects of solution requests. Do you see ways to improve the request itself or how you think about making it?

—⁓—

Before stepping into the office to talk to Scott, James takes a couple of deep breaths and connects with his feelings and needs in that moment. He realizes he feels some trepidation going into the conversation, which is arising out of wanting to be heard and understood. He then walks into Scott's office with the intention to stay present and to hear Scott. James begins by letting Scott know why he is there.

"Scott, I wanted to talk to you about the decision to put Aaron on my team. This decision affected me significantly and you didn't talk to me about it first. I would have liked my perspective to be taken into account. It's important to me that you feel respected and that we have good, honest communication between us, so I'm wondering how it is for you hearing what I'm saying."

"Well, I can't take everybody's input into account in making decisions," Scott says. "That would take much too long and just isn't feasible. I really don't see what the problem is."

James remembers to step into mediator mind when he hears this and takes a deep breath, connecting again with his feelings and needs. He reminds himself of his intention to empathize with Scott and asks himself where Scott might be saying "please." Though he isn't quite sure, simply asking that question helps him remember to consider Scott's point of view.

"So, Scott, is it that you want me to understand what it's like to be in your position, making these kinds of decisions and the time pressures you're under? Would you like some understanding from me about that?"

Scott shrugs. "Yeah, of course. I don't think you understand what I'm dealing with."

James nods. "I do appreciate what you're saying about needing to make a lot of decisions at a high level in the organization, and that they're based on a lot of pressures I don't know about." James decides to let Scott know what is going on for him to see if he can hear it. "And, I'd really like some way of being included in decisions that affect me by having some input. I'm wondering how it is for you to hear that?"

Scott brushes the comment off. "Yeah, well, like I said, I don't have time for things like that. It's your job to make it work."

James knows that Scott needs more empathy if he is going to hear him, and again asks himself if he can hear a "please" in what Scott said. "It sounds like you'd just like to trust that those of us working for you will get the job done and not have to think about it?"

"Sure, I want to be able to rely on people and trust them to get things done." Scott throws up his hands as he continues. "I don't need to be nursemaiding them or tracking or paying attention or making sure everything is getting done."

James tries again to express what is going on for Scott. "I really want you to feel supported and to do everything I can to contribute to that, and I think I have a lot to contribute if I can be involved somehow in decisions that are going to be about my team and my area. I really believe it might be helpful to you, and it would give me a sense of being included in a way that I can feel supported also, which I think is important—that we both feel supported. I think I'll do a better job for you and for the company. Are you willing to let me know what you're hearing so I can see if I'm being clear in what I'm trying to say?"

"Okay," Scott says. "So you think it might help me to include you in these kinds of decisions, and you want both of us to be supported, not just me, and that it might work out better for the company."

"Exactly. And I really appreciate that you have so much respect for me and my work that you trust me to take care of things. I think that being included in some of these decisions will help us both. Would you be willing, even if you don't think my input could change anything, to still let me know before a decision is made, just in case there's something I could say that might make a difference? Like, for example with Aaron, just to let me know ahead of time?"

Scott glances away and crosses his arms. "Well, the truth is that with Aaron, I didn't have much choice. The decision was made higher up that he's too valuable to lose since he's been with the company for so long. They decided my area was the best place to put him, and you had just lost Matt, so I put him with you."

James returns to empathy for Scott before continuing with the request. "I see. So in that situation you didn't feel like you had much choice either?"

"Exactly. Sometimes I don't have as much say as I'd like either. That's just the way it is." Scott shakes his head. "I'm not sure it makes sense to bring decisions to you, even if they're potentially ones you could have input on. It's not going to be a productive use of time."

"So if we do it, you'd like to make sure it's a productive and efficient way to use time?" James asks.

"Sure. We all have a lot of pressure right now."

James continues with his request, hoping Scott feels heard enough to be willing to consider it.

"There may be some times I could contribute something you didn't predict and that actually could be really valuable, or even more productive in the long run. Can we just try it as an experiment for a short period to see if it works? We could see what we can learn from it, and if it doesn't work out, we'll stop doing it. Would you be willing to try it out for three months?"

Scott shrugs. "Okay. We'll try it out for three months."

―⁓⁓―

ADVANCED MEDIATION SKILLS

While a roadmap can come in handy to get to your destination, some additional skills are helpful to more successfully complete your trip. The IPM map is the set of steps to use in a difficult conversation, and the skills give you more of the *how*. They elucidate a limited set of choices you can use as you move through the map to stay connected with yourself, attempt to connect with the other person, and keep the conversation on track to resolution.

If you are in the early stages of learning the map, it may feel overwhelming enough without adding in these additional skills. If that's the case, you are welcome to keep focusing on learning and utilizing the steps of the map and the skills of Empathy and Solution Requests for the time being. As you become more familiar with the steps, you may find you're ready to incorporate more skills into your practice and conversations. When you reach that phase, you can come back to this section and begin mastering the skills outlined on the following pages. If you're not yet ready for these advanced skills, you may wish to move to page 182 and resume with the section, Notes on Having a Map.

As you begin using the IPM map in conversations, you will likely discover certain situations cropping up that you would like to know how to respond to effectively. These additional skills answer the common questions that arise when people try to mediate their own conflicts, such as, "What do I do when ...":

+ the other person doesn't answer my question?

+ the other person isn't listening to me when I express myself?

+ I find I'm having trouble following what the other person is saying?

+ I'm concerned about the way the conversation is going or how the other person is interacting with me?

+ I'm not sure the other person has understood what I've said?

+ the other person becomes triggered?

+ I become triggered?

A list of the advanced skills follows. While you may wonder how you'll juggle the various skills, don't worry—at the end of the chapter, we will talk about multiple ways to practice the framework, map, and skills so you can effectively use them when you are in a difficult conversation "in the wild."

+ Connection Requests

+ Pulling by the Ears

+ Emergency Empathy

+ Tracking

+ Interrupting

+ Self-Empathy

+ Self-Expression

CONNECTION REQUESTS

Connection Requests are those that are not about specific actions or solutions, but are intended to discern how connected you and the other person are to help you decide what to do next. Often Connection Requests are used during Step 4, when you are telling the other person what's going on for you. You use your skills to communicate your observations, feelings, needs, and requests, but you may still want to make sure that they are hearing what you would like them to hear. As such, you may want to pause periodically in what you are saying to check how connected they are to what they're hearing.

There are two types of Connection Requests: Message Sent, Message Received and Quality of Connection.

MESSAGE SENT, MESSAGE RECEIVED

It's easy for a message to be heard by the other person in a way you were not intending. Even if you weren't trying to be critical, blaming, judging, or demanding, the other person may still hear your words that way. To make sure they hear what you intend, you can make a request that will give you this information.

People typically ask, "Do you understand what I'm trying to say?" But the problem with this question is that it elicits a yes-no response, and even if the person says "yes," you still don't actually know *what it is they understood*. They may *think* they understand, but it may be very different from what you wanted them to hear.

To check if the message you sent was received the way you wished, you can say something like, "Just so I can trust I'm being heard the way I'd like, would you be willing to tell me what you've heard thus far from me?" or "Would you let me know what you heard me say?"

This request helps both of you. If the person is willing, you'll know by what they say if they've heard what you desired. If what they say is not what you intended, you have the chance to clarify it. You might say, "Thank you for saying what you heard, but I'd like you to hear it a little differently. I'd like you to hear that _____. Are you willing to tell me what you heard now?"

This request can also help the other person, because in the act of trying to repeat what they've understood, they often become a little clearer on it themselves. Let's face it: it's easy to not listen when someone else is talking; people often get caught up in formulating a rebuttal, disagreeing with what the other person is saying, or focusing on what they want to say next. But when you ask someone to let you know what they heard, it encourages them to pay attention, allowing your message to become clearer in their mind.

Through the tone of their voice as well as what they actually say, you can clarify not only whether they are *hearing* you as you would like, but if they are *reacting* to what they have heard. If they are triggered into a reaction and no longer connected and present with you, it often doesn't help to keep expressing—it's probably time to go back to empathy.

QUALITY OF CONNECTION

The other type of Connection Request is designed not so much to find out whether the other person heard you, but to check how they are reacting to it and what's going on for them in hearing you. The request here is, "How do you feel hearing what I've said?" or "What's your reaction to what I've said?" or any question that asks them to express their response to what they've heard. This question checks the connection in a different way; the information you receive both through body and verbal language is valuable for deciding what to do next. If they give you back a thought, such as,

"Well, I feel like you don't really understand what I'm saying," it may make more sense to go back to empathy rather than continue with expression.

> ## PRACTICE PAUSE
>
> How might you incorporate Connection Requests into your everyday life? Think of a few recent situations when it might have helped to make sure you were heard as you desired or to check how the other person felt about what you said.

PULLING BY THE EARS

What do you do when you have asked the person to say what they've heard, and the person does something else? We use an expression that comes from Marshall Rosenberg—you "pull them by the ears." This phrase refers to a manner of asking the person to say what they heard in a way that focuses their attention on what you want them to hear, particularly the needs you are expressing. This is not intended as a violent or condescending image—what it means is to gently and respectfully direct someone's attention toward hearing you in a way that will create connection.

Let's say you said, "I'd really like you to hear that what you said didn't meet my need for respect. Would you be willing to let me know what you heard me say?" Then they respond with one of the following:

+ The judgment they heard in what you said:

   "I heard you say you think I'm a disrespectful jerk."

   To pull by the ears, you might say:

"Thank you for saying what you heard. I want you to hear that I really want respect. I'm not trying to say you're disrespectful, but when I heard what you said, my need for respect wasn't met. Would you be willing to say that back?"

+ They start expressing instead of saying what they heard:

"Sure, I'll tell you what I heard ... what I heard is you don't get it. I think you're the one who's disrespectful. I was just trying to explain why I thought your idea wasn't going to work."

To pull by the ears, you can say:

"Hold on, I really want to hear what you have to say, but first I just want to know if you'll tell me what you heard me say a few moments ago, then tell me how you feel about it."

Use Pulling by the Ears when you sense there might be a willingness in them to say what they heard, but they either didn't quite understand your request or don't know the distinction between empathizing with you and expressing themselves.

This skill is not about forcing someone to repeat back what you've said, or about making a demand instead of a request. It's a choice that will hopefully create greater connection. If, for example, the person is in too much pain, perhaps a different choice would be likely to create connection.

At times, if you have already empathized and it didn't seem to help, it can be valuable for someone to simply repeat back what they've heard instead of offering more empathy. Pulling by the Ears is about a willingness to be persistent without demanding, and it is often combined with the next skill, Emergency Empathy.

EMERGENCY EMPATHY

Especially in the early part of the conversation, the other person may be in pain and not have the capacity yet to be able to sincerely listen to you. If you've shifted into expression, asked for reflection, and found that the person reacts out of their hurt, it's time for some emergency first aid empathy. Metaphorically, they are bleeding and need some care in order to stay present with you in the conversation and get to a place where they can hear you.

Giving Emergency Empathy is utilizing the same skill of Empathy you use in Step 3 of the IPM map. In Emergency Empathy, you step out of the process—wherever you were—to quickly empathize so that the other person can stay in the process with you. Using the four elements of presence, silent empathy, understanding, and need language, connect with what is happening for the person in this moment. You may find it only takes one or two empathy guesses to meet the person's need before returning to where you were in the process. But to do this, you need another mediation skill: Tracking.

TRACKING

Tracking is the skill of remembering where you were in the map you're using, keeping account of what has happened and what still needs to happen. This skill is used throughout a difficult conversation to note where you are in the map, but it comes in particularly handy when you have stepped out of the map to do something else. In short, Tracking helps you remember where you left off.

For example, if you were expressing yourself and used a connecting request, and the person responded with pain, prompting you to offer Emergency Empathy, you will want to track that you shifted into empathy for them, but that you haven't been heard yet. After giving empathy, you might then shift back into Step 4 of the map to be heard, saying, "Okay, I wonder if you would be willing to share what you heard me say now that I've listened to you for awhile." You might even summarize what it is you want to be heard about, then Pull by the Ears if necessary.

INTERRUPTING

Have you ever given someone the chance to tell you what's happening with them and they go on and on, so long that you begin to lose your focus and interest? When you are using the IPM map in a difficult conversation and this happens, it can cause you to lose connection. The other person could be using too many words for you to feel you can keep up, or the pace of their speech is too fast, or the words they use are difficult for you. This is when you can draw on the skill of interrupting.

Many cultures, including ours, teach that it's impolite or disrespectful to interrupt. We suggest it's also impolite and disrespectful to allow someone to continue when you are no longer able to follow them and be with what they're saying. The skill of interrupting is to break into the flow of their speech in a way that contributes to connection, instead of in a way that would disconnect you further. The intention is not to cut the person off and shut them down—it's to make a choice that you hope will create more connection when you feel it slipping.

You have a couple of options in what you say when you interrupt, in particular where you focus your attention. One option is to keep the focus on the other person and interrupt to use empathy. While the person is still talking, you jump in and say something like:

"Excuse me, excuse me, are you saying ...?" and reflect back your understanding of what they've said.

Another example is to say:

"Excuse me, I'd like to see if I'm understanding what you're saying so far. Would that be okay with you?"

You can also interrupt to express what is going on in you. This might sound like:

"Excuse me, I notice I'm losing contact with what you're saying because this is more words than I can take in right now and I've lost the thread. Would you be willing to say the essentials of what you want me to hear right now in two or three sentences?"

Or:

"Excuse me, excuse me, I'd really like to understand what you're saying, but you're using some language that's really hard for me to hear. Would you be willing to share more about what's really important to you that you want me to understand right now instead of what you think is wrong with me?"

In short, interrupt, let the person know what's happening for you, and make a request that you hope will meet your needs for connection and understanding.

SELF-EMPATHY

As the name implies, self-empathy is using the process of empathy on yourself, but it's different from the Self-Connection Process (the first step of the Interpersonal Mediation map); it's a more expansive look into yourself, using language to connect with what's going on inside you.

The SCP, as the first step of the model, is intended to be done in the moment, quickly reconnecting you to yourself. You may find at times, however, that it is not sufficient; perhaps you are stimulated by what the other person has said and are unable to continue to listen to them. You may then need a break from the conversation to give Self-Empathy, asking the other person if they would be willing to continue the discussion later. You could do this by saying:

"Excuse me, I realize I'm not as present with you as I would like to be—I'm distracted by some reactions I'm having. I want to be able to hear you better than I can right now, so what I'd like is to take a break to clear my head and then come back and talk about this again. Would you be willing to come back in (time frame)?"

Make sure you have a specific request about when you would like to return to the conversation.

In the time you give yourself to offer Self-Empathy, either by yourself or with a support person, go through each of the components of observation, feelings, needs, and requests. What is it that you are observing? Your observation could be either what the other person is saying or doing that's hard for you, or what's going on within you (your thoughts, judgments, etc.). Then ask yourself, *what am I feeling?* Check in with the sensations in your body, and make sure you are actually naming a feeling and not a faux feeling (see *Choosing Peace* if you are unclear about the difference, and use the list in Appendix A to help you name your feelings).

Put language to the internal bodily experience of your emotions by naming and labeling them in a clear way. Then inquire into your needs, exploring as deeply as you can what needs are not being met as you contemplate your observation—hearing the other person talk, experiencing their actions, or noticing the thoughts in your own mind about how the conversation is going.

See if you can be aware of the layering of needs. Sometimes you might tap into a need, such as protection, only to then find that meeting this need is in truth a strategy to meet another need. Finally, check in with yourself about any requests you might have. You could have a request of yourself or of the other person.

As you connect more fully with yourself through inquiry into the observation, feelings, needs, and requests, notice any shift in how you feel. Strive to stay with the process long enough to get the physiological shift of opening and softening that often comes with connecting to yourself.

A more expanded version of self-empathy would be to use the Enemy Image Process that was presented in the previous chapter. When you feel ready, you can then return to the conversation and pick up where you left off in the IPM map, or perhaps make a request of the other person if you came up with one while giving Self-Empathy. In connecting with yourself, you will be better able to listen to the other person and hear where they are coming from to reach a resolution that will work for both of you.

PRACTICE PAUSE

Think of someone you are upset with right now, or a recent situation in which you were upset with someone else. Go through the process of self-empathy.

SELF-EXPRESSION

Expressing yourself as the fourth step of the IPM map involves telling the other person what is important to you about the situation with the intention to create connection. As a mediation skill, however, self-expression is actually the skill of expressing about the *process* that you and the other person are in together.

Remember that you are in dual roles in an interpersonal conflict—the role of the mediator and the role of yourself in conflict with the other person. As a mediator, you have a perspective on the conversation that the other person may not have, including the map of the process as well as behaviors and attitudes that will make the process more likely to succeed. In short, self-expression in this context is about being able to make requests that will facilitate the quality of the mediation process.

As you come into a conversation with the skills and experience you have learned from this book, you are seeking for both parties to be heard in a way that feels satisfying—with the goal of creating a solution that meets the needs of both of you. The skill of self-expression comes in if the process starts deviating from that approach.

For example, perhaps the person you are talking with says or does one of the following:

+ Interrupts you to say, "I don't care what you have to say. I'm not listening to you!"

+ "You're just a jerk!"

+ They start using a lot of swear words.

+ Their voice gets louder than you are comfortable with.

+ They respond in a way that begins to frighten or concern you.

If you experience something in the conversation that you predict will lead away from each person being heard and reaching a mutually satisfying resolution, you may want to express your concern and make a request about how it would work for you to continue. For example, you might say one of the following:

"I would like it if we took turns so that we could really hear each other. Would you be willing to do that?"

"Hold on, I just want to stop the conversation here and say that that kind of language is going to make it hard for me to talk with you the way I'd like. I wonder if you'd be willing to agree that neither of us use name-calling with each other and focus more on how we're feeling and what we really would like from each other."

"I'm feeling anxious when I hear your voice get louder because I would like us to be able to speak to each other with respect. Would you be willing to speak in the same volume I'm using right now?"

"Excuse me, I'm feeling uncomfortable and unsafe here. Would you be willing to sit down?"

"I'm feeling uncomfortable and distressed sensing your urgency, and I'm not able to pay attention to what you're saying when I'm feeling afraid, so would you be willing to lower your voice and sit back in your chair?"

In the skill of self-expression, your requests are an attempt to maintain a frame around the conversation that will support you to connect with each other.

NOTES ON HAVING A MAP

As we said earlier, interpersonal conflicts are some of the most difficult situations because they can be fraught with emotion and habitual triggers. It might seem difficult at the beginning, if not impossible, to even remember you want to use a map, much less remember the steps or be able to track it as you go through the messiness of an actual conversation. Even if you start out feeling centered, getting swept up in the stress response due to something said by the other person can make it difficult to stay in the process.

What we have found, however, is this: if you remember at the beginning of the conversation that you have a map to use (a set of steps that guide you), make a strong intention to use the map, and keep reminding yourself over and over again to use it, then no matter how hard the conversation gets, you can stay with the map. The times we have noticed we get into trouble is when we don't think about it and go into the conversation on autopilot.

Having the map doesn't mean you won't get triggered, have any reactions to what the other person says, or even get lost at times. But with clear intention and commitment to use it, you will be able to return to the map and follow the steps it lays out for you.

The metaphor of a map is very apt here. For example, if you get in your car in LA and have a destination of say, Chicago, in mind, it's quite a different experience whether you use the map to get there, or merely figure it out as you drive. While on a road trip it might be fun to ditch the map and only use your sense of direction to see where you end up, a map comes in handy if you want to arrive at your destination.

In a difficult conversation, especially with triggers and height-ened emotions potentially clouding both your own and the other person's judgment, figuring it out as you go may not lead to the destination you are seeking. Focusing on following the map, look-ing for the next landmark, and using the steps and skills help you stay focused and navigate the territory of a difficult conversation with more success.

PRACTICE PAUSE

How might you prepare yourself to use the Interpersonal
Mediation map before and during a conversation?

Here again are the steps of the Interpersonal Mediation map,
with the skills where they tend to occur in the process.

1. Perform the Self-Connection Process

2. Ask yourself, "Can I hear the message as a 'please'?"

3. Empathize with the Other,
   if you can
   a. Empathy
   b. Interruption

4. Self-Express
   a. Connection Requests
   b. Pulling by the Ears
   c. Emergency Empathy
   d. Tracking

5. Make Solution Requests
   and Agreements
   a. Solution Requests

Self-Empathy
Self-Expression
(these two apply
to steps 3–5)

Though any of the nine skills may be used at various points in
the conversation, the above table lays them out within the step they
are most likely to occur. For example, the skill of empathy is the
third step of the IPM map. Interrupting is also a skill you are likely
to use while empathizing; when you are listening to the other
person, you may find they are saying more words than you can

take in. During the fourth step, Self-Expressing, four separate skills may come in handy.

+ After you express, you may want to make a Connection Request to see how the other person received what you said or to test the connection between you.

+ If you make a request for reflection and they start to express, you might either use the skill of Pulling by the Ears, or if you intuit that they are upset, you might use Emergency Empathy.

+ The skill of Tracking then helps you recall where you were in the IPM map and continue the mediation process.

The skills of Self-Empathy and Self-Expression are shown on the side of the entire process because they are likely to arise at any point in the conversation.

CONNECTING AROUND THE STIMULUS

When we are open to hearing the other person, it is easier to reach clarity about what started the conflict. What often gets revealed in this iterative process of empathizing and expressing is the observation of their stimulus of the conflict—either a thought they had in their mind, or something you or someone else said or did, or didn't say or do. Often with intimate relationships, people become as stimulated by what others did *not* do or say as by what they *did*. The observation of the stimulus is often a key piece; when through the empathy process the observation is revealed, that understanding can help you become more connected.

We have found two ways that the stimulus for conflict often remains hidden: either people hide what stimulates their hurt as a protective mechanism, or the observation gets so tangled up with judgments that it is obscured. In either case, when you can truly be with another person and help them get down to the observation of what happened that stimulated the conflict, it can open the door to addressing that stimulus in a way that can lead to mutual understanding and resolution. When people hear the observation for the first time, it can be like an epiphany—a light of clarity shines into the situation that wasn't there before.

Using James as an example, let's look at a time when he experienced a similar epiphany.

> While on a call with a woman who had volunteered to translate health materials for some of the urgent care centers in his company, James felt frustrated because he was not clear on what she wanted, yet kept empathizing and trying to hear her. When he finally realized what she was trying to convey, it was revelatory: she believed that by her willingness to perform the previous translation for free in order to gain experience, it was setting a precedent that she would never get paid for her translation work.
>
> Once that observation became clear, the whole conversation shifted. James was able to let her know that he had, in fact, recently been able to earmark some money out of his budget for translation of materials, as the company had begun to see the positive impact. After the observation—the thought that was the stimulus for her—was clear, James could share the real situation with her. It was staying with the empathy that led to finding out the observation, as well as clearing up the misconception. Her whole demeanor relaxed after learning her earlier belief wasn't accurate.

As in this case, sometimes the stimulus uncovers a misperception that can easily be cleared up. The stimulus for her was simply a belief that did not match reality. The empathy uncovers the stimulus, which can then lead you to tell the other person how you understand the situation, or to explain how your perception differs from theirs. In doing so, you still use the same skills; that is, your "education" is not about how distorted their viewpoint is, but rather about expressing your own observations, feelings, and needs, and then making a request.

IN-THE-MOMENT CONFLICTS: THE IDEAL VERSUS THE REALITY

People tend to think in terms of ideals—particularly the ideal of how they want to be. When you think of your interactions with others, you might have an ideal of being able to stay connected with yourself, empathize with the other person, express yourself clearly in a way that maintains connection with the other, and find a resolution that will work for both of you. That ideal is what we are pointing to in this chapter; we are giving ideas, here and throughout the book, on how to develop your skills so that you can begin to embody that ideal more and more.

Nonetheless, we think it is important to note the reality. Even after years of practice, both of us still become triggered; we still react, get defensive, and say things that when we look back on them, we think, "I knew better than that!" yet we say them anyway. The interaction ends up at best being unsatisfying, and at worst in a fight where one party ends up walking out of the room. We mess up. We are human.

So are you. Although you may have high hopes for being able to live out of your values and ideals, there will likely always be someone who will trigger you, who will make you momentarily forget all of your training, practice, and skill building, causing you to resort to your most primitive instinct to fight back, flee, or hide.

When it happens, it's okay. It does not mean something is wrong with you or that you failed. You simply didn't meet some needs of yours, and you can learn from it and try again.

So far we've assumed you know that you will be having a difficult conversation, and that you can do your inner work ahead of time and plan for the conversation. Of course, you don't always have warning that a conversation is going to be difficult. You might be in the middle of a conversation, or see someone unexpectedly, and without being able to prepare for it find that you are in the midst of a conflict. This adds a level of challenge to navigating the dispute.

In these situations you may notice bodily sensations that feel like you've been taken over; you may feel a flush of energy, like someone has injected you, suddenly making you a different person. You have numerous thoughts and feel compelled to say and do things that later you wonder what in the world inhabited you to do so. Different parts of your brain are in control of your consciousness at those moments, and it can feel like being possessed.

Simply noticing that you are in this altered state, this different mode of perceiving and interacting with the world, is a first step. You may notice it by your feelings and by the urgency you have to be heard or to get out of the situation. If this occurs, it almost feels like life or death. When you notice these cues, you can learn to stop yourself from taking the action your habitual response is prompting you to take. You might also begin to talk about it, stepping out of it enough to comment on it as an observer. You can use words to get yourself into more of a third-person perspective so you can begin to disconnect from it, and at least not do or say anything further that you will regret.

Here is an example of being "possessed" by something or someone, and two different ways of handling that emotion:

Corey's grades have not been very good lately, and yet when James walks by his room, he sees Corey playing games on his computer instead of studying.

SCENARIO 1

James glances into Corey's room and sees him playing a game on the computer. He storms into the room, yelling at Corey, "What are you doing? You know your grades are in the toilet, and you're here playing games? Your mom and I work long hours to make sure you can have a good life, and you're not going to just throw it away!"

SCENARIO 2

James glances into Corey's room and sees him playing a game on the computer. He feels a flood of anger rush through his body. Tension arises in his core, and his body heats up. He quickly does Self-Connection Process, connecting to his body and his needs. Looking for the "please" reminds him that Corey may want understanding. James knows he is not able to empathize right now, as he's too worked up, so instead he says, "Corey, when I see your grade report and then notice you're playing games instead of doing homework, I feel frustrated, scared, and confused. I really care about your well-being and wonder whether this is the direction you'd like to go. Would you tell me what's going on?"

Here's an alternative way that James might express himself, particularly if he's too agitated to be clear on his feelings and needs:

"Corey, when I see you playing games with your grades the way they are, I get all tight and pissed off. There's all this intensity in me toward you and I don't want to be that way with you. Would you tell me what you're hearing me say?" (or, "How do you feel hearing this?")

Another way to deal with this type of situation when you feel taken over and out of control is to take a break. You simply let the other person know you are taking a break and that you intend to return to the conversation. If you are comfortable doing so, try saying you don't trust that you can stay connected with yourself and with them, and thus are not able to be in the conversation in the way you would like. Or, you can simply say you need to go do something else, and ask to continue the conversation in a little while. This can be a good option if you are aware you want to stop short and not move further into a potential train wreck. Then, you can do the inner work that enables you to come back to the conversation with more connection and presence.

For example, if James is too angry when he sees Corey playing computer games, and after self-connection and looking for a "please" determines that he still can neither empathize nor express in a way that he feels good about, he might say:

> "Corey, I'm really distressed seeing you here playing games instead of doing homework, and I want to talk to you about it, but I need to take a little time and get into a better frame of mind, so I'm going to come back later."

Of course, the other option is to stay in the conversation, striving to stay connected with yourself as much as possible, and following the steps of the IPM map to the best of your ability.

When conflicts arise in the moment, you may find that at first you do not have the presence of mind to realize it is a time to use your skills, or even remember the option to take a break, and therefore stay in the conversation with whatever reactive patterns are operating. You are on the train, and you may not get off it for awhile. You will make a mess. We encourage you to see those times as opportunities for further practice.

When you come out the other side, there are a number of things you can do to bring yourself back to reconnection with yourself and consider what you want to do. In Chapter 7 we will talk about the Mourn Celebrate Learn map, which is a key process for reconnecting with yourself after something has happened. But for now, you can perform the Enemy Image Process from Chapter 4, as well as return to the Self-Connection Process to get reconnected to yourself.

The important thing to know is that the internal work you do will shorten the time it takes you to come out of a reactive place. Thus, while we encourage you to take a time-out from a conversation—if you are able—to minimize the amount of clean-up to do later, taking time-outs is not the goal of learning to mediate interpersonal conflicts. The real hope lies in doing the internal work *outside* the conversation, such that you are able to more and more quickly get reconnected to yourself and stay there longer. It is then that you can be more present, empathize with the other person, and speak from your heart.

A popular story about the founder of aikido, Morihei Ueshiba, illustrates the promise of returning to presence.

> After observing O Sensei sparring with an accomplished fighter, a young student said to the master, "You never lose your balance. What is your secret?"
>
> "You are wrong," O Sensei replied. "I am constantly losing my balance. My skill lies in my ability to regain it."

Similarly, the more you practice, the more you are able to return quickly to presence when you have been triggered. Initially, it may take weeks or days, then hours, then minutes, until finally it is only seconds before you realize you are disconnected and then can reconnect. The place to focus your practice is not on some kind of "maintaining" of presence, but in developing the skill to regain presence quickly so that you can choose how to respond.

DEALING WITH "NO"

If making requests is a fundamental part of mediating your life, then so too are negative responses to your requests. Hearing a "no" from someone, especially when in conflict, can trigger all kinds of habitual reactions and send you right back into conflict. Instead of hearing "no" as a roadblock to getting your needs met, we suggest that you hear it as another "please"—as an opportunity to go deeper into what needs can be met and create an even better solution than the request on the table.

When you hear a "no," be sure to listen for the "need behind the no." Why? Because when someone is saying "no," they are saying they think something about the request will not meet their needs. It may be a direct and obvious need that won't be met, or the "no" may indicate profound needs that not only help resolve the conflict, but can also open new levels of understanding within the relationship. So, by saying "no," they are in effect saying "yes" to other needs.

For example, in Chapter 1, when Sally tells James to pick Maggie up and take her to her soccer tryouts and he resists, his "no" might be coming from his need for sustainability through maintaining his position at work. On another level, though, his "no" might reflect deeper fears about the shifts happening in their home with Sally going back to work, along with his needs for predictability. Another possibility is that he's upset because he interprets that Sally always throws these requests at him at the last minute, and then he feels he has no choice, so his needs for autonomy and respect are not met.

Sally hears his resistance as an affront to her, triggering her fight or flight response, and she is not able to listen for the need behind his "no." Even though she gets what she wants, the conflict intensifies.

A simple three-step process to use when you hear a "no" is:

1.   Clarify the request as it's connected to needs.

2.   Empathize with the "no"; you want to be able to hear what needs are keeping the person from saying "yes" to the request.

3.   When you can hear those needs, you can then interpret what they want that would meet their needs, reframing your request or helping them make one that might meet the needs of both of you. Or, you can ask them to help come up with a solution that will work for you both. (We include a full exercise for Need Behind the No in Appendix G: IPM Exercise.)

Let's revisit the Chapter 1 scenario and see how Sally might have used this process when she heard James say, "Whoa, wait a minute, I'm taking the kids to school. I can't just leave work in the middle of the afternoon and stay with her through tryouts."

First, she reconnects to herself since his words elicit a reaction in her, and then she clarifies the request as it's related to her needs.

She says, "Someone has to get Maggie to tryouts, and I'm in a meeting with a potential client at that time, so I'm concerned about impacting my chances of landing the work. Is there any way you can help me with this?"

James says, "Well, it's not a great time for me to leave work. It's the middle of the afternoon."

Sally tries to empathize with what is keeping James from saying yes. "So are you concerned about what's going to happen at work if you take the time to pick her up and get her to tryouts?"

"Absolutely. Not only does it look bad, but I won't be able to get as much work done."

Sally nods. "Right, so it's both about making sure your work gets done and that others know you are there. Can you help me brainstorm some ways we can get her picked up?"

From here, James and Sally are in a conversation together to find a solution that meets their needs. As we heard at the beginning of this chapter, James does leave work to take Maggie, but then has Sally's sister Peg take over so James can return to work.

When someone else has made a request of you and the "no" is coming from *you*, you can guess the need behind the request, and then let them know *your* need that would not be met by the request as it currently stands. This keeps you within the structure above of empathizing with the other person first, which generally increases the likelihood that they will hear you. If you say "no" and they react to it, you can also begin with empathizing with their reaction before expressing your own needs. You can then try to come up with a modified request that would meet the need behind their request and the need behind your "no."

For example, if in the scenario between James and Sally it was James who had the awareness to use this process, he might have heard that Sally was making a request (even though it sounded like a demand) and realized that the "no" was coming from him. The conversation might instead have gone like this:

First James clarifies what Sally would like, trying to connect it to her needs. "So when you ask me to pick Maggie up, is that because you're concerned about landing this client?"

Sally replies, "Yeah, it's my first meeting with them and I don't want to give the impression that I'm always running off to handle other priorities."

James nods. "I understand that you'd like them to know they're important. The thing is, I'm concerned because I'm already taking the kids to school, which means I'm getting to work later than normal, and it doesn't look good for me to take off in the middle of the afternoon and not get work done. Can we take a few minutes to see if there's a solution that will work for us both?"

Again, James and Sally can now collaborate on coming up with the solution.

mediateyourlife.com/need-behind-the-no-video/

PRACTICE PAUSE

What is your habitual reaction when someone says "no" to a request you've made? How will you remind yourself next time to listen for the need behind the "no"?

How to Practice the IPM Map

Being able to perform any process "in the wild" successfully requires consciously practicing it so that the skills and capacities will be readily available to you, even when in a difficult situation. It might seem strange to think about practicing having a conversation, but that's exactly what we suggest. Remember the flight simulator metaphor we introduced in Chapter 3? We want you to likewise set up a situation that models real life, allowing you to practice what it is you want to learn to do in an actual conversation, without the harsh consequences of mistakes you might make.

There are two forms of practice we recommend for the IPM map: the IPM Exercise and IPM Role-Play. The IPM Exercise is a step-by-step process that takes you through three levels of practicing the format and skills of an interpersonal conversation with a partner, whereas the IPM Role-Play is setting up a more free-form conversation with a partner where you follow the structure of the IPM map, using particular skills when you think they will contribute to the conversation.

If you are brand new to the IPM map and the skills, we recommend starting with the IPM Exercise. (See Appendix G for the list of steps for all three levels of the IPM Exercise.) Though all the steps may seem daunting at first, we find that having a highly structured format helps people learn; being able to perform the skills, by following the step-by-step process already laid out for you, allows you to practice the skills themselves without becoming overwhelmed by which choice to make in that moment.

Going through the levels of the IPM Exercise does not yield one smooth conversation—not at first—so we recommend you have the sheet in front of you and move your finger down each step, practicing the skill for each. As you do the exercise a number of times, you will support the embodiment of the skills, and you will gain the experience to naturally develop your own sense of when you want to use each skill.

The Intensity Exercise we introduced in Chapter 2 is a companion to the IPM Exercise in helping you be in a difficult conversation. The simplest way to describe the difference is that Intensity Exercise is about *capacity* building, whereas the IPM Exercise is about *skill* building.

In the Intensity Exercise, you purposefully get triggered into the fight-flight-freeze reaction, practicing becoming aware of that response as soon as possible, then becoming present in it and returning yourself to a more centered state so you can act out of choice instead of habit. The purpose is to support your capacity to be present with yourself in the stress response, manage that response, and choose what you want to do next.

Once you are better able to be present and have the capacity to choose, you may ask what choices you can make to navigate an interpersonal conversation. The IPM Exercise is about the actual choices themselves, developing the skills so that when you make the choice, you can capably execute it. The various levels of the IPM Exercise take you through all the skills and choices that will help you mediate your own conflict with another person, with the goal of creating connection that leads to resolution and agreements. It's a highly structured, step-by-step approach that allows you to practice the IPM map with a partner. In this way, you can begin to embody making the choices and using the skills while in conversation with someone else.

Once you are more comfortable with the map and skills, you might try the other form of practice: an IPM role-play. This is a more free-form type of practice, where you and your partner set up a role-play, based on a real or imagined situation, and practice using the IPM map and the nine mediation skills in the conversation. We suggest when setting up a role-play that you use the steps of the Flight Simulator to create a safe container, enabling you to learn at your optimal level (see Appendix J for the Flight Simulator setup steps). As always, in practice you dial your own difficulty, asking your partner for the level of challenge that is right for you at each point on your learning curve. IPM Role-Play helps make it more natural to use the five steps of the IPM map while you are in a conversation.

Whatever practice you choose, always remember that it is up to you to opt for what you would like to work on and to determine the level of difficulty. If you are in the early stage of learning and want to focus solely on the steps of the IPM map, it's best to set up your practice to focus on that and not worry about the additional skills. If you have the steps down and want to work on a particular skill, such as Interrupting or Connection Requests, then focus your practice time on using that skill. We offer the models of the IPM Exercise and Role-Play to give you some initial structure; feel free to modify that structure so that it meets your learning needs.

In terms of "dialing the difficulty"—or setting the level of challenge you would like in your practice—you can do this through your practice focus and requests to your partner. Here are some suggestions for different levels of challenge:

	Lower Difficulty	Higher Difficulty
Focusing Practice	IPM map steps only	IPM map steps and skills
	One skill only	Multiple skills
	IPM Exercise levels 1 & 2 (following exact steps from Appendix G—limiting your choices each moment)	IPM Exercise level 3 (complete IPM Exercise with all steps and skills)
		IPM Role-Play: free-form conversation in which you make all choices about when and how to use steps and skills
Partner Requests	Respond to requests by doing what I've asked	Respond to requests by doing something different (i.e., if I ask for reflection of my needs, instead say what is going on for you)
	Respond in a way that is intended to create connection	Give responses that are challenging for me to hear or intended to create disconnection (partner may need coaching on what to say)

For both the IPM Exercise and Role-Play, set up three chairs so you can move into a physical chair when you are in the role of the mediator. If you are working with a long-distance partner, whoever is taking the lead can set up two chairs to physically move between. Though this may seem strange, we highly recommend you try it out; it will substantially help you begin to embody the mediator mind when you can physically move to a different chair.

In practice, you will move between the different chairs in a similar manner as you did with the Intensity Exercise. The steps of the IPM Exercise tell you when to move into the mediator chair and when to move back to the "self" chair. If you choose to practice using an IPM Role-Play, you might move between the chairs as follows:

+ Sit in the mediator chair to do Steps 1 and 2 (SCP, Can I hear a "please").

+ Stay in the mediator chair to assess in Step 3 whether you can empathize.

+ Move to the self chair to empathize with the other person or express yourself.

+ Stay in the self chair to hear the response from the other person.

+ Move back to the mediator chair to return to Steps 1 & 2.

The separate chairs, remember, are a way to remind yourself to step into a part of yourself that can hold all perspectives in the conflict and is not triggered or caught in habitual reactions. Eventually, with enough practice and experience, you will find that you can stay in mediator mind for increasing amounts of time throughout a conversation.

PRACTICE PAUSE

What requests do you have of yourself or other
people to practice the IPM Exercise or Role-Play?

STOPPING CONFLICT BEFORE IT BEGINS

The Interpersonal Mediation map we outline in this chapter clearly
applies to situations where you are already in conflict with another
person. It also becomes useful, however, to think of utilizing it when
you are not yet in a conflict, but sense that things might go in that
direction. By using the same overall format, you may be able to
avoid a potential dispute. These types of less intense situations also
provide good practice ground to build your skills in staying connected with yourself and in empathizing with the other person.

Too many situations might fall into the "potential conflict"
category to mention them all; however, we will mention general
examples, as well as a more specific one, to help you begin to
recognize when these show up in your own life.

When you have a definite idea of something you want to do—
to the point where you become less willing to consider other
people's ideas—it sets up the potential for conflict. This can
happen with intimate relationships (partners, children, and close
friends) in a multitude of small ways.

For example, you may want to go to a particular restaurant, or
have a clear idea of how you want to spend the day. You might
have a preference for the way a particular chore should be done, for
how you would like the house kept, or for the way a person should
drive. Though these may only be small irritations, they can build
into larger resentments. You may get your way, but often at the

expense of connection with yourself and the other person. Alternatively, you might simply give in and let the other person have their way, again with disconnection as the inevitable result. Instead, use the steps of the IPM map when you have these types of conversations and notice how you change the dynamics of the situation and the relationship.

The earlier example of James's phone call with the translator is a good illustration of avoiding a conflict. Although the situation was not a full-fledged conflict, it was the type that could eventually lead to one if it wasn't handled with some finesse. If, for instance, James had expressed in the call his frustration about the lack of clarity, and not been willing to listen and be present, the translator could easily have sensed it through the agitation and abruptness in his voice. She might then have closed down and felt hurt about not being heard and cared about. It could have created an estrangement, generally dealt with through avoidance, that involves writing the person off and moving on. Since the whole situation was based on a simple misconception, estrangement would be an unfortunate and unnecessary end.

When you do this kind of work, you are often not seen as a hero; when you avoid what might have happened, most people don't see what you've avoided or the skill implicit in doing so. It's difficult to measure the contribution of being able to be in an interpersonal interaction in this way, yet it is very much a contribution.

As you practice using the Interpersonal Mediation map in this chapter, see if you can find times to use it to *avoid* disconnection and conflict. For instance, if you notice that you are holding a particular idea about what to do as a demand when interacting with another person, step back for a moment and see if you can shift to using the IPM map to connect and find a strategy that works better for both of you.

Though our focus in this chapter is on how to facilitate the conversation when you are in conflict with someone else, we do want to point out that we see the conversation as just one part of a larger framework (which we will go into in detail in Chapter 8 when we discuss the learning cycle). When you are in a conversation, for example, you do the best you can, but there are further ways to practice after the conversation and before the next one to continue creating connection. As such, we encourage you not to put too much pressure on yourself, thinking that it is all about *one* conversation. It isn't.

We find that only a small portion of our success in mediating our own conflicts is what we do in the moment. A greater proportion lies in how we prepare for the first conversation, what we do afterward, and how we prepare for the next. This work "around the conversation" helps us show up in a certain way, allowing the conversation to flow from our ability to be present and centered in our needs.

When interpersonal conflicts are with people close to you, such as intimate partners, children, parents, siblings, or close friends, there is often a sense of familiarity to the conflicts; you tend to get in the same ones over and over, sometimes with no real awareness of being able to track how you become stimulated. As you practice the skills in this chapter and the rest of the book, however, this pattern can change.

While in a conflict, you can start to bring more awareness and try different things both during and after the conversation, including tracking back to when you became triggered and talking to the other person about when they became triggered. This helps you learn more about the conflict and to be aware when it shows up again, giving you more opportunity to intervene in different ways. As a result, these kinds of conflicts can evolve over time to a point where you are aware of when they begin much more quickly, enabling you to make choices that lead to reconnection with yourself and the other person.

—————

James briefly feels some relief after leaving Scott's office. Then his mind gets going and he starts second-guessing what he said and whether Scott was really on board. He calls Sally to fill her in on how it went, catching her just as she drops off Maggie for soccer practice.

After they exchange hellos, Sally says, "Well, did you talk to Scott today?"

"Yeah."

"How did it go?"

James sighs. "I think it went okay, but now I'm wondering whether he's really on board and willing."

"What happened in the conversation? Were you able to hear him and say what was going on for you?"

James's voice has more energy as he replies, "Yes. I was pleased with how I could empathize with him, and I think it helped him to be able to hear me. He finally told me that the decision about Aaron had come from higher up, and since Matt had left my team he'd put Aaron with me. I still asked him if we could do a trial period, like we talked about last night, of him including me in decisions that affect me. He said he's willing."

"That's great!" Sally says with obvious enthusiasm. "It sounds like you got what you wanted. So what's going on that's causing you to wonder about it?"

"I'm not sure. I guess part of me is thinking he just said that to get me off his back."

"Is that about wanting to know you matter?" Sally asks. "That what's important to you is important to him?"

"Yeah, I guess it is. And I'm thinking that maybe we could have made a more solid agreement about it, which I'm now realizing we didn't."

Sally clarifies what she's heard. "So now you're also aware that you made the request and he said yes, but there isn't quite the level of specificity you would like?"

"That's it exactly. It feels a little vague. I guess the next time it comes up, maybe I can talk to him about making it more specific."

"Good. And we can talk later if you want to practice what that might sound like."

"Sounds good. Thanks for listening ... and for your help last night. I know it made a huge difference today in my ability to talk with Scott."

—◦∿∿◦—

Next Up

You've successfully navigated a difficult conversation and re-established connection. In order to fully bring the fruits of your labor into the world, the requests you made in the final stage may not be sufficient. Turning those requests into solid agreements can help both of you to be more confident in moving forward.

6 | PATHWAY TO CHANGE

GETTING TO AGREEMENTS

Unless both sides win, no agreement can be permanent.
—JIMMY CARTER

———∿∿∿———

SALLY REACHES FOR ANOTHER HOMEMADE COOKIE from the plate between her and James. "Nothing like a good cookie to help create connection!" She grins at James as he reaches for one too and they raise their cookies to one another in a mock toast. As Sally reheats some water for tea, she reviews their conversation in her mind. Finally, they'd found time to discuss their argu-ment from a few mornings prior when Sally had asked James to take Maggie to her tryouts. Sharing what each had realized after the argument, Sally let James know how much she wanted care—both for the family and kids, but also for her own dreams—and her fear that going back to work meant she wasn't a good mother. James had told Sally how much pressure he felt at work and his concern about taking off in the middle of the day, and how that tied in with his need for sustainability for their family.

Sally pours the water and sits back down at the table. "I think we're starting to have some clarity about our needs," she says. "One thing I feel a little upset about, though, is that I did tell you the night before that I had meetings and couldn't take Maggie to tryouts."

James shakes his head and says, "Yeah, when we were right in the middle of trying to get dinner together and Mags was bugging us about her teacher. I feel like you sometimes tell me things like that at the worst possible time, knowing I can't take it in right then, so you don't have to discuss it but later you can say you told me. It's like you want what you want and will do whatever to get it, without this being a team effort and considering what will work for me too."

Sally takes a deep breath. Part of her wants to argue with him. Yet, she has a dawning awareness that he is right. The truth feels painful, but it is a welcome pain compared to that of endless fighting.

"That's really hard for me to hear, and this is even harder to say, but you're right. I do that. I guess I'm ... I'm just so afraid that it's always going to be me who's going to have to compromise. I feel like I've given up my own dreams for other people for so long—you, the kids—and now that I've rekindled my dream, I don't want to compromise it. I want to do whatever it takes to give it wings. To give *me* wings."

"I'm hearing that you would really like to have a career again and know you are contributing in that way. Is that it?" James asks.

"Yes, but it's more than that. It's also hard for me when you say things that I hear as diminishing the importance of my work, like that my job is casual. You haven't said it directly, but I sometimes think you see my work as kind of a cute hobby that I'm taking on now that Maggie is older, and that your work is more important, so I should be the one to work around all our family commitments. I heard you say a minute ago that you wanted teamwork, and I want that too. And I would love to know I count, that we really are working together—for all of us to be able to have what we want."

James nods. "Yes, I'm getting that we both really want to work together. And you'd appreciate knowing that I see your work as important too, and that we have some equality when it comes to making compromises that affect our lives."

Sally breathes a sigh of relief, her body relaxing a bit as she feels heard by James. "Thank you for hearing me. It seems like we have so many needs in common here—predictability, sustainability, acknowledgment, support ..."

James agrees. "I know. But this is where I get stuck. I keep feeling like we can definitely get connected about this, but then it seems like there's no way forward. Work is important to both of us. So is our family. I feel like no matter what we do, we'll keep having these same situations come up, and one of us will have to give up and feel like our work is jeopardized in some way." He rubs his hands over his face. "I just don't know where to go from here."

Agreements form the backbone of human interaction. Anytime people do something together, it's likely that some form of agreement is in place, whether it's an explicit agreement, or one implicitly agreed to by their actions.

"Let's go to the movies on Friday!"
"Ok! I'd love to see that new romantic comedy!"

"I'd like to move ahead on the project. Can you get me a proposal by Friday?"

"Sure, I'll have it on your desk by 3 p.m."

"Would you water the plants each week while you're straightening the living room?"

"Yeah, I can do that."

Change in the world starts with a request. You might make a request of yourself to do something or you might ask someone else. Another person may make a request of you and you agree or disagree. We covered making requests and how to distinguish between requests and demands in *Choosing Peace*, and in the previous chapter, we talked about making solution requests in the resolution phase of the Interpersonal Mediation map.

Sometimes, making a request is enough. It can help you be heard about what you desire, and if the other person says yes, that may be all that's needed. In many cases, however, taking the small step from making a request to having an agreement can be helpful; making a request builds the foundation for reaching an agreement.

To be clear, requests are different from agreements in that requests are *saying* you want to do something, while agreements are putting a stake in the ground—with the commitment and intention that you are *going* to do it. In situations where the conflict is long-standing, more emotionally fraught, or where trust is an issue, creating agreements helps increase the likelihood that the needs you both surfaced—and that helped connect you with each other—are actually met. James and Sally can both be clear about their needs and express them to each other, but in order to create the change in their lives they'd both like to see, agreements are a necessary next step.

Understanding agreements—how to make, hold, and support them—is a key skill for navigating relationships and meeting your needs, yet it is not one that most people are trained in. For example, consider the following scenarios:

You make an agreement with your teenager that when he borrows the car, he will contribute to keeping the gas tank filled. After he uses it the next time, you find the tank close to empty. When you ask him about it, he says he left money on the kitchen table for gas, while you meant for him to fill the tank while he was out. You realize that because the agreement wasn't clear, you and he understood it differently.

You and your partner agree that the next time either of you is going to be at the store, you will call to see if the other person wants anything. You go to the store, but it's not until you're on the way home do you remember you had agreed to call. At that point, you realize you need some way to remind yourself of the agreement in the moment.

You and a coworker have a large project deadline looming in a week, and it becomes clear to both of you that the project will not be complete by then. You feel your stress level rising as each day goes by and the deadline draws closer. You're afraid that dire consequences will result from missing this deadline; you also realize you weren't clear when you made the agreement about what to do if you couldn't keep it.

When your teenager comes home at midnight after agreeing she would call if she was going to be later than 10:30 p.m. (and she didn't), you get angry and yell at her. She rolls her eyes and goes to her room. You realize that in making the agreement with her, you had actually turned it into a demand, simply expecting it would be fulfilled.

Do you recognize these types of situations in your own life? If so, you're not alone. Everyone can use some guidelines for how to make effective agreements that are more likely to be kept—and how to stay connected when they are not.

To assist with making and keeping agreements, we have identified three types—primary, supporting, and restoring—that we will describe shortly. We will also cover ways to think about requests and agreements that we find most powerful in creating connection and change. But before we get into the specifics of agreements, let's return to the topic of connection.

CONNECTION AS PRECURSOR TO AGREEMENT

If you are in conflict with another person, it's likely that you don't start out feeling much connection to them. In fact, you may not feel any care for them at all, and even want to punish them out of your anger and belief that they don't care about you. You want what you want; you're right and they're wrong. When disconnected from yourself and others, it's common to approach resolution from the viewpoint of "What can I get for myself?"

Through the process of the IPM map—getting connected to yourself and seeking to understand the other person while being understood yourself—you hopefully begin to shift out of this state of disconnection. Ideally, you'll begin to gain a rapport with the person, adopting a broader view in which you realize that in order to get what *you* want, it makes sense to help them get what *they* want. As such, you begin to care about getting needs met for both parties instead of only for yourself.

As we've said throughout this book, the primary intention of the approach we are offering is to focus first on connection. When you begin by creating a connection with someone you are in conflict with, the resolution will oftentimes emerge organically out of that connection. When dealing with challenges, people often want to leap straight to figuring out solutions and conclusions, but we offer a different pathway. Instead of taking a path that attempts to go straight for solution, we recommend an approach that to some people seems like a deviation—one that goes through connection first, then to solutions.

We have found from years of personal experience in mediating between others and in our own lives that this seeming detour is actually not a detour at all. The solutions arrived at when we take the path through connection are qualitatively better than those we come to when we do not connect. They are often unexpected, more satisfying, and since they take into account the needs of everyone, each person feels good about them. What's more, the solutions are more likely to be fulfilled.

Connection is a bit ephemeral and mysterious. One way to think about it is that you can experience a continuum of connection, one that goes from intellectual understanding of where the other person is coming from, to seeing that you share the same needs as human beings, to feeling a sense of underlying oneness with them. These specific phases along the continuum can be checkpoints for you during a conflict conversation, particularly when coming to the resolution phase. Some level of connection is helpful to reach a strong resolution, one that takes the needs of both of you into account. You can tap into how connected you are to the other person by where on this continuum you are.

Check in with yourself during a conversation for any of these states:

+ Feeling a sense of rapport and understanding with the other person

- ✦ Seeing that getting your needs met is going to include addressing the other person's needs

- ✦ Feeling like you want to contribute to the other person out of care and compassion for them

We encourage you to see this as a checklist of possible ways you could experience connection, *not* another way to be self-critical. If you find you're not experiencing a sense of connection, you can choose to stay in the connection phase—the first four steps of the IPM map—to try to become connected. Alternatively, you can test the waters by moving toward solutions, suggesting strategies that you hope might work for the other person and that you imagine will work for you. The reactions you receive from the other person to your suggestions will indicate whether to pursue a solution now or to remain in the first four steps of the IPM map.

Remember, it's not about forcing a state of connection or trying to feel something you currently don't; it's about staying in the conversation, continuing to reconnect with your needs wherever you are, and then seeking to hear where the other person is coming from. It requires trust that these steps will naturally lead you to experience some level of connection with the other person. Then, in the resolution phase, this connection can develop into concrete actions that resolve the issue between you.

Giving and Receiving

One way to know when you are connected is that you want to give to the other person; there may even be a natural shift into making sure all needs are met, regardless of whose needs they are. When you're connected at this level, the two roles you've been playing—mediator mind and disputant—meld into one, and the needs that are uncovered are collective (not *my* needs vs. *your* needs). The question then becomes, how can you both give and receive so that all needs between you are valued and cared for?

It is now that you shift from "What can I get?" to the natural enjoyment of giving and receiving. This shift may happen regardless of where on the continuum of connection you are, and it is especially sweet when you are so connected that the lines blur between giving and receiving. This is when you can actually get lost in the giving and receiving; it becomes unclear who is the giver and who is the receiver. What we mean by this is that even if you're the one giving, it feels like the other person is actually giving to *you* by the way they are receiving what you're giving. It's a poignant state to achieve, particularly when you may have started from a state of anger and wanting to be right.

We want to be clear: we're not suggesting you see the giving and receiving we're discussing as a hard rule or a "should." Instead, merely think of it as a question you can ask yourself during a conversation: "Do I feel like I want to contribute to this person out of my care for them, or not?" The answer should serve as a benchmark, a way of noticing where you are in your relationship with this person, and choosing what you want to do next to create a resolution that would make you happy and be in harmony with what you value.

You can also hold yourself accountable to the following questions:

+ Am I willing to hold the intention to act with compassion and kindness?

+ Am I willing to shift into giving and receiving?

+ Am I willing to use the skills, tools, and distinctions I know to help myself get to the place where I can act out of compassionate lovingkindness?

At times, perhaps because you are still in pain or for some other reason, you may not feel willing to take on the intention to give and receive, and that's okay. What we believe is important here is that if you're going to reach an agreement with the other person, you approach them in some way that their needs are also met. It's a practical reality that the best way to get what you want is to help the other person get what they want as well.

Once you move into the resolution stage, you begin making requests that can lead to agreements. Let's turn now to the types of agreements you might make.

Primary Agreements

Conflicts arise when your strategy to meet your needs differs from someone else's strategy to meet theirs. In uncovering these needs, however, you can create an agreement that strives to satisfy both of you.

> primary agreements *n. pl.*
>
> the strategies designed by you and the person you are in conflict with that you both believe will meet the needs that surfaced during the connection phase

Primary agreements can be anything; there may be requests and agreements from both of you, or just one person. The simplest types, though, are when one person agrees to do something for the other. For example, you agree to pay the other person a specific amount of money by a certain time, or the other person agrees to talk to someone on your behalf in the next few days.

More complicated primary agreements involve changes in interpersonal behavior patterns, which are common in family and work partnerships where people have history with each other and are interested in an ongoing relationship. The conflict may arise out of a pattern of behavior that isn't meeting your needs, and when those needs become clearer through the IPM process, the shift in behavior you desire might also become clear. In this case, you can formulate an agreement that when a particular situation comes up again in the future, the other person will respond in a different way. Or, you may be the one behaving in a way that the other person is finding difficult, and therefore agree to respond in a new way.

The solution requests you make form the primary agreement. Once you and the other person have both made requests that the other person is willing to say "yes" to, the last small but important step is to clarify and make sure you are both on the same page about the primary agreement.

Sally nods. "It sounds like you feel hopeless and would like to have some clarity about what we can do so that we don't keep coming back to the same issue. Is that right?"

James laughs. "I'm hearing Shawn's voice in my head say, 'Well then, make a request!' So maybe that's a start. What request could we make of each other that would help?"

Both ponder James's question for a few moments, then James says, "Here's one idea. Would it be possible for us to take time on the weekend to talk about the schedule for the week—what commitments we each have and what's going on with the kids? That way we can at least discuss it without things always feeling so last minute."

"I like that idea. We can figure out then who will take care of what. And it might be a good idea to include other house-hold tasks on it too, like grocery shopping," Sally adds.

"Ok," James confirms, "so we agree to set aside time on the weekend to discuss schedules for the week and decide who will take care of what."

"Yes, but ... I'm still concerned about how those conversations will go, like if I ask you to do something I used to do and your concerns about work come up, I would like to empathize with you instead of reacting out of my own fears."

"I appreciate that ... and if I start to feel that way, what could I do? Maybe the Self-Connection Process would at least interrupt that pattern and get me connected again. And if something does come up during the week, would you be willing to ask me first if I can talk about it instead of just springing it on me?"

"Yeah, absolutely. So we have an agreement to set aside time each weekend. I agree to ask you first if I need to talk to you about something during the week, and I'll empathize with your response when I ask you to do something ... and you'll do the Self-Connection Process when your concerns about work come up."

James smiles. "That sounds good!"

		Sally	James
Primary Agreements	Actions	Set aside time on weekend to discuss schedules/tasks	
	Behavior Patterns	Empathize with James when his concerns arise Ask James first if he can talk	Perform SCP when fears come up

With primary agreements, either person may have concerns about the agreement being kept. This is where the next two types of agreements become important.

SUPPORTING AGREEMENTS

At times you may need some help to fulfill a primary agreement.

> supporting agreements *n. pl.*
>
> agreements to support the fulfillment of the primary agreement

A supporting agreement can be as simple as agreeing to put an action on a to-do list or schedule it in a calendar. If the primary agreement is to talk to someone, the supporting agreement might be to send an email to schedule the phone call.

Once you've made a primary agreement, the easiest way to approach supporting agreements is to say:

"Now that we have this agreement, is there anything either of us might need to put in place to ensure that we fulfill it?"

If the primary agreement involves a change in behavior, you might bring up supporting agreements by saying:

"I'm a little concerned that this agreement we've made is about new behavior, and at least for myself I'm kind of worried about being able to do it. I'd like to talk about what we can do to support each other—or ourselves—to keep the agreement we made. It means a lot to me to follow through on what we said, so can we talk about what agreements we could have with ourselves and each other that would help us keep the primary agreement?"

These types of agreements are helpful when two people have a history with each other—especially when one or both people may lack trust that the other will do what they say. For example, if Sally and James have agreed that James will call Sally when he's going to be late coming home from work, Sally may not trust, due to her past experience, that James will follow through. Putting a supporting agreement in place, such as that James will set an alarm on his phone to go off at 6 p.m., reminding him to call her if he's not on his way home yet, can help both parties.

Likewise, the person agreeing to the request may be aware that fulfilling the request could be difficult. For example, James might know that when he gets involved in his work, he often doesn't notice the time until it's well past when he should have called. He knows he needs some support to keep the agreement, so he agrees to enlist the help of someone else in his office, perhaps an assistant, to track the time and remind him to call Sally. When primary agreements involve changes in behavior, enlisting the support of a neutral third party can be extremely helpful.

―――∿∿∿―――

Sally smiles back. "Yeah, I think that can work. Do you think there's anything we need to put in place to support us in keeping these agreements? I mean, I know how our weekends can get with the kids, and these other agreements might be hard to remember in the moment."

James chuckles. "So true. Remember last weekend? Felt like Friday night to Monday morning happened in about two hours. Between seeing your mom and Peg, Corey's game, Maggie's science fair, and taking the kids to the play, I'm not sure I had a moment to take a breath."

"No kidding!" Sally agrees. "I think it's a good idea to schedule it, maybe even try to have a regular time if we can. Sunday seems like a good day. What do you think?"

"I'm willing to try that. It may be too hard to do the same time each Sunday, but we could at least commit to that day, put it on the calendar, and rearrange things so we make sure there's time to do it."

"I like it." Sally grows thoughtful. "But what about the other agreements we made? Is there anything I can do to support you to do the SCP?"

James sighs. "That wouldn't just trigger me more?" He pauses, drumming his fingers on the table. "Well, maybe if I start to react, you could ask me, 'Are you connected to yourself?' That will remind me I value choosing instead of reacting."

"Ok," Sally says, "I'll ask, 'Are you connected to yourself?' if you react when I ask about doing something. I think for me, before going into any of these conversations, I would like to ask myself, *Am I willing to hear a "no"*? Since I've agreed to empathize, I think that would help remind me."

James summarizes their supporting agreements. "So we're going to schedule time in the calendar on Sunday to plan the week. You're going to ask yourself, *Am I willing to hear a no?* before these conversations, and if you see me begin to react, you're going to ask me, 'Are you connected to yourself?'"

		Sally	James
Primary Agreements	Actions	Set aside time on weekend to discuss schedules/tasks	
	Behavior Patterns	Empathize with James when his concerns arise Ask James first if he can talk	Perform SCP when fears come up
Supporting Agreements	Actions	Put appointment on calendar for Sunday; rearrange schedules to fit in	
	Behavior Patterns	If James starts to react, ask "Are you connected to yourself?" Ask "Am I willing to hear a 'no'?"	

Restoring Agreements

Even with supporting agreements in place, sometimes agreements are broken.

> **restoring agreements** *n. pl.*
>
> agreements that address what will happen if the primary agreement is not kept for whatever reason

After discussing any supporting agreements you've made, you might ask:

"What are we going to do if one of us doesn't keep to the agreement? We're talking about changing our behavior, and since it can take some time to learn a new way of doing things, what's our agreement if either one of us perceives we're not keeping the original agreement?"

Without these kinds of conversations, people often immediately assume a negative motive on the part of the other person when agreements aren't kept, and therefore jump to judgment, often ending up more disheartened than if they had not made the primary agreement in the first place. If, however, people have discussed the possibility that things may change, they are more likely to check in about their intentions and remind each other of agreements in a way that is supportive instead of critical. Restoring agreements encourage people—by connecting with needs—to step out of the conclusion that things should have happened a certain way. They set the stage for how the parties will interact in the event that the primary agreement does not play out as anticipated.

We encourage you to decide what you will do if the primary agreement is not kept immediately after feeling the satisfaction of having agreed to it. This is when you are usually full of hope and trust in the intentions on both your parts, and are therefore more likely to plan a better relationship-restoring proposal than if you wait until after the primary agreement has been breached.

When the primary agreement is a one-time action planned to occur by a certain date, a restoring agreement might simply set a consequence for the agreement being broken. For example, if your partner has agreed to have the car back by 3 p.m. because you need it to get to an appointment, a restoring agreement might be that if he doesn't have it back, he will pay for you to take a cab to your appointment, and he will pick you up afterward.

In a case where the primary agreement refers to a change in behavior on someone's part, the restoring agreements might lay out what both parties would say or do in the case that the person forgets or behaves as usual. This could include specific words and actions.

Using our example of James calling Sally if he's going to be late:

> Let's say James doesn't call Sally one evening because he was in a meeting with Scott that ran over, and he didn't hear the alarm on his phone. Without a restoring agreement in place, Sally would likely get angry and disconnected again from James. If she has agreed, however, to empathize with the need he was meeting, it can short-circuit her own pattern of behavior. When they talk after James gets home and he tells her why he forgot to call, she might empathize with his need to be effective and productive at work, meeting a further need for sustainability. She might then be able to express her own needs for predictability and planning of how to manage the kids around dinnertime, homework, and bed in a way that James can connect with, instead of reacting in a blaming manner. James can mourn the cost of the needs not met, both for himself—he didn't meet his need for integrity—and for Sally. It can also be connecting if both parties can empathize with the distress that the other may be feeling about the agreement not being kept.

If the skills are not in place to be able to empathize, another restoring agreement can be for each person to have a call with someone who can empathize, or even a call together with someone who can help facilitate the conversation. When a conflict has been difficult and emotions are strong on either side, this is sometimes a good option as it can help the parties become reconnected.

James picks up the last cookie and splits it in half, handing one to Sally. "I'm already feeling so much better from this conversation. And the cookies don't hurt!"

Sally pushes James's shoulder playfully.

"I'm thinking now about those other agreements," James continues, "the ones to make for when you don't remember to do what you planned. I know we can both beat ourselves up when that happens. Is there anything we can do if, say, another Sunday comes around like last weekend and we miss our scheduled time?"

Sally muses while chewing her cookie. "I think what you said is key, about beating ourselves up. So maybe what we could do is acknowledge what needs we were meeting in whatever we made a higher priority than our scheduled time. So in other words, to empathize with ourselves for what *did* happen."

"Yeah, and then maybe commit to set a new time as soon as we can," James adds.

"Exactly. And maybe that same idea would work if either of us forget and react—maybe taking a time-out as soon as one of us notices we're disconnected, do the SCP, and then come back and empathize with each other."

"And keep Shawn and Alicia on speed dial in case we need them!"

James and Sally both laugh.

———

In mediating your life, supporting and restoring agreements are often crucial. If you notice some distrust in yourself about an agreement being kept (either on your side or the other person's), you can suggest supporting and restoring agreements. These fortify your ongoing relationship with the person, whether or not the agreement is kept. The more important your relationship with the person is, the more helpful these types of agreements become.

		Sally	James
Primary Agreements	Actions	Set aside time on weekend to discuss schedules/tasks	
	Behavior Patterns	Empathize with James when his concerns arise Ask James first if he can talk	Perform SCP when fears come up
Supporting Agreements	Actions	Put appointment on calendar for Sunday, rearrange schedules to fit in	
	Behavior Patterns	If James starts to react, ask "Are you connected to yourself?" Ask "Am I willing to hear a 'no?'"	
Restoring Agreements	Actions	Commit to a new time as soon as possible	
	Behavior Patterns	Empathize with needs met/not met in prioritizing something else over scheduled time Take time out if either react, perform SCP, then empathize with each other	

PRACTICE PAUSE

Thinking back to the primary agreements you've made recently, did you make any supporting or restoring agreements? If so, what were they? If not, what supporting or restoring agreements do you imagine might have been helpful?

PRESENT TENSE NATURE OF AGREEMENTS

When you have made an agreement with someone, how do you then think about it? Do you assume it must happen as agreed? *Well, of course!* you may think. *We agreed to it. Obviously it should happen as agreed to!*

Yet, you can never guarantee what you will do in the future; all you really have is this moment, and whatever occurs in this moment will pass. In other words, when you sit with other people and make agreements about the future, none of you can guarantee that future activity will occur—all you can say is that in the present moment, you intend to do something in the future and that you are not aware of anything that will keep you from doing it. But as you know, numerous things intervene in human affairs that keep you from doing what you agree to, even if you are fully committed to it. There's also the possibility that you will change your mind; conditions might shift such that you no longer want to fulfill the agreement.

United States law and its antecedents in English law recognize that in breach-of-contract cases, people cannot guarantee what will happen in the future; there is no requirement that contracting parties will fulfill a bargain as a duty. The parties, therefore, have the right to breach a contract, though there may be consequences for doing so. It's no surprise that this system has been in place for over 800 years, as the realities of human interaction have always been a struggle. Hence, since agreements may not be kept, stating what the parties will do in that event is vital.

A more realistic way, then, to hold agreements is to consider them *present tense intentions* rather than guarantees of future action. While this doesn't mean you shouldn't take a commitment seriously, viewing agreements this way gives you more choice. If, for example, you believe that because someone has said they will do something in the future it is a guarantee, you are holding the agreement as a demand. In other words, you believe they *should* keep it. If they don't, you may disconnect, even seeking revenge or punishment.

Instead, when you hold agreements as present tense intentions, each moment is an opportunity for connection and contribution—even the moment when the agreement has clearly been broken (we'll talk more about what to do when this occurs shortly). You may notice a freedom and acceptance that comes from living this way, a peace that is not disturbed if things don't happen the way you thought they would. With this mindset, it's easier to stay connected with yourself and other people, making the best of whatever happens, whether the agreement is kept or not.

For example, the two of us (Ike and John) were in Australia a few years ago with another trainer, Sigal. We were hanging out for a few hours in Sydney before catching a train to the retreat venue. This brief interlude was our time to be tourists and enjoy the city a bit before we started teaching. Well, due to a mix-up on the location of the station, we ended up missing our train. In my mind (Ike's), I interpreted it as my misreading of the tickets, concluding it was my fault. Because I had stimulated disruption for other people, I believed everyone should be blaming me for being late. To me, we had an *implicit* agreement that I was the logistical director, responsible for our arrival to the retreat location on time. This wasn't an *explicit* agreement, but it was my reaction nonetheless.

Fairly quickly, however, I noticed that John and Sigal were not acting in a way consistent with blame; in fact, they reacted with a kind of openness and spaciousness, an attitude of "Okay, this is what's happened, but let's just enjoy our time together and move on to the next moment, focused on how we can be in connection now."

Although we're not suggesting that considering an agreement "present tense" is a way to let yourself or the other person "off the hook," we *are* suggesting that you have greater choice, and therefore greater power, when you are in reality about what people can and cannot guarantee. The bottom line: when you hold your agreements less tightly, it makes for a more pleasant experience for everyone if the unexpected happens.

PRACTICE PAUSE

Notice how you hold agreements you've made. If you find that you tend to think agreements *should* happen the way they are stated, try taking some period of time, maybe a week or so, and see if during that time you can hold agreements differently. What opens up in your world when you do?

INTEGRITY AND AGREEMENTS

Invariably when we discuss the topic of holding agreements as present intentions, someone will say, "But wait, I *do* want the agreement to be kept, otherwise I wouldn't have made it!" Once again, we are not suggesting that holding agreements as present intentions means that you completely let go of your needs and your desire that they be met through the agreement. We're pointing to something much more subtle—that it helps *your own experience* when you can have some clarity about not holding an agreement as a "should."

Some self-empowerment courses talk about the integrity of your word, suggesting that the more you keep your word, the more trust and power you build with others. In our experience this is also the case—the more we do what we say we are going to do, the more it contributes to trust with ourselves and other people. So while not holding agreements as demands may seem contradictory to this, we actually see the two as compatible.

Ask yourself this question: Can I simultaneously hold that the more I act on my word, the better, and that if agreements don't happen as stated, then that's what simply *is*? Honoring your word, after all, includes tracking that you made an agreement, who is going to be affected if there is a change in plan, and letting them know at an early opportunity if that plan won't be fulfilled. Integrity also includes accepting the consequences that flow from any change in decision, including being with any distress the decision may stimulate in others. When you honor your word—even if that means informing someone that you can't keep an agreement you made—you are willing to be heard and understood, even by yourself, about not doing what you said you would do. In doing so, you connect with the needs you are meeting by changing the plan, and mourn the needs you will not meet. With this internal clarity, it is more likely you can be considerate of the reaction from others who are impacted by your decision.

For example, let's say two friends, Mack and Fred, decide to go into business together. They spend three exciting months working on the idea and preparing, and then a few weeks before launching, Fred is offered a lucrative position at his ideal company. Torn between his commitment to his friend and his amazing new opportunity, he approaches Mack as soon as possible to talk about it.

> Mack is understandably upset about the possibility of Fred pulling out at the last minute. Since Fred has the Mediate Your Life tools and skills available, he empathizes with Mack and is also able to express his own distress and the needs he is meeting by accepting the new position. Though a difficult situation and conversation, the ability to create clarity about his needs allows Fred to be in integrity while making a decision and staying in connection with Mack as they work out a plan for the business.

THE ITERATIVE PROCESS OF BEHAVIORAL CHANGE

When agreements are made concerning changes in behavior, it becomes especially important to understand the present tense nature of the agreement. Behavioral changes are not easy to make; we can almost guarantee that the first few times someone attempts to change their behavior when the particular situation arises, they will not do it. This "failure" has nothing to do with their intention and everything to do with the process by which behavioral change occurs.

To accomplish this type of shift in yourself, you first have to become aware within the exact moment you want the change to happen, then know you have another choice available, then choose it. It is likely that both the awareness and making the new choice will take a number of tries before you succeed. But don't berate yourself. It's human nature to initially run on your habitual way of doing things. Significant changes take time and practice.

It's a common pattern to make these types of agreements with someone concerning behavioral change, then simply continue living your lives. It's not until the situation comes up again that you see if you can deal with it differently based on the agreement. If not, it is an opportunity to revisit the agreement, seeing if there's a way to adjust it to find a strategy that will work more effectively and meet more needs.

At one time, James and Sally had a conflict about the use of powdered garlic in cooking: Sally doesn't like powdered garlic, and James used it because it was easier and he couldn't tell the difference between that and the real thing.

When Sally asked James not to use it, they made an agreement that James wouldn't put it in a recipe that Sally would be eating, or he would separate out a portion for her without it before sprinkling it on the food. One night, James was in a hurry cooking dinner for the family and threw in powdered garlic without thinking about it. When Sally got upset, James knew the issue wasn't really about the powdered garlic; it was about Sally's need for care and consideration. From her perspective, those needs would be met if James were willing to use real garlic simply because she wanted it, even if it made no sense to him.

They talked further about strategies that would help James in these situations, both with the awareness (putting tape over the powdered garlic so he'd have to pause before using it) and the new choice (using garlic-infused oil or pre-chopped garlic to meet his needs for efficiency). Now they're in another period of living with those agreements until another situation crops up.

These types of conflicts are generally frequent in close relationships. While they can seem like trivial issues, they're what intimate relationships are built upon. Does James care enough to deal with the powdered garlic issue? If Sally cannot trust him about that, her needs for care and consideration are not being met. These are the seemingly small issues that, because the underlying needs are still fundamental and important, can lead to major resentments and rifts in the relationship.

When the issues are more important, such as the agreements Sally and James make about managing schedules for their family and household, understanding how behavioral change happens becomes even more critical. Even with the supporting agreements they made, both are likely to forget when situations arise that call for those behavioral agreements. Sally will ask James to do something when he cannot take it in, and James will forget to perform the SCP and react. As a result, they may get into another argument. The bottom line: making agreements is not a panacea—the work of making behavioral change is real and ongoing.

We find it helpful to remind ourselves that making agreements is an iterative process, especially in an interpersonal conflict with someone we interact with frequently. For example, you may connect with yourself and come up with a strategy that you think will fulfill your need. If it involves someone else, you have a conversation and make the request, and they agree to it. In the carrying out of that request, however, you find that it didn't meet your need the way you thought it would. This does not necessarily mean you were wrong or that they didn't fulfill the request the way you asked them to; it might simply mean that you now have more information, can reassess your needs and the strategies that might meet them, and request a modification of the agreement.

Mediating your life sometimes becomes a series of conversations that focus on the modification of agreements as both you and the other person learn more about what will meet your needs. Sometimes what you initially agree to isn't actually the best strategy; it's merely the first iteration. It may be the tenth iteration that makes you both happy. The truth is, it can take awhile to get through different layers of experimentation with various strategies. The first agreement may be a "good enough" agreement, but it can evolve as you both learn more about what will meet your needs.

In Chapter 8, we'll see how James and Sally mess up and continue to work through their situation, changing the agreements as they find what will contribute to their lives.

WHEN AGREEMENTS ARE NOT KEPT

Successfully navigating a broken agreement, especially when a restoring agreement is not in place, requires awareness of your attitude about the agreement not being kept, as well as your communication with the other person. How you hold the situation and how you communicate can either hinder or assist the process of working toward the change you want to see.

In the moment of a broken agreement, you have a set of possible choices you can make, including going into the norm of blame, shame, and punishment. If *you* didn't keep the agreement, then perhaps you judge yourself or try to place the blame somewhere else, such as on "outside circumstances" that kept you from fulfilling it. If the *other* person didn't keep it, you might blame them and think they're a bad person. You might also feel hopeless, believing the previous conversation and agreement was a waste of time.

How does this choice play out in the moment? Let's take the example of James agreeing to call if he's going to be home late.

One evening, James forgets to call. Sally expected that because they made the agreement, it would be kept as stated, as if it were written in stone and punishable by death. Her underlying attitude is, James should do it and there's something wrong with him if he doesn't. She has framed the agreement as a demand.

When James comes home, he will notice on some level that she is upset. Even if she is using the components of Observation, Feelings, Needs, and Requests to talk about it, he will get the message of blame, shame, and punishment that she sends. James then reacts to what she says: his need for autonomy comes up, and the needs *he* was meeting in not calling aren't seen. Since with Sally James tends to go into a flight pattern, he will likely close down. They enter a downward spiral that results in neither of them getting their needs met, and the possibility of reaching an even better strategy than the original agreement is lost for the moment.

If you find yourself in judgment after an agreement is broken, check whether you were holding the agreement as a demand. Do you have any sense of "Well, you agreed to it, so now you should do it" or "I agreed to it and now I have to do it"? Admitting that you had the agreement as a demand is not an invitation to judge yourself further. It's a chance to stop, perform the Self-Connection Process to connect with yourself, and step into mediator mind.

From mediator mind, you can recognize that the broken agreement has already happened and cannot be changed—it's in the past. The bottom line is this: if an agreement is not kept and you think it should have been, then you are fighting what *is*; the agreement hasn't been kept, so that's the reality of that moment. The question then is, do you want to be present and connected with yourself and others in that moment, or do you want your reaction to *what is* to take you out of showing up and being present for your life? Though being "right" can feel wonderful in the moment—stamping your foot and saying, "You agreed. You said you would do it!" can feel like a victory—it isn't likely to get you what you want in that moment.

Instead of becoming increasingly upset about it, you can start with "what is" *now*. Ask, "What will better meet my needs in this moment?" Using the SCP and accessing mediator mind, you can see all perspectives and more of the choices available to you.

It's important to point out here that when one of you has not kept the agreement, you are again in mediation with them. Using the IPM process, start with connecting to yourself, and then proceed from the point where you are now, with whatever upset occurred from the broken agreement. How you continue will depend on whether it was the other person or you who didn't fulfill the agreement.

If the other person broke the agreement, we've already said that they were meeting some needs by not doing what they said they would do. But let's now look at how empathy plays a role. In empathizing with them in the third step of the IPM map, it can be particularly helpful to focus on what they were saying "yes" to when they didn't keep the agreement. In other words, in not keeping your agreement, they are choosing to do something else instead (assuming they didn't simply forget); focusing on empathizing with the "yes" can begin to shift you into connection with them.

When you express in the fourth step of the IPM map, you might talk about what needs of yours were not met. In the resolution phase, you can both consider whether the agreement itself ought to change, or whether new supporting or restoring agreements would help in the future.

If you are the one who didn't keep the agreement, you are likely to have some internal conflict about it. You said you would do something and you didn't, so you might have an internal voice judging you. Try not to let that overtake you. (We will talk in the next chapter about a process you can use in this situation to help you reconnect with yourself, allowing you to be more clear in deciding how you want to communicate with the person about not fulfilling your side of the agreement.)

In talking to the other person, we want to remind you that you are in the realm of interpersonal mediation. They are likely to have some distress about the agreement not being kept; empathizing with their upset helps open up some space for them to be able to hear what was going on for you when you didn't do what you said you would. Using the IPM map, you can stay in the connection phase, using empathy and expression until you have re-established connection with the person. Then, in the resolution phase, you can have a discussion with them about how to adjust the original agreement (and add in supporting and restoring agreements) to better meet the needs of both of you.

Now let's consider what happens when Sally deals in the moment with James forgetting to call when he's late coming home from work.

> Instead of going into blame, she uses tools that she knows will help. Before he gets home, she might perform the Enemy Image Process. When he does come home, she uses the IPM map. Starting with the SCP to connect with herself, she then asks herself whether she can hear a "please," then she mediates the needs that kept James from fulfilling the agreement, as well as the needs she would like to be met. The conversation allows them to find a new synthesis, a fresh agreement that might better contribute to their well-being. From James's perspective, being heard as well as hearing Sally may prompt him to recommit to the original agreement with a new supporting agreement in place. Instead of a downward spiral of disconnection and blame, they are in an upward spiral of mutual enhancement and benefit.

COMING BACK TO CHOICE

Being connected to yourself and your needs means all your choices become clear. One of those choices may be to decide in the future not to have the same kind of relationship with someone. If you've sought to have your needs met through agreements with that person, and over time find that you don't have the confidence to meet them by making those agreements, you may choose to have your needs met in other ways. You may either choose to end the relationship, or to be in it in a different way.

Remember that the point of using these tools is always to bring you back to choice. Agreements are a key place where "shoulds" easily creep into our thinking. "I said I would do this, so I should." "He said he would do this, so he should." "I should keep the agreement I made." As we've said, we're not encouraging you to *not* keep your agreements. What we're emphasizing is the power of stepping out of the whole "should-should not" duality completely.

As best you can, stay connected with your needs at each moment. Use the tools presented thus far, especially the Self-Connection Process, which helps you step into mediator mind and see your choices, and the Enemy Image Process if you find that you have enemy images based on an agreement not being kept. Use the IPM map to have a conversation with the person about the abandoned agreement, or, if *you* didn't keep the agreement, you will benefit from the process called Mourn Celebrate Learn in the next chapter. By utilizing these tools and practices, every moment is an opportunity to connect with yourself and the other person, even—and especially—in the moments when agreements don't go as you expected.

NEXT UP

People naturally go into a process of evaluation after something happens. Whether your evaluation supports you in moving toward what you desire, or reinforces past judgments, depends on how you go through the process. In the next chapter, you'll learn how to evaluate in terms of needs instead of judgments, resulting in greater connection with yourself.

7

From Rumination to Reflection

Transforming Post-Conversation Judgments

*When you stop ruminating about what has already
happened, when you stop worrying about what might never
happen, then you will be in the present moment.
Then you will begin to experience joy in life.*
—Thích Nhất Hạnh

———✺———

"WE'LL SEE YOU IN A FEW MONTHS, DAD." JAMES HANGS
up the phone and breathes out a mixture of relief and
gloom. He made it through that conversation, for now at least.
He'd called Dan to try to clean up the mess he'd made the week
earlier when they talked and to finalize the travel plans for him,
Sally, and the kids to visit.

The Enemy Image Process he'd done right after the
previous call had been so helpful in kindling a feeling of hope
that he believed the connection he longed for with his father
might be possible. After performing the EIP, he was going to
ask Sally to do the Intensity Exercise with him and Shawn to

role-play the conversation, but since he and Sally had their own issues to talk about, he instead asked Alicia to help him with the Intensity Exercise. More quickly than he had imagined, the triggers of Dan calling him "boy" and then "Jimmy" were both defused through the exercise. Then, when he and Shawn role-played the conversation, James practiced by asking Shawn to react using both names, as well as saying other phrases typical of Dan that James would find difficult to hear. Following the conversations with both Alicia and Shawn, James felt solid going into the call with his dad.

Now that he has talked to Dan, he attempts to refocus on work only to find his mind recalling the conversation. Bits of their call replay in his mind, each triggering a different emotion —frustration, apathy, dejection, bitterness. *What did I do wrong?* he thinks. *I was so sure I'd be able to talk to him. Why couldn't I be more present? Maybe how I tried to empathize with him wasn't good enough. I hate how I feel so small and insignificant when I talk to him! Why does it seem like my only options are to be a doormat and take what he dishes out, or lash out at him and then feel bad about it?* James grits his teeth as he stares out the window. "I was such an idiot to think that anything would ever change," he says out loud.

In the wake of their conversation, the spark of hope James had felt after doing the EIP quickly fades back into hopelessness.

—⁓—

Evaluating what happened in the past is a characteristic of being human. It's woven into many settings, such as the military and the workplace, in the form of a "debrief" whereby people get together to talk about—and hopefully learn from—the past so that they can affect the future. These debriefings often focus on strategies, like what ought to change the next time around to achieve a different result. The majority of the time, people tend to expect these sessions to emphasize who is to blame or be punished for whatever went wrong.

You might notice that you have an internal version of these debriefings. For example, have you ever left a conversation with someone and felt terrible afterward? You carry that feeling around for a few hours, a day, or even longer, eventually noticing that you have all sorts of thoughts and judgments about yourself and the conversation. Like James, many of these thoughts are reproaches, blaming yourself or the other person. Remembering one thing you said, you think, *Why did I say that? What was I thinking?* Then you recall something the other person said, feel angry, and decide that "when he said that I should have retorted with ...." Feelings might range from anger and frustration to sadness, disappointment, or shame.

When these intrusive thoughts and feelings get in the way, what do you do? Most people ruminate on them, going over and over what happened in the mistaken belief that doing so will somehow change what happens in the future, when actually they are gnawing on something that has no value. The other go-to option is to ignore these intrusive thoughts and get on with the day. Either way, you miss out on the gift that is available when you're able to find what's going on underneath the spin cycle of judgment that has captured you.

In this chapter, you'll learn a map that will allow you to emerge from the discomfort and pain of continuously chewing on what went wrong and how you should have been or done something different.

PRACTICE PAUSE

Think of a recent interaction or situation you felt
bad about afterward, judging yourself or someone
else. Take note of how you felt, what you were
thinking, and what you tend to do in those situations.

Debriefing Yourself

While you might reflect after an event about things that went well,
the thoughts that often follow tend toward the negative and what
went wrong. These thoughts indicate needs that were *not* met,
while those that focus on what went well indicate that certain
needs of yours *were* met. Thus, we use a process we call Mourn
Celebrate Learn (MCL), a map that enables you to mourn the
needs not met, celebrate the needs that were (or at least that you
were trying to meet), and then learn from what you've uncovered.

This process is a powerful way to debrief yourself that is
especially helpful when you notice you feel awful after a conversation and have thoughts you don't enjoy. The name of the map
outlines the three steps:

1. Mourn

   Empathize with your needs that were not met by what happened.

2. Celebrate

   Empathize with your needs that were met by what happened.

3. Learn

   Reflect on new possibilities that have emerged. Plan and practice
   what you would like to do to better meet your needs.

Below we'll go through these steps in detail, but first let's touch on our discussions in previous chapters about how the maps and exercises relate to mediator mind.

As you've learned, the Self-Connection Process (SCP) helps you become present and step into a space that is outside determined points of view. Then, in the Intensity Exercise, you move into mediator mind to perform the SCP and make a new choice about how to respond when you are triggered. In the Interpersonal Mediation map, you use mediator mind to mediate your own conflict, being both the mediator and someone in the conflict.

Mourn Celebrate Learn (MCL) is a map similar to the Enemy Image Process (EIP), wherein you take the mediator position to empathize with two perspectives within you. In EIP, the two perspectives you are mediating are your own needs and those of the person with whom you have an enemy image (without that person being present). In MCL, you are empathizing with the part of you whose needs were not met, and the part whose needs were met.

When you become aware of feeling unsettled after an interaction, we recommend first performing the SCP to put yourself into mediator mind, enabling yourself to choose what to do next. Then, as you go through the Mourn Celebrate Learn process, you'll stay in mediator mind to empathize with all that is going on for you.

MOURN CELEBRATE LEARN

MOURN

As people are usually most aware of judgmental thoughts after something has occurred, we generally suggest starting with Mourning. (We'll discuss exceptions to this a bit later.) To mourn, you'll go through the components of NVC, beginning with observations on what actually happened—what you or the other person specifically said or did. It helps to remember that observations are what a video would show of the situation.

You might also be aware that you have strong interpretations of what went on, choosing to focus on your thoughts and judgments. In this case, your thoughts may boil down to some version of *You really screwed that up. You're such an idiot.* You might also notice judgments of the other person. As these thoughts are generated, take note of them and name them. Simply observe what it is you are thinking.

Then, turn to tapping into how you feel. You might feel hopeless, scared, depressed, sad, angry, or some combination. These feelings may also vary over time, especially as you begin to get in touch with them and name them. If you've identified more than one observation, you might also notice different feelings that go along with each one.

From feelings, check in with your needs and ask:

+ What needs are not met by having those thoughts?

+ Or more generally, what needs were not met in the situation?

In this process you translate the thoughts that are about judging yourself or others—what went wrong and what was good or bad—and try to find the needs behind those thoughts. Then, you deepen into those needs, imagining what it would feel like for them to be met.

As you name and experience these needs, you might notice that a natural mourning or sadness comes up. If your needs weren't met through your own actions or words, you may also feel some regret about what you could have done differently. If your judgments were triggered by what the other person did or didn't do, you may feel disappointment or sadness. Allow yourself to feel those emotions as you sink into your needs.

A recap of these steps is as follows:

1. MOURN

   a. Identify observations of what happened or the judgments you have in your mind after the conversation.

   b. Notice how you feel when you recall what happened or think those thoughts.

   c. Ask what needs of yours are not met by what happened or what unmet needs are you seeking to express with your judgmental thoughts.

⸻⁓⸻

James recognizes his internal distress and remembers his conversation with Shawn. When he had expressed his hopefulness about the upcoming conversation with his dad, Shawn suggested that James also set aside time after the conversation to connect with himself, reminding James of the Mourn Celebrate Learn map. At the time, James thought he wouldn't need it, but now he sees the value, having several thoughts and judgments about what went wrong in the conversation.

With too many thoughts roiling in his mind to focus well, he decides to write out the process so that he won't get lost in the chaos. To help keep things straight, he imagines himself sitting in a mediator's chair, with the chair on his left representing the part of himself that has unmet needs, and the chair on his right representing the part that did have some needs met.

He can barely visualize the chair on the right because the unmet needs are so loud and insistent, so he starts listening for what that part of him is saying.

The first thought that comes is, *What did I do wrong?* James writes down the observation, "I'm thinking I did something wrong," and then checks in with his feelings. Immediately, he feels despair. *What needs am I meeting by having that thought?* he wonders. *What comes to mind is competence. I'd really like to be effective in what I'm doing, to have some success with it.*

As soon as that thought is complete, another leaps in. *Success? Who are you kidding? You're an idiot to hope for change here.* James sighs and writes that thought down as another observation. When he taps into his feelings, he notes anger, disgust, and some disappointment as well. Finding the need behind that thought proves to be a little tricky. At first he can't think of any possible need, and his mind keeps following well-worn pathways about what didn't go well. He keeps pulling himself back to the question and eventually it hits him. *I'd really like to have the power to create change, and to know I have that power as well as the skill and capacity. And I'd like to have the trust and faith that my efforts will have some impact.* A wave of energy passes through him as he writes down those needs.

Desiring to have an impact triggers a recollection of a segment of the conversation. James had said to Dan, "When you call me 'boy,' I get a little ticked off. I'm a grown man, a father myself, not a boy anymore. Would you be willing to call me James?"

Dan had responded by saying, "Well, you'll always be my boy. Doesn't matter how old you get. And I called you Jimmy all the time you were growing up—not likely I'll be able to get that name out of my head." Dan chuckled as he continued, "Well, except for when we called you Jambo. Remember that?" Dan went on to reminisce but it didn't even register with James. He felt his entire body get heavy and exhausted, a thick fog of despair settling over him. Simply remembering this exchange re-creates that feeling again, and James checks in with his needs. "I'd still like respect and a sense of equality with him," he says, realizing that these same needs he came up with when performing the EIP still ring true for him now.

As James looks over the observations, feelings, and needs he has down so far, he perceives that the biggest observation is missing—the sense that he desires a different outcome than what happened. Sadness rises in him with this realization, and he notes that his needs to connect, be heard, and be understood are not met. The sadness prompts James to go further into the mourning of his needs not being met, and he takes a few minutes to be with those needs. As he does so, the sadness shifts subtly and he feels a release in his chest, allowing him to simply be with all of it—his disappointment and despair, along with the needs for trust, respect, equality, connection, competence, and power to create change—with greater ease and kindness.

Mourning helps you shift out of blaming or judgmental thoughts about what you did or how you did it; however, it does not provide the whole picture. There were likely also occurrences that met your needs—or you attempted to meet them in what you did—that you can uncover through celebrating.

CELEBRATE

As you've probably observed and experienced yourself, people in most cultures tend to ruminate on what is wrong, what didn't work, and where things need to be fixed. It's important, however, to also acknowledge what went well. Not only does it provide an antidote to the tendency to focus on the negative, but recognizing where needs were indeed met also prompts you to focus attention on how to continue to achieve that.

The steps to this segment are as follows:

2. CELEBRATE

    a. Identify observations of what happened that you liked.

    b. Notice how you feel when you recall those instances in the conversation.

    c. Ask what needs of yours are met by what happened.

Celebration begins the same way as mourning—by identifying your observations. Examples would be focusing on:

+ observations about what actually happened in the conversation

+ thoughts you have about it now

+ *how you were* in the conversation

+ celebrating the intention you had going into it (less tangible)

+ how you were able to do something differently than you did before

Perhaps there was a moment you were triggered by something the other person said and you were able to reconnect with yourself in a way that pleased you. Maybe you responded to something the other person said that prompted them to soften, or you expressed yourself with honesty and care for the other person despite your concern about how it would land. You can also note observations about what the other person did or didn't do that you liked.

When you have the observations in mind, turn to how you *feel* in remembering them. You'll notice that your feelings are almost always positive in celebration, generating emotions of gratitude, appreciation, joy, satisfaction, or pleasure.

Now, look at what needs were met during those positive times in the conversation, both from what you or the other person said or did (celebrations can be based on what happened between you and the other person, or on your internal assessment of what you did and how you felt).

You can also celebrate the intention you acted from in the conversation. Because everything you do is a strategy to meet needs, you can celebrate the underlying motivations that prompted you to act that way, even when those actions didn't ultimately meet your needs. For example, perhaps you made a comment during the conversation that was intended to lighten the mood, but it didn't go over as well as you would have liked. You can still celebrate that you were acting from a need to contribute, even while you mourn that it didn't have the intended result.

When you deepen into these needs, it can be quite liberating and exciting; you realize there were strategies that worked, things you said that you were pleased about, moments you stopped yourself from reacting and took a breath instead, or times you simply listened and heard the other person in a new way. Allow yourself to be energized by what did go well.

It's important to note here that many people go back and forth between the first two parts of the map—mourning and celebrating —multiple times before they feel complete. In the process of celebrating, for example, you might identify certain needs that still weren't met. Allow yourself to fluidly follow what comes up for you. If you're celebrating and find another judgment arises, note it and switch back to mourning. Track where you were in celebrating when the judgment came up so that after you mourn that judgment, you can go back to your celebration. We recommend staying in these first two steps of the MCL process until the intrusive thoughts and feelings have lightened considerably, no stray memories of the situation cause you to go into distress, and you feel complete and ready to move into learning.

—◊◊◊—

Feeling a little better from going through the process of mourning, James looks forward to celebrating. Even so, he flounders getting started, searching to find something, anything, that had gone well. Finally, he realizes he can celebrate what he did regardless of what happened afterward. He feels lighter as soon as he recognizes that one of the first things he said to Dan is something to celebrate—that he regretted what he'd said at the end of their previous conversation.

Before he can go further in celebrating that, however, he feels the heaviness creep back in. Dan had not responded at all to James's admission of regret, and James interprets that his father sidestepped it out of denial and discomfort. Going back to mourning for a moment, James feels the need for recognition of his attempt to make amends. Being with this need supports him to go back into celebration, as he gives himself the recognition for opening the conversation with honesty, meeting his needs for care and integrity. *That's who I want to be in the world,* James thinks to himself, *a person who acknowledges when I haven't acted in the way I'd like.*

The appreciation he experiences for himself makes the next celebration come to mind much more easily. When Dan responded to James's request about not calling him "Jimmy" and "boy," James had identified what was going on in his body pretty quickly. *I wish I'd been able to do something more with it,* James reflects. *I could have done the SCP right then and asked if I could hear a "please," but I didn't even think of that.* James switches back to mourning again, feeling a little disheartened at not having been able to shift what he was feeling in the moment. He states out loud, "I'd really like the awareness and capacity to be able to notice and then do something right away so I can respond more effectively." He notes that at least he had not reacted as he might have in the past, and marks this change as a celebration. He feels encouraged and thankful that he was at least aware of what was going on, meeting his needs for growth and learning, not to mention dodging making a further mess!

Prompted to look at other ways he's pleased with how he handled himself, James recalls his preparation for the conversation. He and Shawn talked about James's distress when he interpreted that Dan was telling him how to raise his kids, and what request he might make. Though it brought up a lot of fear in James to even consider saying something about it, he recalls what he managed to say and how Dan responded.

"It's hard for me when you try to tell me how to raise my kids. I'd like to think I'm doing a decent job on my own. I'm wondering if you could tell me what you heard me say." When James asked this, he felt his whole body shake.

Dan had said in return, "Well, I just don't want to see him go downhill. I know you're having some problems with him and he's just at that age where things are only going to get more difficult." Even though James knew his father had not responded to his request, he decided to empathize.

"It sounds like you really care about Corey and would like to support him. Is that it?"

"Sure," Dan said, "he's a good kid. I'd like to see him stay that way. So easy these days for them to go astray."

James feels proud of himself for letting his dad know it bothered him when Dan gave him advice, and for making a connecting request, again recognizing his needs for growth and competence that he met in doing so. He also celebrates that he chose to empathize with his father instead of getting frustrated, which gives him a sense of accomplishment. James actually feels appreciative of what his father said, knowing he came from a place of care and concern for Corey, and it opens James up to feeling more expansive about what he sees as Dan's interference. He still doesn't like the way Dan shows his care, and he wasn't able to make a request that Dan not give advice about raising Corey, but he feels encouraged both by his own efforts and by the clarity he's gained about where Dan is coming from.

James feels his body get lighter and lighter as he notes what happened in the conversation that meets his needs.

———

Celebrating is a close cousin to gratitude practice. The more you can celebrate when your needs are met, the easier it is to be grateful for what is showing up in your life. You might consider using this part of the MCL as a practice on its own—make it a ritual each day to celebrate the good things that happened and the needs that were met. You may be surprised how much it expands your life.

LEARN

Once you have mourned and celebrated the needs met and not met, you can learn from the experience. Of course, if at any time in this step you find more comes up to celebrate or mourn, feel free to return to the first two steps before continuing. While the first two steps shift you out of judgment and into connection with yourself, the step of learning is designed to prompt you to take the shifts you experienced and integrate them into your life in the present and future.

This step actually has three parts to it: learning, planning, and practicing. In learning, you will consider the following guiding questions:

+ What have you learned in going through this process?

+ How do you feel different now than you did before you began?

+ How can you better meet your needs going forward?

In learning, you reflect on the process of mourning and celebrating as well as on the situation. As a result, you might have insights now about how you can shift out of blaming yourself for something you did, or how you can change from feeling your heart closed to holding the other person with care and consideration. You might likewise discover the power of being able to shift out of judgmental thoughts and into connection with needs. You may also be more in touch with your needs, and able to consider how to better meet them in the future, which leads you naturally into planning.

When you plan, you consider what you would like to be or do differently—either in general or in a specific situation—to meet your needs. Both mourning and celebrating can help you tease out more ideas about how to experience what you desire. For example, after uncovering needs that were not met during mourning, you might ask yourself, "What could I do differently next time in order to better meet my needs?" After revealing needs that *were* met through celebration, you can ask, "What might help me meet those needs again?"

Planning can lead you to ideas about how to move forward in the situation you are working with, and it can also prompt you to consider more generally how to meet your needs in life. To make plans in relation to your current situation, you might ask:

+ "What do I want to do, if anything, to move forward with this situation?"

To consider the needs you've uncovered in the larger context of your life, you might ask:

+ "What new patterns or habits of thought and action can I create to better meet these needs in my life?" or

+ "What can I learn from this situation that will help me in general to better meet these needs?"

When your planning leads you to desired actions, such as having another conversation with someone or interacting with them in a new way, practicing is a helpful next step. Set up a role-playing session with a partner, or rehearse what you would like to say or do in your own mind.

To recap, the steps to learning follow.

3. Learn

    a. Learn through reflecting on how you feel different now that you've gone through the process.

    b. Plan what you would like to do from here, either in the current situation or in general, to meet your needs.

    c. Practice anything that will help you embody your learning so you will have it available in a similar situation in the future.

mediateyourlife.com/mourn-celebrate-learn-video/

James is inspired to dial up Shawn and thank him. When Shawn picks up the phone, James fills him in on the conversation, how he felt afterward, and how he remembered Shawn's words about performing the Mourn Celebrate Learn process. He then quickly runs through the mourning and celebrating he did.

"Cool," Shawn says, "so what about learning? What did you learn from going through the process?"

James laughs. "Oh yeah, I was so excited about feeling better that I haven't done that part yet!"

Shawn shares the laugh.

"Well, the first obvious thing is that I see the conversation differently now. Before I only saw what went wrong, and now I don't think it was as bad as I thought."

Shawn reflects back what he's heard. "First, you only saw what didn't go the way you wanted, and now you're seeing it in a different way?"

"Yes. I get that there are things I can be proud of and satisfied with, even though I'm still sad that I didn't feel like he could really hear me or understand me." James sighs deeply as he rubs his forehead. "It seems I'm going to be mourning that for quite some time, actually."

"So it sounds like you're feeling some satisfaction about how you were in the conversation, and would still like to have some of the needs met that you uncovered in the mourning part of the process?" Shawn says.

James pauses before answering. A new realization is struggling to emerge fully into his awareness, and he stumbles in his attempt to verbalize it. "Hmm, hearing you say that, I'm getting that … it's like there's some way I'm stuck here. I guess I'm wanting *him* to meet those needs … but then, is that confusing need and strategy? But I *do* really want him to meet those needs … he's my dad, and I long for his respect and acknowledgment."

Shawn responds with another question. "Are you sensing that you were tying the needs to a strategy of his meeting them, and that that was keeping you stuck and not able to shift fully out of your judgments about the conversation?"

"I think so! And it's keeping me stuck in all the judgments of him—and of me. It's like I so want to be seen, understood, respected—all of it—that I forget or don't see at all that getting those needs met some other way could even be valuable. It's like there's this deeper need for a simple, pure connection with him that clouds everything else. But now I'm beginning to get that maybe I'll never be able to get those needs met from him. I guess I can mourn that but also realize they can be met elsewhere. Even just understanding that, I feel a little better."

"So it gives you some relief to understand the distinction between needs and strategies more fully, and to see that you can get those needs met in other ways, even as you still wish he would meet them?"

James stands with rising enthusiasm. "Yeah, relief and just some space." His voice grows more excited. "Like I can allow myself to be me and have these particular needs, but also allow him to be himself with whatever capacity he has or doesn't have, without it all meaning so much."

Shawn thinks for a moment. "What I'm hearing is that you would like to keep making requests to him to get these needs met, but not have it as a demand that he meet them. Is that right?"

"Yes!" James exclaims. "I hadn't thought of it that way, but that's exactly what I mean. Sure, it would be really nice if he'd be willing to call me what I'd like to be called. I can keep working on that not being a trigger for me, but it would also be great if he'd be willing to shift. So I can keep making the request, and make sure it really is a request and not a demand. I think having more role-playing conversations would probably help me with that. I'd like to be able to have these conversations and get more skilled at dealing with my own reactions and staying connected, regardless of how he is."

"So one thing you'd like to practice from here," Shawn confirms, "is to be able to have these conversations and stay connected to yourself?"

"Exactly," James says. "I think this has helped me see that I'd like to keep my focus on my own internal state and process rather than having so much focus on some kind of external outcome I can't control."

Shawn summarizes what James said he learned from going through the Mourn Celebrate Learn process. "I'm hearing that you see the conversation very differently now and are able to be satisfied with what happened, even though the outcome wasn't what you wanted. You now see that you can get your needs met elsewhere, which has given you more space for both you and your dad to be who you are, and you'd still like to try to make requests to him while not turning them into demands. You'd also like to practice more so that you can stay connected and focused on your internal process instead of the outcome. Did I get all that?"

James nods. "Yeah, that sounds about right. You know, as painful as that conversation and how I felt afterward was, it feels worth it to get to where I am now."

Shawn agrees. "Yes, even if you can't see it early on, it's often worth the experience to get to the awareness you have afterward!"

———❀———

Not only does it feel better to shift out of the guilt, blame, shame, or anger in going through this process, you might also notice a "settling into" feeling that's peaceful and calm. This is what happens when you connect with needs, even when you're connecting with needs that weren't met. The learning piece that comes out of considering needs also gives you a better sense of what to do next than trying to "learn" through avoiding the bad feelings you started with.

Now that we've gone through the description of the Mourn Celebrate Learn map, here are the detailed steps again, in order. You can also find these in Appendix I.

1. MOURN

    a. Identify observations of what happened or the judgments you have in your mind after the conversation.

    b. Notice how you feel when you recall what happened or think those thoughts.

    c. Ask what needs of yours are not met by what happened or what unmet needs are you seeking to express with your judgmental thoughts.

2. CELEBRATE

    a. Identify observations of what happened that you liked.

    b. Notice how you feel when you recall those instances in the conversation.

    c. Ask what needs of yours are met by what happened.

3. LEARN

    a. Learn through reflecting on how you feel different now that you've gone through the process.

    b. Plan what you would like to do from here, either in the current situation or in general, to meet your needs.

    c. Practice anything that will help you embody your learning so you will have it available in a similar situation in the future.

mediateyourlife.com/mourn-celebrate-learn-video/

PRACTICE PAUSE

Take the situation you thought of in the previous practice pause or a similar one and go through the Mourn Celebrate Learn process. How does it change your view of the situation, yourself, and any other people involved?

STARTING WITH CELEBRATION

Have you ever been so caught up in your thoughts and judgments that it's difficult to find a way to even begin changing your thinking? If so, you're not alone. But the good news is that the first step is to simply remember that you have a map to use when you notice judgments after something has happened. If you can remember the first step of that map, you can take the step and then remember the next one. All Mediate Your Life maps can most effectively help you when you have clarity about when to use them and which step to start with.

Generally, for any kind of self-debriefing process, we suggest beginning with mourn, then moving to celebrate, then to learn. Mourning is often the natural place to start because it's where the mind tends to go—to what went wrong or to the judgments about the situation. Starting there is the quickest route to escaping from those judgments.

However, there are times when it works even better to start with celebration, even if feeling bad is coming up in your mind first. The process is the same except for reversing the order of the first two steps of the map.

Sometimes, starting with celebration makes it easier to mourn. Why? Because maybe you're so filled with guilt or shame that it's too painful to face those difficult emotions initially, and you don't even want to do the process. But if you start with celebrating needs that *were* met, it can give you some fortitude and capacity to then tackle the harsh judgments of yourself and the unmet needs. In short, celebrating first allows you to get into the process by increasing your capacity through an initial connection to needs.

Celebration is also a good first step when you have conversations with other people. For example, if you want to follow up with the person who prompted your judgments during a conversation, you can use this same map to discuss what happened. Or, if you are debriefing with a team of people about a past event or product launch, you can similarly use this map as a way to discuss what went well and what did not.

As we've said, we tend culturally to focus on the negative. As such, in contexts where you are talking with others, even if you're talking about needs, mourning can be heard as who messed up and who's to be blamed and punished. When you would like to create a feeling of safety and trust to talk about what didn't go well, it helps to start with what was successful—or the celebration step.

Focusing first on what worked helps overall learning, as well as connecting you and others. Begin with appreciating what happened and the needs that were met, and then move into talking about the things that didn't work so well. If someone still reacts to what didn't go well by hearing judgment, you can treat it as an opportunity to empathize.

PRACTICING MOURN CELEBRATE LEARN

The best way to practice MCL is to utilize it often. When you pay attention to your intrusive thoughts about something that happened in the past, you can use those to walk through the process. Likewise, if you know you're going to be in a difficult conversation, you can anticipate doing MCL afterward, planning the time to go through the process as Scott suggested to James. Set aside some uninterrupted time, as close to the conversation as you can, for this quiet reflection on what happened in the conversation. If you suspect you'll desire support, you can also set up a call in advance with a support partner who can help you go through the process.

After you have mourned and celebrated, make part of the learning step an evaluation of what you got out of using MCL. Ask yourself at the end:

+ "What benefit did I get from doing this?"

+ "Did this enhance my life?"

+ "Is it nurturing me and supporting me to make my life better?"

When you build in a self-reflective aspect of the process, it embeds the value of doing it. In other words, consciously considering the benefits makes it more likely you will remember to use the process the next time than if you simply complete the process without reflecting on the value you received from it.

Once you've practiced and internalized the map, you'll find you will be able to do it more quickly and in the moment. One way to think about this is to combine it with the SCP. For example:

1. If you just had an interaction you want to debrief, start with performing the SCP and reconnecting to your breath, body, and feelings.

2. When you get to the needs segment of the SCP, consider both the needs that were not met and those that were in the interaction.

3. Ask one of the questions from Step 3 (Learn), such as "What would I like to do to move forward?" and plan what you will do next.

This is a quicker way to do MCL where you can flow from one map right into another in a way that doesn't take a lot of effort. As this is a more advanced technique, we recommend you try this exercise *after* you've had some experience going through MCL step by step in detail so that you begin to embody the process and the shifts that it brings.

PRACTICE PAUSE

How will you prompt yourself to remember to use MCL? How will you practice it so that you have easy access to it?

Both mourning and celebrating are important; we encourage you not to skip either one of them. Mourning helps you break out of self-blame and judgment, training you to think about how you can better meet your needs. Celebration provides the antidote to focusing only on what you think went wrong in a situation, training you to look automatically for what you were satisfied with and what you would like to improve upon. When you learn through the lens of needs met and unmet, you focus your attention on how to meet your needs in the future more effectively, hence creating more of what you want in your life.

NEXT UP

Now that you've debriefed after a conversation or event, you might have ideas about having a subsequent conversation or moving ahead in some way, which means you are now looking forward. The tools and maps in this book can be experienced in a cycle that always leads you toward meeting your needs. The next chapter explores this cycle and how to integrate all the maps and skills in this book into the ongoing flow of conversations in your life.

8 | LIVING BEYOND JUDGMENT

INTEGRATING YOUR LEARNING INTO YOUR LIFE

*Out beyond ideas of wrongdoing and rightdoing
there is a field. I'll meet you there.*
—RUMI

———

JAMES AND SALLY BOTH COLLAPSE INTO BED EXHAUSTED. It's Sunday night, and the day has not gone as planned. Sally groans, not even bothering to open her eyes as she says, "We didn't get a chance to schedule the week today."

James doesn't respond for so long that Sally assumes he is already asleep. Finally, he whispers, "I'm way too tired now. Let's do it in the morning."

The week before, they had set time aside on Sunday as agreed and looked over the week. Both had felt good about how the conversation flowed and the week had been smooth, so they were excited to continue with their new plan. But today, life had intervened.

First, Sally got a call from Maggie's best friend Charlotte's mother, who was in a panic. A single mom, her older son had just broken his arm falling off his skateboard, and she asked if Charlotte could come over while she took her son to the hospital. As soon as James and Maggie returned with Charlotte, Sally's sister Peg called, concerned about their mother, Doris. Sally rushed over and spent most of the day with Peg, chasing down doctors to get Doris's medication adjusted. Their day had been hijacked, and now they were both too tired to even think about the week ahead.

In the midst of the usual morning bustle the following day, James and Sally attempt to talk about the week's schedule. Juggling her calendar and the sandwich she is making for Maggie's lunch, Sally glances over her shoulder at James. "I have two meetings this week—one tomorrow morning and the other on Thursday, later in the afternoon. So I need you to take the kids to school tomorrow, and if you could get Maggie on Thursday, that would be great. Oh, and you have Maggie's parent-teacher conference on Friday in your schedule, right?" Sally slaps the sandwich together and puts it in Maggie's lunchbox.

James flips the hash browns he is cooking for himself and the kids. "I can take the kids to school tomorrow, but Thursday and Friday aren't going to work. We've got presentations at the new clinic from Wednesday through Friday. You'll have to figure something else out."

Sally grips the edge of the counter and barely stops the retort ready to fly out of her mouth. Her anger simmering, it is all she can do to keep quiet and not react. The silence in the kitchen grows heavier until she manages to get out, "We'll have to talk about this later."

James merely shrugs as he serves up breakfast and pours himself a cup of coffee.

You've done your inner work, using the Self-Connection Process and Enemy Image Process to connect with yourself and the other person, and the Intensity Exercise to defuse your triggers, perhaps several times. You've been able to have the difficult conversation using the Interpersonal Mediation map, and you've made solid agreements about moving forward. You've then done more inner work, mourning and celebrating the conversation and learning how to better meet your needs. You're finished, right?

While it's tempting to think that your toughest interpersonal conflicts might be resolved that swiftly, one time through these processes is most often just the beginning. It's not easy to change ingrained reactive habits, so go easy on yourself; any number of situations can occur that are completely normal. A few examples are:

+ After living with the resolutions and agreements you came to, you may discover where you have difficulty fulfilling a request or how an agreement didn't meet your needs the way you thought it might.

+ New situations will arise that test your commitment to changing your habitual response.

+ The other person may realize an agreement doesn't work for them and come back to you with changes.

+ Either of you may forget completely or react from an old trigger.

The tendency, when any of these happen, is to think that something has gone wrong, that you or the other person is bad, or that these processes are useless and change is impossible. Sally is likely to go into blaming James, believing that their previous conversations have been a waste of time and that he will never change, while James resists what he perceives as Sally's usual way of dictating what will happen without considering what will work for him. Despite previous conversations and the best of intentions, typical patterns can reassert themselves in a flash.

What do you do then?

We hope you now understand that going into the judgments of who is wrong and to blame is not the only option available to you. There's another pathway you can take, one that leads you to deeper connection with yourself, to clarifying what is important to you and the people close to you, and to finding the ways to contribute to your own and each other's well-being, thus enriching both your lives. This is the pathway that leads you toward the field that Rumi is talking about in the quote that begins the chapter, the field beyond ideas of wrongdoing and rightdoing.

Have you ever experienced being in that field? Can you imagine living your life there, even some of the time? With concepts like what Rumi is describing, the "how" often feels elusive. Our hope is that the maps, skills, and tools we've given you in this book will help you find this field in your own relationships.

In this chapter, we are stepping out of the narrower view that focuses on a particular map, and into the big picture of how to integrate what you've learned across the ongoing flow of conversations and situations that constitute your life. In doing so, we hope to provide you with that elusive "how"—an accessible way to put all the pieces together to find your way to the life-enhancing path that leads to the field beyond wrongdoing and rightdoing. When you're on that path, everything that occurs—each interaction, mess-up, missed opportunity, triggered reaction, and perceived judgment—opens up new possibilities for you to live the life you desire.

THE LEARNING CYCLE

The power of the Rumi quote lies in the contrast from how people typically live. After all, wrongness is entrenched in most cultures. It's even embedded in how people are taught to learn.

Have you ever noticed this pattern in your own life?

+ You take some action in the world.

+ After taking that action, you evaluate it and the results.

+ From your evaluation, you then learn what to do in the future.

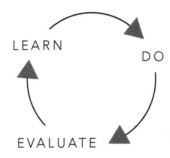

We call this pattern of do-evaluate-learn the Learning Cycle.

To take a simple example, let's say you are in a meeting at work. You and a colleague have to report to the whole department that the campaign you created did not get the hoped-for response. You take some responsibility and assume your colleague will as well, but instead (in your view) your colleague throws you under the bus and implies that the entire failure rests on your shoulders. You see your colleague as a jerk for not admitting to their part; you likewise decide to avoid working with them in the future if possible, that you should have known ahead of time they would do this, and to next time let the other person talk first so you know how to respond to protect yourself. You also plan how to perform damage control, particularly in the eyes of your boss and other respected coworkers.

This example is the typical way—adopted from cultural training —people go through this cycle. That is, after doing something, people evaluate it in these terms:

+ "Did I do it right or wrong?"

+ "Did I or somebody else screw it up?"

+ "Did I do a good or a bad job?"

+ "Does someone else deserve to be blamed and punished?"

+ "Do I deserve to be punished?"

+ "Who is guilty of wrongdoing?"

You may not ask these questions directly, but for most people the tenor of their evaluation is along the lines of blame, shame, and punishment. This tendency in most people is so reflexive that it seems hardwired into them. People turn defensive easily, learn to deflect blame early in life, and may even deny having done something entirely (even when everyone knows they did). In the example above, by the time of the meeting the colleague had already gone through this learning cycle in their mind (evaluating the failure of the campaign) and decided, perhaps unconsciously, that avoiding blame was their best option.

After evaluation comes learning. This is when you develop some ideas and decisions about how to perform the next iteration of whatever happened (such as what to change if a similar situation occurs again, or what to do next in the current situation). You can certainly learn in this process, but *what* do you learn when you evaluate through the lens of blame? If you look back at the example, you'll notice that the learning was about reinforcing where you and the other person stood on the spectrum of right-wrong, protecting yourself in the future, and digging yourself out of the damage done while avoiding your colleague. Evaluating in this way only leads to learning and planning how to avoid future blame and punishment, as well as what to do to be seen as—and rewarded for—being "right." So, inherent in this do-evaluate-learn cycle is, in reality, doing, assessing right and wrong, and planning to avoid punishment.

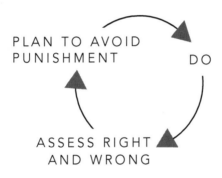

"Well," you might ask, "isn't avoiding blame and punishment a good thing?" On one hand, sure; nobody wants to be blamed and shamed for what has happened. In fact, if you think about it, it's probably ingrained in you to elude any hint that you're at fault. If so, you're likely conditioned—as many people are—to feel that way through upbringing and societal expectations. The problem with that, however, is this: when you're planning how to avoid what you *don't* want to experience, you often miss focusing on how to experience what you *would* like. This can place you in a never-ending cycle of avoidance.

PRACTICE PAUSE

Think of a recent situation in which you evaluated something that happened. What was the tenor of your evaluation, and what did you learn from it?

Even the habitual patterns that run so many of our interactions with others can be traced to this dysfunctional learning cycle. Let's look at when you were a small child for a typical example.

Your parent told you to get in the car seat. You said "no" in the forceful way kids can to something they don't want to do. Your parent then used force to get you into the car seat. With this pattern—your parent using force to get you to do what you didn't want to do—repeated over time in a variety of situations, you may have learned any number of lessons that continue to affect you as an adult, such as:

+ That what you wanted didn't matter
+ That force was an acceptable way to get people to do what you want
+ That you would be punished if you spoke directly against an authority
+ That it was better to manipulate people into doing what you want

Now, as an adult, you might find one or more of these patterns still in effect. Perhaps you've become so accustomed to *not* knowing what you desire—out of the hopelessness that your needs will ever be met—that you still have trouble making requests or even knowing what it is you actually want. Perhaps you use force to get others to do what you'd like, or you find ways to manipulate them that don't always meet your needs. Perhaps you still have trouble speaking clearly to someone who has authority over you, such as your boss. Each time a situation arises that even resembles the pattern, what you learned in your childhood takes over and pushes you into this same cycle, thus reinforcing the pattern again.

AVOIDING THE CYCLE OF AVOIDANCE

Though it may seem like these ingrained patterns are set forever, the good news is they're not. You can learn in a much more powerful manner that helps you step out of the cycle of avoidance. While the Do, Evaluate, Learn cycle is natural and expected, you can tweak it slightly—away from evaluating through assessing right/wrong and learning through avoidance—so that it becomes a more functional and empowering Learning Cycle.

When you evaluate in this version, instead of seeking who is right or wrong, you ask:

+ What needs of mine and of others were met?

+ What needs of mine and of others were not met?

+ How might I better meet my needs next time?

In other words, you still assess what happened and what you can learn from it, only from the perspective of *needs* instead of blame, shame, or punishment.

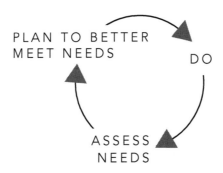

PLAN TO BETTER
MEET NEEDS   DO

ASSESS
NEEDS

With your colleague, the assessment might focus on your needs for safety in the workplace; to trust the people you work with; or on honesty, integrity, and a shared reality with your colleague about responsibility for the outcome. When you think about what needs were met or not, you are primed to learn about and plan how to better meet them. Instead of being in avoidance, you are homing in on how you can improve your life and well-being.

PRACTICE PAUSE

See if you can apply this more functional learning cycle to the situation you thought of in the previous Practice Pause. How does it change your experience to think in terms of needs?

In this book, we have given you processes to help you at each step of the Learning Cycle when it comes to interpersonal relationships. Let's break them down simply.

The first part focused on all the practices to use before a conversation in the preparation stage:

+ Self-Connection Process (SCP)

+ Intensity Exercise

+ Enemy Image Process (EIP)

Next, to support you in the "doing" phase of the conversation, we gave you:

+ The Interpersonal Mediation (IPM) map and the mediation skills

Then, in the previous chapter, we talked about the process to use afterward, when you find yourself in the evaluation stage that so commonly equates to beating yourself up.

✦   Mourn Celebrate Learn (MCL)

MCL gives you an option that is kinder and leads to learning that makes a real difference in your life through focusing on needs.

Mediator mind also plays a role throughout the cycle, providing the space for you to interact with yourself and others in the way you desire, and is especially important in the IPM map when you are both the mediator and a part of the conflict.

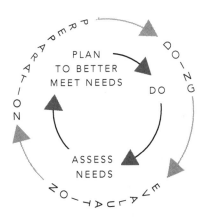

HELP! WHICH MAP DO I USE?

The maps we've presented in this book are sets of steps to use when you are in a particular type of interpersonal situation and would like to be able to shift your internal state so you can choose how you would like to act in the world. We just broke them down simply for you, but here's a brief recap of each map and when to use it:

SELF-CONNECTION PROCESS

Use SCP any time you want to reconnect with yourself, at any point before, during, and after a difficult conversation, or any time you feel disconnected from yourself. This process puts you into mediator mind, from which you can make new choices and learn from them.

ENEMY IMAGE PROCESS

Use EIP to prepare for a difficult conversation with another person when you find you have enemy images of them. This map helps you empathize with yourself and the other person, transforming any judgments so that you can be in a conversation with the intention to connect.

INTERPERSONAL MEDIATION MAP

Use the IPM map to have a difficult conversation with another person. This process gives you the roadmap to follow anytime you are in a conversation in which you would like to make sure both you and the other person are heard the way you desire.

MOURN CELEBRATE LEARN

Use MCL when you want to learn from an interaction that has already happened and to care for yourself. This map supports you to come out of judgment of yourself and move toward meeting your needs instead of avoiding punishment.

We know from personal experience, however, that living your daily life is messy, and it can be far less clear when in the midst of a sticky and uncomfortable situation to know which map to use. What do you do then?

When feeling flooded by emotions and thoughts, people often feel overwhelmed. As such, it's important to realize that you can pare down your options to two:

+ Where do you focus your attention?

+ What are you going to do?

Any choice you make can be put into one of these two categories: attention and action. So when you find yourself swimming in the muck after an encounter, these two choices can help you orient yourself.

We have suggested that the place to focus your attention initially is on yourself through the Self-Connection Process—the go-to map whenever you begin to feel the slightest bit of disconnection, discomfort, stress response, or even simply want to feel more grounded. Use it anytime and anywhere, so that it becomes natural to you to reconnect with yourself. Every part of the Learning Cycle process, from doing to evaluating to learning, can be punctuated with numerous Self-Connection Processes.

Then, when you find yourself in a situation where you feel out of sorts, after performing the SCP simply ask yourself, "Is there a map I could use right now?" and "What map would most help me in this situation?"

These questions may seem so obvious they border on silly, but don't underestimate the importance of asking them. We teach these maps, and we still sometimes find it challenging in the moment to remember we have these maps and to use them. Both of us have experienced times when we've made a mess of a situation, forgetting entirely to use a map. We've had whole conversations only to realize afterward that we had no awareness during the conversation that this was a time to use one. Since everyone (including us!) experiences these hiccups, we offer the following advice.

Part of choosing what to do is simply being able to name the choices you have. You can set yourself up for success by following this simple formula:

✦   Where are you in this moment?

✦   Use SCP to connect with yourself and your needs right now.

✦   Ask, "Which map would most help me in this situation?"

✦   Walk through the steps of the map, or seek support from
     someone if you find it challenging to do on your own.

NAVIGATING A CYCLE OF CONVERSATIONS

As we've shared, the Learning Cycle gives one potential path to
follow when you are in a cycle of difficult conversations with
someone close to you. Once again, that path would follow the cycle
in a circle, as in the graphic below.

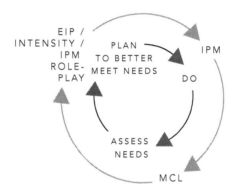

One way to choose a map is to think about where you are in
the learning cycle. Are you getting ready for a conversation or
assessing the situation after one? Does that help you choose a map?

While using the Learning Cycle is one possibility for choosing
which map to use, you might choose a different sequence of maps
and exercises depending on what is going on for you in any given
moment. With this in mind, let's see how James and Sally both
follow up from their conversation that begins this chapter.

During a break in her day, Sally reflects back on the morning conversation with James. Knowing she is still upset about it, she goes through SCP and asks herself which map might help. Mourn Celebrate Learn process comes to mind as a good place to start. She mourns that she thinks they are still not on the same page and her need for collaboration is not met. She also feels sad that she wasn't willing to empathize with James, but is able to celebrate that she stopped herself before she said anything that would have escalated the conflict. The observation she keeps returning to is the phrase James ended with: "You'll have to figure it out." Every time she thinks about that statement, she feels her anger intensify. She knows that hearing it keeps her from being able to hear anything else.

Recognizing that this statement is a trigger for her, Sally decides to ask Shawn to do Intensity Exercise with her, using this statement as the trigger. During their session, Sally feels successful in largely defusing the stress response she experiences upon hearing it, but she still has some lingering judgments about where James is coming from. She believes he is taking his typical hands-off, you-deal-with-the-home-front attitude and is not following through on what he said about valuing teamwork.

In order to shift these judgments, Sally next chooses to perform the EIP. She connects again with her own needs for support, integrity, and collaboration that are behind her judgments of James, and when she feels more open, she considers what James's needs might be. She guesses he might like some ease in the situation, not only in working something out for that week, but also more generally with their transition to her going back to work. She also supposes he might want pre-dictability in knowing that he can fulfill his work commitments.

Though she doesn't feel entirely confident that her guesses are accurate, she still experiences a change in herself as she connects to those needs, realizing she also wants things to work out well and go smoothly all around. Feeling better, Sally knows she is more likely to be able to talk with James, and she asks Shawn to role-play with her so she has some practice being in the conversation the way she desires.

"Business as usual," James mutters under his breath as he drives to work, his mind still on the morning conversation with Sally. *She has meetings and expects me to drop everything to fill in. Doesn't matter how much we talk about it, she always has to railroad me into doing what she wants.* After a few minutes of internal ranting, James recognizes how disconnected he is and performs a quick Self-Connection Process so he doesn't take his angst into work. Since he is most aware of his judgments of Sally, he decides that when he has a break, he will go through the EIP.

During lunch, James takes a walk and performs the steps of the EIP in his mind. He feels upset and resistant when he interprets he has no choice and connects to his need for auto-nomy. The need for understanding also comes up, and he deepens into it, seeing how much he longs for acknowledgment of all the ways he contributes, as well as the limitations on what he can do. He guesses that Sally is feeling pressure, both to make sure household tasks get done and to stay committed to her fledgling business. He softens as he taps into their shared needs to care for their family and to be fulfilled professionally.

Awareness of their shared needs prompts a feeling of sadness to well up in him as he remembers their conversation, specifically how he responded to what Sally said by digging in his heels. He shifts into Mourn Celebrate Learn as he mourns the missed opportunity to empathize with Sally. His actions met his need to care for himself, which he can celebrate, but not his need to care for their family as a whole. James experiences the settling within himself that indicates he is connected, feeling complete for the moment. He makes a mental note to ask Alicia to role-play a conversation with him to prepare to talk with Sally.

After work, James and Alicia role-play by phone. At one point James dials the difficulty up a little higher by asking Alicia to say, "I need you to pick up the kids," so he can practice how he wants to respond. When she delivers this trigger, though, he immediately moves into his typical stress response and is unable to continue. They switch to the Intensity Exercise and use as the trigger, "I need you to do what I want—what you want doesn't count," as this is what James interprets when he hears Sally say, "I need you to ...." James is pleased that he reaches a point where he doesn't react to this statement anymore. They switch back to the role-play and James is able to choose his response to hearing Sally say, "I need you to pick up the kids." He practices a few responses, trying both empathy and expression.

As James drives home, he has a few niggling judgments about Sally thinking her work is more important than his. He quickly runs through the EIP one more time, finishing as he pulls into the driveway.

The path Sally follows after her conversation with James—to process what came up for her and to prepare to have another conversation—is shown below:

Now she feels ready to have another conversation.

James uses the same maps and exercises, only in a different order:

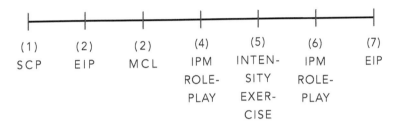

Now he's ready to have another conversation.

Sally and James both choose the next map based on where they are in the moment. It's a practice to keep checking in with yourself, asking what is going on, whether there's a map that can help, and if so, which one. To guide you in recognizing how to choose which map will be most helpful to you, we've created the following reference table.

If you ...	Try this map or exercise
Are stuck in a set of judgments and diagnoses of another person	Enemy Image Process (EIP)
Notice a particular phrase or action that another person does that triggers your stress response	Intensity Exercise
Would like to prepare to talk with someone about a topic that is difficult for you	IPM Exercise or IPM Role-Play
Are beating yourself up for something that happened in the past	Mourn Celebrate Learn (MCL)
Find yourself in a conversation and feel stressed, challenged, or confused	Interpersonal Mediation (IPM) map
Become aware of feeling out of sorts without being sure what it's about	Self-Connection Process (SCP)
Dread a future event, such as a work meeting or family gathering	Enemy Image Process (EIP)
Feel shame, anger, depression, agitation, or guilt	Self-Connection Process (SCP)
Find yourself yet again acting out of habit, even though you know you want to make different choices in that situation	Intensity Exercise
Feel distracted and not present with yourself and others	Self-Connection Process (SCP)
Are in a conversation with a person or discussing a topic that is difficult for you	Interpersonal Mediation (IPM) map
Don't enjoy how you feel about a past situation	Mourn Celebrate Learn (MCL)

Finally, remember that the cycle of conversations that create your relationships is a fluid process; hence the maps and exercises you use to support you can also be flowing and flexible. You may, for example, decide to begin with EIP, and in the process it morphs into MCL, or vice versa. You may have a conversation using the IPM map, then do the Intensity Exercise to work on something that triggered you, and then walk through MCL. What is going on within you at each moment is the truest guide to what you choose next. Allow each moment to be an opportunity to engage with yourself and other people from connection and choice.

Daily Practice

Being able to use the maps and exercises in a fluid way requires practice; we've suggested numerous ways to do this in each of the preceding chapters. And while many of the practice suggestions involve finding a partner, it also helps to have ways of rehearsing on your own.

As we've said, one of the most difficult things about learning a new way of communicating is to remember that you have new tools and skills and to utilize them in the moment. If you practice on a regular basis on your own, you have a constant reminder that you know these maps and what the steps of the maps are, and therefore have confidence in using them. This type of daily repetition and rehearsal makes it more likely that you will not only remember the maps in the moment, but also that you will more effectively be able to apply them.

A great way to incorporate a daily practice that will reinforce the maps and skills—and help you become aware of what's going on for you to make choices about what to do next—is to use the Interpersonal Mediation map as a daily meditation routine.

The IPM map is the most difficult map to remember to use in the heat of the moment, and it is also one of the most comprehensive. It begins with the Self-Connection Process and includes empathy, expression, and requests, as well as the mediation skills. So far we've only presented ways to practice this map with another person, all of which are valuable, but you can also walk through it on your own, and here's how.

Set aside some time to practice the IPM map daily. You might incorporate it into your daily meditation, or reserve another time during the day. The important thing is to make space in each day for it as part of your routine.

One way to proceed is to journal, which can be helpful for focus and to reinforce your learning. For example, write out the steps of the SCP as you walk through that process, and then list the rest of the steps of the IPM map as a reminder. Then, think of someone you are in conflict with, or even someone with whom you had an unpleasant interaction, and imagine having a conversation with them using the IPM map. How would you go through the steps with that person? Writing out your actual dialogue can be beneficial in keeping yourself on track. Once you are familiar with the steps, you can also play out the conversation in your mind.

While this practice can help solidify the steps of the IPM map in your mind and give you additional practice on your own, you may also find that it leads you in various directions in terms of the other maps. As you try to imagine the conversation, for example, you may notice you can't empathize because of enemy images, or you realize that you're stuck on a past interaction with the person. As you go through the conversation, pay close attention to what is going on in you, and use what you're aware of as the impetus to continue making choices.

For example, if you imagine the other person saying something that you know triggers you, then switch to doing Intensity Exercise in your mind. If you notice you are having a hard time even imagining having a conversation with them because you are so upset, you might decide to walk through the EIP. You may likewise remember an interaction that happened with them already, prompting you to use the MCL. You might find you just need a lot of self-empathy and therefore choose to focus your time there.

In other words, let your current experience be your guide in what map you choose, and see if you can avoid making it a rule that you have to complete the IPM map before moving on to something else. Since you are doing this practice daily, you can begin again the following day by imagining a conversation with this same person using the IPM map and seeing how it's different. You might find you get further in the conversation, or new things come up and different maps present themselves as helpful. Allowing yourself to notice the shifts you make during the practice bolsters your learning.

Practiced in this way, two important benefits accrue. First, you reinforce the steps of the maps and gain more experience using them. Second, the IPM map becomes a portal into what's going on for you as you think about a particular person, thus leading you to choose what you can do to shift how you are in a relationship with yourself and with them.

———

That evening after dinner, Sally and James have a chance to talk about the morning conversation.

"I felt angry this morning when you said, 'You'll have to figure it out,'" Sally says, "because I'd like to know that we're in this together. Instead, I heard you saying it was all on me."

Though James wants to share his own upset, he catches himself and reflects what he heard from Sally. "So you'd like to know that I'm with you in working out what to do when there's some conflict in schedules?"

"Yes. I know we've both said that collaboration and teamwork are important to us, but it still seems like we haven't quite gotten there yet. What was going on for you?"

James takes a deep breath. "I agree with you about that. For me, I felt irritated this morning when you said 'I need you to ...' and then just went on without asking whether it would work for me. I heard an assumption that because you had meetings, I had to fill in the gaps regardless of my commitments at work. I realize that hearing those words from you is a major trigger for me. I actually worked on it today with Alicia."

Sally guesses what is going on for James. "So when you hear me say that, you feel angry. Is that about wanting consideration for what would work for you?"

"Yeah, and what also comes up is I'd like to feel I have a choice, and I'd like acknowledgment for the ways I do contribute." James remembers his guesses about Sally's motivations and asks, "I was wondering if you feel pressure to make sure everything is handled both at home and at work?"

Tears come to Sally's eyes and her shoulders drop. "I do. All these things need to happen ... I mean, we can't have the kids not being picked up. It might get easier once Corey starts to drive in a couple years, but for now, we're it!"

"I know, and it's important to me too. This is where I get hung up, though. I had this thought on the way home about you thinking your work is more important than mine, so I did the EIP. What I got was how much I actually feel my work is more important because it's paying the bills. So yes, the kids need to be picked up, but my job pays for the maintenance on the cars we drive to pick them up. My work also pays for the groceries, and the kids' expenses, and the mortgage. I get stuck because I don't see a way around how much we rely on my job financially ... and the pressure I feel to make sure I'm not jeopardizing it in any way."

"Right ..." Sally says slowly, her face beginning to light up. "So you keep thinking your job is more important because it's paying the bills, which keeps you thinking that I should be taking care of more, or maybe all, of the household stuff. And I sense that and feel defensive, then resist it by not wanting to ask you what would work for you, and not being willing to empathize or hear a 'no' from you!" She chuckles and shakes her head, realizing the ridiculousness of it all. "And I would like my work to be contributing financially, so I try to push stuff onto you so I can work toward that goal, which then causes you to resist because you believe your work is more important. It's like we're caught in this crazy-making feedback loop of impossibility!"

James reaches over to rub her shoulders. "Wow, yeah, I guess you're right. I hadn't seen it that way. We're like two little kids both going, 'My work is more important!' 'No, my work is more important!' 'No, MINE is more important!' 'NO, MINE IS!' and on and on."

Sally nods in agreement as James adds, "And I know I also get stuck in feeling like I have to figure out a solution—and I don't see one."

Sally sighs and takes James's hand. "Just visualizing that whole insanity makes me feel a little better. I'd really love for it to just disappear magically because we've named it! But I suppose that's not likely. Maybe it will get easier to spot, though, when it comes up again."

They sit in silence for a few moments, each being with their own feelings and needs, until Sally breaks the silence. "Well, one thing that's clear is that trying to have that conversation this morning was not a good idea. We were too distracted. So we know that doesn't work!"

James laughs. "No kidding! There was just no way it was going to happen yesterday, though. We need to have that time be a priority and for both of us to be centered."

"Maybe we just need to move it to an earlier day or time. Not Saturday night—that's our date night and I want that to be fun—but what if we did Friday night? If we planned it, and something came up or we had plans, at least we could re-schedule on the weekend and still have some leeway."

"Hmmm. I'm a little concerned about bandwidth on Friday night. We can both be pretty tired by then." James pauses. "Hey, maybe we could start it as a celebration of the week, like do a Celebrate Mourn Learn process. We can look at what went well, mourn anything that didn't go well, see what we can learn from it, and plan the coming week. That way maybe we'll both have the energy for it, and it will keep us reflecting on how our plan went during the week—we didn't make time for reflection before."

"Ooohhh. I like that. And we can start with the SCP so we're both grounded."

James reiterates the new agreements. "Ok, so we'll make our scheduling time a priority, do the SCP at the beginning, and then structure it as a Celebrate Mourn Learn, planning the next week at the end. And we're going to do it Friday night, or as soon after that as we can if we have other plans. Is that right?"

"Yep!" Sally nods. "That sounds good."

MOURN CELEBRATE LEARN OR ENEMY IMAGE PROCESS?

We understand it takes time to become accustomed to the various maps and when to use which, but one of the biggest confusions people have is when to use Mourn Celebrate Learn and when to use the Enemy Image Process. As such, we want to give you some tips on which is the appropriate choice for a given situation.

These two maps have similarities—they both use the same basic NVC processes, but the purpose for them is different, as is their place in the Learning Cycle.

The EIP is used when you have an enemy image of somebody that's less focused on the past and more of a generalized image you have in the present. For example, when you are seeing an image of someone with all your judgments and analyses embedded in it, and you want to relate to that person differently, you use the EIP. Though the judgments may be based on what happened in the past, those events have been translated into a present-time image, and going through the process focuses you on how to shift this image so you can interact differently with that person in the future. The EIP is also useful when preparing for a future event you are dreading, even if you aren't aware of specific judgments of a person. Performing the EIP can uncover those judgments and shift your feelings going into the event.

With the MCL process, the focus is on a past event—something that happened that you may be replaying, resenting, and/or beating yourself up over. The event does not feel complete but continues to trigger you in the present. As we stated earlier, when you evaluate through judging and blaming, as in the cycle of avoidance, it's hard to learn from the experience in a way that will contribute to your life. The MCL is a process of completing the event and reconciling the past, healing from what happened and learning from it. If you want to learn in a different way from something that happened in the past, MCL is a beneficial process to use.

The other primary distinction between the two processes is whom you are judging. When you are aware of judgments of yourself, MCL is helpful to stop beating yourself up for what happened. When you are aware of judgments of someone else, use the EIP to shift how you see that person.

What process to choose depends both on whom you are judging and where you see yourself in the cycle. Here are two useful rules of thumb:

- ✦ Use the EIP when you are preparing for a future event, action, or conversation, or when you have judgments of another person.

- ✦ Use MCL when you are remembering an event in the past that does not feel complete or that you have intrusive thoughts about, especially judgments of yourself.

Let's take the earlier example of your colleague who you feel "threw you under the bus" in the meeting.

- ✦ If you primarily feel upset about what happened in the meeting and are blaming yourself, you might use Mourn Celebrate Learn to shift how you hold that event.

- ✦ If you have been told you will be working with that colleague again on another project and are aware of how many judgments you have of that person, you could walk through the Enemy Image Process to get clear about how you want to work with them in the future.

Of course, in that kind of situation, you might find that both are the case: you are stuck on what happened in the past *and* you still have to interact with someone you are judging. One process can directly follow from the other. In this case, MCL will be helpful to learn from what happened in the meeting; and as part of the final step of learn, plan, practice, you use the EIP (and maybe even Intensity Exercise) to work with your judgments of your colleague.

Here's an example of how Sally experienced the MCL flowing into EIP in an interaction one day with Corey:

James and Corey had a brief exchange about Corey's grades that triggered him; Sally could see Corey was upset and went to his room. She knocked on his door, opened it slightly, and stuck her head in. "Are you okay?" she asked. "Seems like you're upset. Do you want to talk about it?"

Corey didn't answer, waving Sally off with an angry look. Sally closed the door and left, but she didn't feel great about it. In her mind she was thinking, *Well, to hell with you then.*

Sally performed the Self-Connection Process to feel more connection with herself, then decided to go through Mourn Celebrate Learn. She mourned that she was annoyed with Corey and that her response to his actions wasn't the best; she wanted care and connection for Corey, but also for herself. Pondering what needs of hers were met and could be celebrated, she realized that just by knocking and trying to connect with Corey, her need for connection had actually been met a little, if only in the act of asking.

As Sally moved to the learning stage of MCL and considered how she saw the situation now, she felt a little more open, but as she thought about it she heard, *Corey was being such a jerk.* Recognizing this for the enemy image it was, Sally went right into the EIP.

Remember that the steps of the EIP are:

+ Self-Empathy
+ Empathy for the Other
+ New Possibilities: Learn, Plan, Practice

Sally asked herself what needs she was meeting by having that judgment. She determined that she wanted to be seen for her intention to connect and for the care that she had tried to give. She also longed to contribute to her son. Meeting her own need for empathy allowed Sally to be more open about what was going on for Corey—to consider what needs he was trying to meet by not talking to her.

Sally then put herself in Corey's shoes. She imagined Corey thinking that she wouldn't be supportive of him in the way he desired, and therefore was protecting himself from more pain. His actions toward Sally weren't personal; it was simply his way of meeting his need to care for himself. Talking to Sally in that moment wasn't a strategy he wanted to use.

Sally felt the enemy image of Corey dissolving and her heart opened. She decided she would find a way to connect with Corey later—they had a family activity night planned after dinner, and she made the intention to engage with Corey during the evening, not so much as her son, but as a human being. Her goal became being present with him, outside of their roles as mother/son, and simply being with him and enjoying him. Focusing on that intention during the evening, she appreciated her interactions with Corey and found herself learning more about her son.

As we near the end of our dialogue between James and Sally, so far you've witnessed how they've been working to resolve their issues by using the Mediate Your Life maps and skills. Though they have some new ideas about tweaking their primary agreements to help with managing the family schedules, they still have the looming issue of how they each react out of their past patterns in moments of tension. Let's see how they work together to take the next steps toward resolution.

—⁓—

"So that just leaves this other issue," James says, "our pattern you uncovered of reacting to each other's assumptions about what we want and whose work is more important."

Sally looks thoughtful as she responds. "You know, I don't think we're going to figure that out right now. I think we're going to have to live with it, as uncomfortable as that may be, and stick to our earlier agreements we made about how to interact with each other. We didn't do any of those this time—we didn't empathize with what happened on Sunday that kept us from scheduling ... and I didn't ask myself if I was willing to hear a 'no.'"

James nods. "And I didn't do the SCP when I noticed I reacted. It *is* uncomfortable just "living with" that pattern right now, but I do like reconfirming those agreements we made. I'd also like to make some request of myself, like when those thoughts come up, I connect with myself and ask the question, 'Is there something I'd like to do to meet my needs in this moment?' Maybe that will help me feel less hopeless about not being able to figure out a solution."

Sally smiles. "I like that. And we do know that our agreement can work. After all, last week went great! We planned, things worked out, we felt good about it. It's only when there's some conflict between all our schedules. And ... one thing we've always shied away from is getting outside help."

"Yeah," James says, "but we can't really afford that right now."

"I know, but I'm not just thinking about paying someone. There's Peg—she's around since she's living with Mom now, and she's willing to step in occasionally and help, like she did with Maggie's soccer tryouts—and she'd get to hang out with the kids more. Alicia and Shawn have offered too. They really enjoy the kids. And sometimes I could ask one of Maggie's friend's moms to pick them up together if need be."

James shifts uncomfortably. "Yeah, I just hate to do that. I don't want to impose on other people. I felt so bad calling Peg that day and asking her. And since I just did, I feel like we can't ask her again anytime soon."

Sally makes a face. "I know, asking for help isn't exactly a strength for either one of us. But maybe we should reconsider it. Peg, Alicia, and Shawn have specifically said it wouldn't be an imposition, and we can trust them to let us know if it is. And with Maggie's friends, we can reciprocate. Hopefully it's all temporary and when I start bringing in more income, part of it can go toward hiring someone if we need to."

James throws his hands in the air in mock defeat. "Okay, Okay! I give up! If we need to, I'm open to asking someone to help us out."

Sally and James then discuss who to ask to pick up Maggie on Thursday, and whether to reschedule the parent-teacher conference on Friday—since James can't make it—or for Sally to attend on her own.

They end the night not only feeling pleased with the ideas and new agreements they've generated, but also with a plan for the week that both of them feel good about. "You know," Sally reflects, "as difficult as today was, and as upset as I was this morning, being on the other side of all of it after talking it out and feeling closer to you ... somehow it all seems worth it."

"I feel the same," James says, squeezing Sally's hand.

Below is a table with the updated set of agreements between James and Sally, following their conversations about what didn't work on Sunday. Old agreements are crossed out, new agreements are in bold, and recommitted agreements are in italics.

		Sally	James
Primary Agreements	Actions	~~Set aside time on weekend to discuss schedules/tasks~~ **Prioritize scheduling time on Friday night** **Start with SCP** **Structure as Celebrate Mourn Learn** **Ask others to help by picking up kids if needed**	
	Behavior Patterns	*Empathize with James when his concerns arise* *Ask James first if he can talk*	*Perform SCP when fears come up* **Ask "Is there something I'd like to do to meet my needs in this moment?"**
Supporting Agreements	Actions	Put appointment on calendar for ~~Sunday~~ Friday, rearrange schedules to fit in, **if already have plans then schedule for as soon after as possible.**	
	Behavior Patterns	*If James starts to react, ask "Are you connected to yourself?"* *Ask "Am I willing to hear a 'no'?"*	

Restoring Agreements	Actions	*Commit to a new time as soon as possible*
	Behavior Patterns	*Empathize with needs met/not met in prioritizing something else over scheduled time.* *Take time out if either react, perform SCP, then empathize with each other*

PRIMARY EXPERIENCE AND CHOICE

Throughout this book, we've striven to present the maps and skills with clarity about how and when to use them. If you are just beginning, as with any new learning, it helps to follow the instructions as closely as you can so that you begin to experience the shifts that can happen. The steps of each map or exercise, and the tips for when and how to use the skills, are offered as a support for you to learn in an effective and efficient manner.

However, the experience of living—with all the thoughts, judgments, feelings, hopes, and habits—is never quite as neat and clean as the instructions we've presented imply. As you practice and gain some mastery with these tools, you will find what works *for you* to create connection with yourself and others. When the learning becomes a part of you instead of something you are practicing, you may find that you utilize these maps and skills differently.

Although the guidance and specific steps we've provided have proven results, we also want you to feel some flexibility in utilizing them—the goal is to put you in touch with your primary experience and help you find its value and meaning. We hope that presenting what we have found to be beneficial and significant will help you become clear too.

As you know from reading this book, each of the individual processes we've given you is designed to help you shift out of your stress response and habitual ways of reacting when in a difficult interaction. They help you connect to a constructive way of relating to yourself and others; once you get there, you can see more clearly what you want to do. They change your perspective so that you have choice.

Each individual map is important in and of itself, but it's in putting them all together and using them as needed in the cycle of conversations that you will truly see the impact on your life. Each time you make a choice to use a map, and each time you then make new choices in interactions with yourself and others, you build new neural pathways that strengthen those new choices. The old choices slowly become less desirable and available until you eventually realize that the hold they have over you has diminished.

With each new choice, we hope you will begin to reap the benefits of acting in ways that lead to connection. In connecting with yourself, you move beyond the patterns of self-judgment that keep you stuck in old habits. In connecting with others, you create new possibilities of contributing to each other's well-being. Eventually, you will emerge from the ingrained path to walk in the desired field beyond wrongdoing and rightdoing.

NEXT UP

You now have all the maps, exercises, and skills you need to navigate the cycle of conversations in your life! We'll finish off with expressing what is possible when you are able to be present and in a place of choice, and our hope for these skills to impact the world.

CONCLUSION
ONE CONVERSATION
AT A TIME

*Choice is more than picking "x" over "y." It is a responsibility to
separate the meaningful and the uplifting from the trivial and the
disheartening. It is the only tool we have that enables us to go from
who we are today to who we want to be tomorrow.*
—SHEENA IYENGAR

How many conversations do you have every day? When those
interactions go smoothly, your life feels more flowing and
joyful. When discord and disconnection occur, you likely find your
productivity declines, your mood sinks, and life feels more difficult.

In this book, we've explored the territory of interpersonal conversations. We've shown you how to navigate this territory by
connecting to yourself before you have a conversation, eliminating
triggers and transforming judgments so you can interact from
choice and presence. We've provided you with the maps and skills
to be in a conversation in a way that can keep you connected with
yourself—and help you connect to the other person—so that you
can both gain understanding that leads to strong resolutions and
agreements. If you have thoughts after the conversation about how
it went, you also know the process to use that will give you a more

balanced view of what happened and what you can learn from it. We've also shown you how to use these maps and skills in the cycle of conversations that typically occurs in ongoing relationships at home and at work.

Take a moment to reflect on what you've read. What is possible for you out of these maps and skills? In reading the stories and examples, have images or thoughts popped into your mind about what you would like to create and experience in your life and your relationships? Imagine for a minute how your life would be different if you were living those changes.

Remember that this work is not merely about handling conflict; we hope this book will help you in any area where you are not experiencing what you desire. Is there a part of your life where you feel stuck, in pain, or unfulfilled? If so, you're like many people who can point to some aspect of their life that is simply not working the way they'd like. This is why we wrote this book: to offer a way of having conversations so that you can have positive, enjoyable, productive interactions and contribute to the world in the way you desire, giving you a sense of power in creating your life.

We hope that in reading this book, you will now:

+ have more choice about the relationships in your life

+ be able to work through challenges with others

+ find the contribution that people have to make, to you *and* to the world

+ act from the knowledge of your own and others' contributions instead of from judgment

As we said early in the book, the value of a world that is compassionate, caring, loving, peaceful, kind, collaborative, and cooperative is widespread in many traditions, and yet, *how* to bring these into your life and act from them is often missing. As such, we hope that in these pages you've begun to see and experience how to relate to yourself and others in a way that brings all of these positive qualities into your life. When you can embody them, you are part of creating a world that is a little more peaceful, compassionate, caring, and collaborative.

These maps work. Think of them as a guide—a predictable, reliable, consistent guide to being successful with any aspect of interpersonal relationships. Use them and you will begin to create connection with yourself and others that then provides a platform for you to generate more of what you want to experience in life.

We'd like to end the book with a few final comments about our dreams for what this work can do for you and for the world at large. First, however, we'd like to share with you a bit about how the skills and maps have impacted our relationship and those of people who have been in our trainings. Through these stories and comments, we hope to transmit to you the possibilities for your own life and relationships. As you read through the following personal examples of this work's impact, keep in mind what you would like to create for yourself.

WALKING OUR TALK

When there is one or more persons, there is the potential for conflict. That's true as much among those of us involved in Mediate Your Life as it is anywhere else. We not only teach these maps and skills, we use them.

We have, as with any business, gone through times of turmoil. A few years ago, Ike resided outside the United States for several years as we were forming Mediate Your Life. Since we lived nine time zones apart and were not doing trainings together as frequently, we had many disagreements about all levels of the business, from where to go with it to how to do the trainings. It was a very stressful and intense period when both our business relationship and friendship could have suffered, or even ended, over our disagreements.

As we both actively used the tools in this book and the rest of the series, we continued to overcome our differences. Coming back to connection with ourselves and with each other, we could acknowledge our varying viewpoints and then refocus on the commonality between us. Both of us had to catch ourselves before the downward spiral started, reconnect with ourselves, and then reconnect to each other.

Even when we are not in that level of conflict, the two of us have differences in how we see things and how we think they ought to be done. It's easy to become irritated because the other person doesn't see it the same way, and then interpret that the other doesn't appreciate what we have to offer. Old patterns—not being good enough, not being valued or appreciated, a compulsion to be heard and to be right—rear their heads, and if we're not careful, we can easily run with those reactions and ruin any kind of partnership.

When we can work with these patterns, going through the processes in this book, what appears is a greater capacity to be willing to allow things to unfold. We each are open to understanding where the other person is coming from instead of assuming that our initial interpretation ("He's wrong and I'm right!") is correct. As a result, there exists more curiosity to be in the process of communication and more trust that everything will be revealed in due course, that the way through will become clear if we simply use the tools and keep returning to connection with ourselves and each other.

Every time we've been able to use the tools and return to connection, it takes us further into what we have to contribute together. In our differing perspectives we can interpret that we are working against each other, but when connected we can get to a place where we see that our differences are synergistically complementing each other and creating a larger whole than either of us could create alone. Ultimately, doing the internal and interpersonal work of coming back to connection brings out the best in both of us.

What does this way of being lead to in a partnership? Our relationship is characterized by qualities such as deep care, tenderness, appreciation, openness, love, and trust that we can each be ourselves and be met by the other with the intention to understand. Respect is another key quality—particularly respect that the other person is living this work too, and that even if one of us doesn't quite grasp an idea the other has hatched, we strive to understand it because we've so often experienced that the other person comes up with ideas that move our work forward.

Every project, indeed the collaborative creation of anything new, is a series of conversations to create what you'd like to see in the world. That's true of a business, and it's also true of this book. With three primary people working on creating it—John, Ike, and Julie—plenty of opportunities arise for misunderstandings and conflicts. The process of writing often entails Ike and John getting on the same page about what they are actually saying, then coming to some agreement about how to present their work in the midst of their varied perspectives and ways of thinking. Julie's task extends beyond taking their perspectives and weaving them into a readable book; it includes mediating the process of getting the book done, making sure that Ike and John stay on track, and managing the editing and production process with the editor and designer.

At all points in the process, conflict can—and does—arise. What should be included, and how? What's the title going to be? Who are we hiring to do the editing and design? How are we going to promote the book? Any project is comprised of thousands of decisions, and when multiple people are involved, any of those decisions might involve different perspectives. The skills in this book can help smooth the process of getting everyone on the same page when points of view differ about how to proceed on a project.

Moving Forward in Connection

Besides using these skills in our own personal and business relationships, we also hear stories from people who have been in our trainings and used these maps and skills, moment by moment, conversation by conversation, to create significant change. Below are the types of stories we hear from those who have taken this work to heart, and who have, sometimes over long periods of time, shifted estranged relationships until they are characterized by care and hope. While based on actual stories of people we know, these examples have been modified to protect anonymity.

DIFFICULT DIVORCE

"My ex-wife of twenty-five years and I went through a difficult divorce a few years ago, with so much hurt on both sides. For the first few years after the divorce, it was difficult. Things got so bad at one point that she said she never wanted to talk to me again. I live not too far from one of our two grown children, and she said that when she was visiting, she wanted me to leave. She wanted nothing to do with me and never wanted to be in the same room again.

"Today, things are much different. My ex-wife has said recently that she wants us all to be together for holiday celebrations. Our daughter is being honored for work contributions at a large gathering, and both of us will be at the event sitting at the same table.

"Don't get me wrong—it's been a very long and difficult journey! For about a year, I've been using every tool and map I can. Much of the time I felt like I was fighting against my own reactions, which, had I indulged them, would have been like pouring gasoline on a fire. I needed the regular support of other people to get out of my judgments, to empathize with myself and with her, and to practice having conversations in a way that I could show up with her and be present enough for her to have her needs met too. I'm so grateful, both for these tools and for her willingness to come to the table with the work I'm certain she's undertaken on her side as well. I feel much more hope than I have in a long time. To have some peace between us, to not have our children feeling like they have to choose sides, and to be able to move forward in connection are all priceless."

BOARD CHAIR

"As chairperson for a board of directors, I'm often managing conflict. Recently, one of the board members called me very upset about a proposal in front of the board. She wanted me to hear her views and proceeded to rant, hurling label after label, judgment after judgment.

"I noticed I was triggered by what she was saying. Before learning the Mediate Your Life tools, I would have argued points with her, but this time I empathized and tried to listen for what she felt was important, which was difficult with so much story and judgment to wade through. When she spoke up at the next meeting where we discussed the proposal, she still said things difficult for people to hear, but I continued to listen and reflect her underlying concerns. As a result, we were able to develop a revised proposal that everyone was pleased with, in part because I had taken the time to hear what she really cared about.

"When I reflect on this whole experience, I realize that from performing the practices I learned in the Mediate Your Life trainings, I now notice when I am being triggered in the moment. A few years ago, I would have either argued with her or not engaged at all; however, this time I was able to notice my reaction, breathe, and abandon my typical ways of reacting. Over time, my capacity to be with what is happening in the moment has increased. While I don't want to be in that kind of intense conversation every day, I can now recognize that I'm triggered quickly and then reconnect enough with myself internally to be able to be with the other person."

BRIDGING MARITAL DIFFERENCES

"Before I started using these tools, my wife and I were thinking about separating. We knew we loved each other, but we simply kept landing in a place where we felt like we were too different. We had many conversations about our incompatibility, each time determining it was too painful and difficult to be together, that we just weren't right for each other. In using these skills, though, I began to see how we would both get hurt or irritated over a little thing the other person said or did, causing us to go into a combative state where the situation would escalate.

"The first step for me was getting to a point where I could catch myself and not say anything to make it worse. I learned that if I could be aware and stop before the toboggan surpassed the rim of the hill, I would have more choice about what to do. Now, both my wife and I can more easily get back to feeling connected and aligned with each other—and to the love that's truly there between us. When we come back to that loving space, we can find ways to bridge the differences and collaborate with each other."

We offer the example of our own and other people's stories so you know that even in situations where it feels difficult or impossible, even when you still have hurt and lack trust that your needs will be met, there is always a way. It may take a little time, it may require some work on your part, and it may demand asking for some help to go through various processes. But it is possible to work through situations and emerge with relationships not only intact, but also strengthened.

What Is Success?

In many of the examples in this book, particularly the family story with James and Sally, both people know and are using the Mediate Your Life toolbox. Success, however, is not dependent on both parties knowing the skills. In the three examples above, only one person was coming to our trainings and incorporating the knowledge into their life, yet they were still able to effect significant change.

Based on the stories above, it might seem like success means that the conflict is resolved to everyone's satisfaction, people are reconnected in a loving, compassionate embrace, and all is wonderful in the world. While that is possible and delightful when it happens, it's not an appropriate scale by which to measure success. Similarly, success is not living in a constant state of peace and connection in which disagreements and misunderstandings never happen. So how do we define it?

In our view, success lies in:

+ cultivating your awareness of what is going on for you moment by moment

+ increasing your skill to return to presence, regardless of what is happening

+ nurturing your ability to choose what to do instead of react

+ learning from whatever happens so that your skills, experience, and effectiveness expand over time

Notice that each of these markers of success reflects something occurring in you, that these tools are never about changing someone else, but rather about changing *you*. The target is to shift how you feel internally and your capacity to act in ways that contribute more to your own and other people's lives.

When you use the maps and skills with a realistic view of success, you can find success in each encounter *regardless of the outcome*. If a conversation doesn't go the way you hoped, you can learn from what *did* happen. Even if you choose to no longer interact with a certain person—an outcome that by one point of view might be viewed as failure—if you've used the tools and come to that choice with conscious awareness, that is actually a success.

The Mourn Celebrate Learn process is an especially helpful tool to begin to see your success, regardless of what happens in any interaction. Celebrate when you use the tools. If you forget that a map is available in the moment, celebrate when you remember, even if it's a week later. Change will not come through using these tools as another way to judge yourself; it will come when you can emerge out of judgment again and again.

A WAY OF LIFE (NOT A QUICK FIX)

When you begin to use the tools in this book, you will likely see some immediate benefits, even if they're small. Perhaps you are in pain about a situation and begin to find some relief. You might notice that you enjoy connecting with yourself on a regular basis and find that connection helps you interact in the world in a way that you enjoy.

People often approach new learning with the hope that they will see an instant payoff, a quick fix or magic bullet that will create ease in their relationships for all time. The real hope of this book, however, lies not in quick fixes, but in practice and repetition that leads to incorporating these skills into who you are. The goal is to arrive at a point where you live the skills on a daily basis, knowing they are readily available when those sticky situations arise. In utilizing the skills and tools regularly, you change. People around you often change too, not because you are forcing them to, but because their responses reflect the change in you.

We've talked about mediator mind in the context of each map, but we also want to stress that it's a state of mind you can access at any time, not only when you are using a map or exercise. Once you have a sense of that state within yourself where you can hold multiple perspectives, mediator mind can become a practice throughout the day.

After all, how often do you find yourself stuck in a story, whether one about you and your inadequacies, or about other people and what's wrong with them? Remembering mediator mind can help you shift away from believing in those stories and living your life from the judgments in them. It's a way to come back to the present moment, detaching from the thoughts that keep you stuck. As you practice accessing mediator mind regularly, you will find that it keeps you connected to yourself and more able to access happiness and well-being, regardless of what is happening outside you.

CHOICE AND SELF-KNOWLEDGE

With most of the tools in this book, you are connecting again and again with your observations, feelings, needs, and requests in the moment. This practice is a powerful form of learning about yourself. When you know what stimulates you into reacting and identify the needs that are motivating you, you gain greater capacity to change it.

As you use the maps in this book over time, you will find that you become less reactive. This means that those habitual patterns of fight or flight, the normal ways you react when you encounter stress or conflict that lead you into deeper trouble, have less of a hold over you. Initially, you will likely find that each time you are triggered, you have to work through your reaction to return to a present, centered, connected state. By doing that over and over again, however, you will find that you begin to go less deeply into reaction before catching it. Eventually, you will notice the reaction but have immediate awareness that you can do something different.

The key result of reducing reactivity? Choice! When you develop trust and confidence that you can manage your emotional responses to the world and choose what you do instead of reacting, you change your relationship to your emotions. Instead of being powerless over them, you have compassion for yourself and others, giving you the space to see new possibilities.

Self-knowledge and the capacity to choose allow you to be more effective in your life and interactions with the world. If you become aware of your reactions and mitigate them, you can avoid being blindsided by your personal history as situations come up. For example, instead of acting out of habitual responses based on your early experience (that essentially re-enact your past), you are able to see those responses in contrast to new ones that give you more of what you desire. When you can see multiple options and be disengaged even a little from emotions, you are able to choose.

Each time you choose, it gives you new information to then make more choices in the next moment. Imagine how much more effective you can be when you are consciously choosing in each moment instead of being triggered into a choice-less and reactive state!

So often in both family and work environments, however, people operate from a sense of *no* choice, believing things like, "These are the people in my family. I just have to put up with them." or "Well, he's my boss, he can fire me and I have to go along with what he says no matter how idiosyncratic it is." When people finally do make a choice, it is sometimes drastic, resulting in schisms that get passed down for generations in a family, or in actions that sabotage productivity and career advancement at work.

We see these same patterns writ large on the world stage. Communal rifts and sectarian divides exist across the planet: religions pitted against other religions, tribal groups and ethnicities at war, class against class. Because these conflicts are pervasive and involve many people, the tendency is to feel hopeless about creating change in this larger arena.

It's important to remember, however, that even these long-standing, large-scale conflicts begin the same way: people interacting with each other out of their past hurts, being hijacked by the stress response, and acting in ways that do not meet their own or other people's needs. When each side does this, the inevitable result is disconnection, violence, and suffering. People then feel justified and "right" in their perspective of how "wrong" the other side is, passing that point of view down to their children who continue the conflict, generation after generation.

Whether we're talking about individual conflicts in families or national-scale conflicts, how they begin and end is the same: *one conversation at a time.*

Peace starts right here and right now, with the conversation you are in with yourself and the people in your life. Do not underestimate the importance of coming back to choice again and again, choosing the response that leads to connection as much as possible. Your choices create a ripple effect, touching people you may not even know as they flow outward. When other people experience and witness your choices, you also open the possibility for them to begin choosing differently in their relationship to themselves and others.

We hope the maps and skills in this book, and in the rest of the Mediate Your Life series, will contribute to people having conversations that lead to peace. We would like everyone to be able to bring themselves and their concerns to the table, and to have conversations characterized by shared understanding and mutual care. In sum, we encourage you to use the skills and tools in this book so that every conversation becomes one in which you are creating the world you would like to live in.

Whether you're a stay-at-home mom or a Fortune 500 CEO, a school janitor or the President of the United States, every relationship, every change, and every new possibility for a better world happens one conversation at a time. What will you create with your next conversation?

APPENDICES

A | Feelings List

Feelings are bodily felt experiences and tell us about our needs being met or not met, and about what we are observing, thinking, and wanting.

PEACEFUL	LOVING
tranquil	warm
calm	affectionate
content	tender
engrossed	appreciative
absorbed	friendly
expansive	sensitive
serene	compassionate
loving	grateful
blissful	nurtured
satisfied	amorous
relaxed	trusting
relieved	open
quiet	thankful
carefree	radiant
composed	adoring
fulfilled	passionate

GLAD	PLAYFUL	INTERESTED
happy	energetic	involved
excited	effervescent	inquisitive
hopeful	invigorated	intense
joyful	zestful	enriched
satisfied	refreshed	absorbed
delighted	impish	alert
encouraged	alive	aroused
grateful	lively	astonished
confident	exuberant	concerned
inspired	giddy	curious
touched	adventurous	eager
proud	mischievous	enthusiastic
exhilarated	jubilant	fascinated
ecstatic	goofy	intrigued
optimistic	buoyant	surprised
glorious	electrified	helpful

MAD	SAD
impatient	lonely
pessimistic	heavy
disgruntled	troubled
frustrated	helpless
irritable	gloomy
edgy	overwhelmed
grouchy	distant
agitated	despondent
exasperated	discouraged
disgusted	distressed
irked	dismayed
cantankerous	disheartened
animosity	despairing
bitter	sorrowful
rancorous	unhappy
irate, furious	depressed
angry	blue
hostile	miserable
enraged	dejected
violent	melancholy

SCARED	TIRED	CONFUSED
afraid	exhausted	frustrated
fearful	fatigued	perplexed
terrified	inert	hesitant
startled	lethargic	troubled
nervous	indifferent	uncomfortable
jittery	weary	withdrawn
horrified	overwhelmed	apathetic
anxious	fidgety	embarrassed
worried	helpless	hurt
anguished	heavy	uneasy
lonely	sleepy	irritated
insecure	disinterested	suspicious
sensitive	reluctant	unsteady
shocked	passive	puzzled
apprehensive	dull	restless
dread	bored	boggled
jealous	listless	chagrined
desperate	blah	unglued
suspicious	mopey	detached
frightened	comatose	skeptical

For a printable version, visit:
mediateyourlife.com/from-conflict-to-connection

UNIVERSAL HUMAN NEEDS / VALUES LIST

The needs below are grouped into categories of core needs, three meta-categories and nine subcategories.

WELL-BEING

SUSTENANCE/ HEALTH	SAFETY/ SECURITY	BEAUTY/ PEACE/PLAY
abundance/thriving	comfort	acceptance
exercise	confidence	appreciation
food/nutrition	emotional safety	gratitude
nourishment	familiarity	awareness
rest/sleep	order	balance
relaxation	structure	ease
shelter	predictability	equanimity
sustainability	protection from harm	humor
support/help	stability	presence
wellness	trust	rejuvenation
vitality	faith	simplicity
energy		space
		tranquility
		wholeness
		wonder

CONNECTION

LOVE/ CARING	EMPATHY/ UNDER- STANDING	COMMUNITY/ BELONGING
affection/warmth		cooperation
beauty	awareness/clarity	fellowship
closeness/touch	acceptance	generosity
companionship	acknowledgment	inclusion
compassion	communication	interdependence
kindness	consideration	harmony/peace
intimacy	hearing	hospitality/welcoming
mattering	(hear/be heard)	mutuality
importance	knowing	reciprocity
nurturing	(know/be known)	partnership
sexual connection	presence/listening	relationship
respect	respect/equality	support/solidarity
honoring	receptivity/openness	trust
valuing/prizing	recognition	dependability
	seeing (see/be seen)	transparency
	self-esteem	openness
	sensitivity	

SELF-EXPRESSION

AUTONOMY/ FREEDOM	AUTHEN- TICITY	MEANING/ CONTRIBUTION
choice	adventure	appreciation/gratitude
clarity	aliveness	achievement
congruence	discovery	productivity
consistency	honesty	celebration/mourning
continuity	initiative	challenge
dignity	innovation	efficacy
freedom	inspiration	effectiveness
independence	joy	excellence
integrity	mystery	growth
power	passion	learning/clarity
empowerment	spontaneity	mystery
self-responsibility		participation
		purpose/value
		self-actualization
		self-esteem
		skill/mastery

For a printable version, visit:
mediateyourlife.com/from-conflict-to-connection

C | SELF-CONNECTION PROCESS (SCP)

BREATH *(Awareness: being in the present moment)*

1. Focus attention on your breathing, following the in-flow, extending the out-flow.

2. Observe your sense perceptions (sight, sound, scent, touch, taste).

3. Shift attention from thoughts and "stories" back to breath and sense perception.

BODY *(Presence: being with feelings, and accepting what is)*

1. Put attention into your body.

2. Feel the sensations and animating energy and aliveness.

3. Name your sensations, emotions, and fight or flight reactions, then go back to experiencing.

NEEDS *(Choice: choosing thoughts, beliefs, and actions to meet needs)*

1. From awareness of your thoughts and feelings now, ask yourself, "What are the needs underneath?"

2. What needs do you choose to focus on now? What inspires, uplifts, and empowers you?

3. Repeat the needs to yourself, feel your body, and experience the needs met within you through your imagination, self-talk, or taking action.

We encourage you to set aside at least five minutes a day to practice SCP, and also to practice throughout the day, in as many moments as you can, even when you're not in a fight-flight-freeze reaction.

SELF-CONNECTION PROCESS: EXPANDED VERSION

BREATH

1. Slow and deepen your breathing.
2. Count to the same number on the inhale and the exhale.
3. Extend your exhale longer than your inhale.
4. Breathe in, hold breath, breathe out—all to the same count.
5. Practice relating to thoughts with kindness, humor, and friendliness.

BODY

1. Feel your feelings without naming, analyzing, or thinking about them.
2. Focus attention on three body centers—belly, heart, head ("triune brain": reptilian/instinctual, mammal-ian/emotional, neo-cortex/intellectual/intuitive).
3. Relax your muscles; allow openness, softness, and flexibility in your posture.
4. Mind-body practices
   a. Relax your muscles (e.g., eyes, tongue, jaw, shoulders, arms, belly).
   b. Open your posture (e.g., open chest and arms, say "Ahhhhh").
   c. Align and balance around your spinal core.

NEEDS

1. Breathe into three body centers (spinal "chakras"—belly, heart, head).

2. Connect core needs to the body centers.

   a. Well-being (peace)—sustenance, safety, order

   b. Connection (love)—care, understanding, community

   c. Self-expression (joy)—freedom, honesty, meaning

3. Focus on a "chemistry-changing" positive image for each body center.

4. Imagine the needs fully and completely met.

5. Gratitude practice: Celebrate how needs are met in your life; "mourn" any ways needs are not currently met.

6. Tonglen—breathe in suffering of self, others, the world; breathe out peace, love, joy, happiness, well-being, connection, self-expression.

For a printable version, visit:
mediateyourlife.com/from-conflict-to-connection

D | INTENSITY EXERCISE

LEVEL 1A: PRACTICING WITHOUT CONTENT

1. The receiving partner performs the Self-Connection Process, then asks the delivery partner to present the trigger.

2. The deliverer says a neutral phrase, such as "Water is wet" or "Snow is white" in a conversational tone, pauses, then repeats it, gradually increasing the volume, intensity, and aggression level of the words, amping it up slowly.

3. *As soon as* the receiver notices their body reacting to the intensity level, they raise their hand as a nonverbal way to ask their partner to stop delivering the trigger.

4. The receiver then physically moves into the mediator chair and performs the Self-Connection Process out loud until they feel calm, physically relaxed, and no longer in a fight-flight-freeze reaction mode.

5. The receiver moves back into the receiving chair and asks the delivery partner to begin again.

6. The deliverer starts by saying the same words as before at a lower intensity level than what triggered their partner, and again incrementally amps it up in intensity.

7. Repeat steps 3–6 until the receiver has practiced to the degree they desire or notices not being triggered anymore, no matter how intense the delivery.

8. Share with each other what came up for you.

LEVEL 1B: PRACTICING WITH CONTENT

1. The receiver tells their partner what words they want to use for the practice, giving instruction on how to weave them together with specific tone, volume, or body language. For example, if the words are from another person and often come with a particular gesture and tone of voice, the delivery partner can incorporate that gesture and tone along with saying the words.

2. The receiver performs the Self-Connection Process, then asks the delivery partner to begin.

3. The deliverer begins presenting the trigger at a low level of intensity, gradually increasing.

4. *As soon as* the receiver notices their body reacting, they raise their hand as a nonverbal way to ask their partner to stop delivering the trigger.

5. The receiver physically moves into the mediator chair and performs the Self-Connection Process until they feel calm, physically relaxed, and no longer in a fight-flight-freeze reaction mode. When they feel they have choice about how to respond, they are ready to continue.

6. The receiver moves back into the receiving chair and asks the delivery partner to begin again.

7. The deliverer presents the same trigger as before, starting at a lower intensity level than what triggered their partner, and again incrementally amps it up in intensity.

8. Repeat steps 4–7 until the receiver has practiced to the degree they desire or notices not being triggered anymore, no matter how intense the delivery.

9. Share with each other what came up for you.

LEVEL 2: RESPONDING TO A FIRST TRIGGER

1. The receiver tells their partner what words they want to use for the practice, giving instruction on how to weave them together with specific tone, volume, or body language.

2. The receiver performs the Self-Connection Process, then asks the delivery partner to begin.

3. The deliverer begins presenting the trigger at a low level of intensity, gradually increasing.

4. *As soon as* the receiver notices their body reacting, they raise their hand as a nonverbal way to ask their partner to stop delivering the trigger.

5. The receiver physically moves into the mediator chair and performs the Self-Connection Process until they feel calm, physically relaxed, and no longer in a fight-flight-freeze reaction mode. When they feel they have choice about how to respond, they are ready to continue.

6. The receiver says out loud (still sitting in the mediator chair) how they want to respond to this person now, choosing between empathy or self-expression.

7. The receiver moves back into the receiving chair, responds accordingly, and asks the delivery partner to begin again.

8. The deliverer then presents the same trigger as before, starting at a lower intensity level than what triggered their partner, and again incrementally amps it up in intensity.

9. Repeat steps 4–8 until the receiver has practiced to the degree they desire or notices not being triggered anymore, no matter how intense the delivery.

10. Share with each other what came up for you.

LEVEL 3: RESPONDING TO A SECOND TRIGGER

1. The receiver tells their partner what words they want to use for the practice, giving instruction on how to weave them together with specific tone, volume, or body language.

2. The receiver performs the Self-Connection Process, then asks the delivery partner to begin.

3. The deliverer presents the trigger at a low level of intensity, gradually increasing.

4. *As soon as* the receiver notices their body reacting, they raise their hand as a nonverbal way to ask their partner to stop delivering the trigger.

5. The receiver physically moves into the mediator chair and performs the Self-Connection Process until they feel calm, physically relaxed, and no longer in a fight-flight-freeze reaction mode. When they feel they have choice about how to respond, they are ready to continue.

6. The receiver says out loud (still sitting in the mediator chair) how they want to respond to this person, choosing between empathy or self-expression.

7. The receiver moves back into the receiving chair and responds accordingly.

8. The deliverer presents another trigger by reacting to the choice, saying something that would be hard for the receiving partner to hear.

9. The receiver physically moves again into the mediator chair and performs the Self-Connection Process until they feel calm, physically relaxed, and no longer in a fight-flight-freeze reaction mode. When they feel they have choice about how to respond, they are ready to continue.

10. The receiver says out loud (still sitting in the mediator chair) how they want to respond to this person now, choosing between empathy or self-expression.

11. The receiver moves back into the receiving chair, responds accordingly, and asks the delivery partner to begin again.

12. The deliverer presents the same trigger as before, starting at a lower intensity than what triggered their partner, and incrementally amps it up.

13. Repeat steps 4–12 until the receiver has practiced to the degree they desire or notices not being triggered anymore, no matter how intense the delivery.

14. Share with each other what came up for you.

In Levels 2 and 3, after making a choice and moving back into the Self chair:

1. For empathy with the other, remember the four elements of empathy—presence, silent empathy, understanding, and need language.

   a. If you'd like, you can use the empathy template:

      i. "Are you ____ [FEELINGS] because you want ____ [NEEDS]?"

2. For self-expression, first connect with the needs you want to express, then let your words flow naturally, owning your observations and thoughts as your own, from *your* subjective frame of reference, and connecting your thoughts, feelings, and what you would like from this person back to your needs. Also, try to speak from presence with the other person while you talk.

b. If you'd like, you can use the expression template:

    i. "When I see/hear you _____ [OBSERVATION], I feel _____ [FEELINGS], because I want _____ [NEEDS].

    ii. Would you _____? [CONNECTION REQUEST: e.g., "How do you feel hearing this?" and "Would you tell me what you're hearing me say?"]

For a printable version, visit:
mediateyourlife.com/from-conflict-to-connection

E | ENEMY IMAGE PROCESS (EIP)

You can do this process with yourself, in your head or written down, or with an empathy or practice partner.

PART I: EMPATHY FOR YOURSELF

1. Observations of:

   a. What the other said or did that triggered your reaction

   b. Judgments, "enemy images," "stories" you have about yourself or the other

2. Feelings: sensations and emotions in *your* body. Watch for "faux feelings."

3. Needs: *your* universal human desires, not specific to any "strategy." Take time to feel and experience the feelings and needs in your body.

CYCLING: As you go through the steps, you may notice you have more reaction in you with which to empathize. Continue to cycle through steps 1–3 until you feel complete for the moment, connected to your needs, and feeling a degree of inner calm, relaxation, and centeredness.

PART II: EMPATHY FOR OTHER

In this step, you connect within yourself to the other person's experience:

1. Observations of

    a. What *you* said or did that might have been triggering to the Other

    b. What their thoughts about you and the situation might be

2. Feelings: sensations and emotions in *their* body

3. Needs: *their* universal human desires, not specific to any "strategy"

CYCLING: As you move through these steps, continue cycling through all three until you feel complete for the moment, connected to the Other, and more peaceful and non-reactive. Also, as you attempt to empathize with the other, you may get triggered into more of your own reactions. If this happens, go back to Part I and cycle back and forth between Part I and Part II as needed.

PART III: EMERGENCE OF NEW POSSIBILITIES

Ask yourself about your:

1. Learning from doing Parts 1 and 2. Do you now see any new ideas, insights, or possibilities that have emerged?

2. Plan of action (specific) for how to meet your needs now that you are on the "other side of connection."

See if you can form a specific, doable, action-language (what you do want) request of yourself, which may be to make a request of the other person or someone else.

3. Practice: After forming an action request and a plan, you may want to practice whatever you came up with. If this involves a conversation, you can practice what you might actually say and also practice dealing with challenging ways they might respond. One way to do this is to role-play a practice conversation (e.g., with a coach, practice partner, or through journaling).

Cycling: As you go through these steps, you may notice more conflict reactions coming up in you. You could then go back to Parts I and II, and cycle back and forth between Parts I–II and Part III until you feel ready to complete Part III.

For a printable version, visit:
mediateyourlife.com/from-conflict-to-connection

F | INTERPERSONAL MEDIATION (IPM) MAP

The IPM map is a guide for helping you navigate difficult conversations between yourself and another from the perspective of the inner third chair of "mediator mind."

THE 5-STEP IPM MAP

1. Perform the Self-Connection Process (SCP)

2. Ask yourself, "Can I hear the message as a 'please'?"

3. Empathize with the Other, if you can

4. Self-Express

5. Make Solution Requests and Agreements

MORE DETAIL OF THE IPM MAP STEPS

1. Perform the Self-Connection Process (SCP)—breath, body, needs

2. Ask yourself, "Can I hear the message as a 'please'?"

   a. "Please" meaning that the Other is saying, "I'm in pain. I have unmet needs."

3. Empathize with the Other (if you have capacity)

As mediator of your own conversation, you choose from moment to moment where you want to direct the focus of empathy, toward yourself or the other person, to create connection. We suggest first giving empathy to the Other, if you have the capacity to do so, then seek to be heard yourself.

4. Self-Express

Now it is your turn to be heard by expressing what's going on in you (speaking from connection with needs). As your own mediator, you are in essence directing empathy (rather than seeking agreement) toward yourself. We recommend ending your self-expression with a Connection Request. Stay with steps 1–4 until there is empathy and connection between you, then go to step 5, Solution Requests and Agreements.

   a. Two types of connection requests:

      i. For reflection, e.g., "Would you say what you're hearing?"

      ii. For expression, e.g., "How do you feel about what you're hearing?"

5. Solution Requests and Agreements

   a. Specific present, positive, action language (emergence from needs/connection)

   b. Request vs. demand (choice)

   c. Interdependence—seeking to get everyone's needs met

   d. Need Behind the No process

      i. Clarify the request and the needs behind it.

    ii.   If there is a "no," empathize with the no and find the needs prompting it.

    iii. Ask the one saying no for a request that would meet the needs of self and other, or the initial requestor could offer a new request.

e. Agreements

    i.   Primary—what you mutually agree to do to meet the needs between you

    ii. Supporting—agreements of what to do to support the primary agreements

    iii. Restoring—agreements about what to do if the primary agreements are not kept

For a printable version, visit:
mediateyourlife.com/from-conflict-to-connection

G | INTERPERSONAL MEDIATION EXERCISE

IPM EXERCISE LEVEL 1
EMPATHY, SELF-EXPRESSION, AND CONNECTION REQUESTS

From the Self chair:

1. Tell your practice partner who they are and one observation of something the person says or does that is challenging for you.

2. Start by expressing something to the Other (practice partner) to begin the conversation

3. The Other expresses a challenging statement back to you.

Move to the Mediator chair, and:

4. Perform the Self-Connection Process (SCP).

5. Ask yourself, "Can I hear the message as a 'please'?"

6. Choose, as the mediator, to direct the focus of empathy toward the Other, if you have the capacity. If you don't have capacity, stay with the previous steps until you feel ready to make this choice. Your practice partner can shift out of role and support you with empathy for yourself.

Move to the Self chair, and:

7. Empathize with the Other. Give empathy to the Other (remember the four elements of empathy), *with the intention to create connection*. Continue giving empathy until the Other indicates they feel heard as they would like. You can ask, "Is there more you want me to hear?" [Remember, at any time you can pause and move to the Mediator chair and repeat steps 4, 5, and 6.]

8. Self-Express. Now, focus the empathy toward yourself (in essence, you are asking the Other to hear and empathize with you as you).

9. Express your honesty and inner truth and reality to the Other. This is your chance to be heard and to practice courageously expressing perhaps "scary honesty." First, silently self-connect with your needs, then speak from those needs while being present with the Other. Express *with the intention to create connection*.

   • Use this self-expression template if it's helpful to you:

      "When I see/hear [OBSERVATION], I'm [FEELINGS] because I want [NEEDS]."

10. End your self-expression with a Connection Request for reflection, e.g., "Would you let me know what you hear me say?"

11. The Other gives empathy to you until you say you feel heard as you desire.

12. Now ask the Other the Connection Request for expression, e.g., "How do you feel about what I said?"

13. The Other at this point expresses *with the intention to create connection.*

14. Give empathy to the Other (elements of empathy), *with the intention to create connection,* until they indicate they feel heard. You can ask, "Is there more you want me to hear?" [Remember, at any time you can pause and move to the Mediator chair to perform the SCP.]

IPM Exercise Level 2
Adding Solution Requests and Need Behind the No Process

Do all of Level 1, and then add what follows after Step 14:

From the Self chair:

15. Make a Solution Request of the Other, seeking to meet both your needs *and* theirs.

16. The Other says some form of "no" to your request.

Move to the Mediator chair, and:

17. Perform the Self-Connection Process (SCP).

18. Choose Empathy for the Other.

Move to the Self chair, and:

19. Give empathy to the Other, trying to get to the needs behind their "no," the needs keeping them from saying "yes." Stay with empathy until they say they feel heard.

20. Ask the Other if they have a request that tries to meet both their needs *and* yours. The Other does their best to think of a request, but if they can't, you can offer one.

IPM EXERCISE LEVEL 3

THE FULL MONTY

From the Self chair:

1. Tell your practice partner who they are and one observation of something the person says or does that is challenging for you.

2. Start by expressing something to the Other (practice partner) to begin the conversation.

3. The Other expresses a challenging statement back to you.

Move to the Mediator chair, and:

4. Perform the Self-Connection Process (SCP).

5. Ask yourself, "Can I hear the message as a 'please'?"

6. Choose, as the mediator, to direct the focus of empathy toward the Other, if you have the capacity. If you don't, stay with the previous steps until you feel ready. Your practice partner can shift out of their role and support you with empathy for yourself.

Move to the Self chair, and:

7. Give empathy to the Other (remember the four elements of empathy) *with the intention to create connection*. Continue giving empathy until the Other indicates they feel heard as they desire. You can ask, "Is there more you want me to hear?" [If at any time while empathizing you become triggered, you can pause and move to the Mediator chair and do steps 4, 5, and 6 again.]

8. Self-Express. Now, as mediator, focus the empathy toward yourself (you are now asking the Other to hear and empathize with you as you).

9. Express your honesty and inner truth and reality to the Other. This is your chance to be heard and to practice courageously expressing perhaps "scary honesty." First, silently self-connect with your needs, then speak from those needs while being present with the Other. Express *with the intention to create connection.*

   a. Use this self-expression template if it's helpful to you:

      "When I see/hear [OBSERVATION], I'm [FEELINGS] because I want [NEEDS]."

10. End your self-expression with a Connection Request for reflection; e.g., "Would you let me know what you hear me say?"

11. The Other self-expresses instead of saying back what they heard.

12. Continuing to self-express and direct the focus of empathy toward yourself, use the mediator skill of Pulling by the Ears, e.g., "I want to hear you," and "First would you let me know what you heard me say?"

13. The Other reflects back judgment instead of needs.

14. Maintaining self-expression and the focus of empathy toward yourself, use Pulling by the Ears again, e.g., "Thank you for saying what you heard. I'd like you to hear ..."

15. The Other self-expresses in a triggered way that is challenging and difficult.

Move to the Mediator chair, and:

16. Perform the Self-Connection Process (SCP).

17. Ask yourself, "Can I hear the message as a 'please'?"

18. Choose to focus the empathy toward the Other by using the mediator skill of Emergency First Aid Empathy.

Move to the Self chair, and:

19. Give empathy (elements of empathy) to the Other, *with the intention to create connection*, until they say they feel heard. [Move back to the Mediator chair and perform the SCP if you become triggered.]

20. Choose the mediator skill of Self-Empathy.

21. Tell the Other that you would like to take a break and come back to the conversation.

22. Your practice partner now steps out of their role and helps you do a quick Enemy Image Process (EIP) with yourself.

23. Come back to the conversation with the Other when you're ready.

Continuing the Conversation with the Other:

24. Use the mediator skill of Self-Expression; e.g., "I would like for us to both be heard and to get to a solution we both feel good about. Could we take turns talking and listening to each other?"

25. The Other says, "Yes."

26. Use the mediator skill of Tracking and return to the Pulling by the Ears, e.g., "I wonder if now you'd be

willing to let me know what you heard me say earlier in the conversation?"

27. The Other reflects back understanding and needs, *with the intention to create connection.* The Other continues reflecting until you say that you feel heard.

28. Thank the Other for hearing you.

29. Now, use the other Connection Request for self-expression, e.g., "How do you feel about what I said?"

30. The Other self-expresses, continuing to talk until you interrupt them.

31. Use the mediator skill of Interrupting (with empathy).

32. Offer a Solution Request that seeks to meet your needs and the Other's.

33. The Other says a version of "no."

34. Empathize with the "no," getting to the needs behind the no that are keeping the person from saying "yes."

35. Ask the Other if they have a request to meet the Other's needs and yours.

36. The Other offers a Solution Request.

37. Say "yes," or offer another Solution Request.

For a printable version, visit:
mediateyourlife.com/from-conflict-to-connection

H | NINE MEDIATION SKILLS

1. EMPATHY

   a. Presence

   b. Silent empathy

   c. Understanding

   d. Need language

2. CONNECTION REQUESTS

   a. Message Sent, Message Received
      "Would you say what you heard?"

   b. Quality of Connection
      "How do you feel about what you heard?"

3. PULLING BY THE EARS: Re-requesting that the other person reiterate what they heard if they self-express, or restate their judgments instead of reflecting understanding or needs

4. EMERGENCY (FIRST AID) EMPATHY: Giving empathy when you've asked the other person to repeat what they heard but they are too triggered to do it

5. TRACKING: Where the conversation is in terms of the 5-step Interpersonal Mediation map

6. INTERRUPTING: Using empathy to interrupt when the other person is saying more words than you can hear or that are disruptive to the process

7. SELF-EMPATHY: Giving empathy to yourself during the conversation

8. SELF-EXPRESSION: Expression related to the process of the conversation

9. SOLUTION REQUESTS: Making specific, doable, action-language requests

   a. Need Behind the No Process

      i. Clarify the request and needs.

      ii. Empathize with the needs behind the "no."

      iii. Ask for or suggest a new request that seeks to meet needs for both people.

   b. Three Types of Agreements

      i. Primary: What you mutually agree to do between you

      ii. Supporting: What to do to support the primary agreements

      iii. Restoring: What to do if the primary agreements are not kept

For a printable version, visit:
mediateyourlife.com/from-conflict-to-connection

I | MOURN
CELEBRATE
LEARN (MCL)

PART I: MOURN

Empathy with needs *not met* for you by what happened in a conversation or interaction with another.

1. OBSERVATIONS

    a. What happened that did not meet your needs?

    b. Do you have any negative thoughts, judgments, or "stories" about this?

2. FEELINGS: Sensations and emotions in your body

3. NEEDS: Connecting your observations, thoughts, and feelings to your needs

CYCLING: Move through the three steps in whatever order works for you. Continue to cycle through the steps until you feel an inner calm and are connected to your needs.

PART II: CELEBRATE

Empathy with needs met for you by what happened in the conversation or interaction.

1. Observations

    a. What happened that met your needs, including good
        things that might happen in the future from what
        occurred?

2. Feelings: Sensations and emotions in your body

3. Needs: Connecting your observations, thoughts, and
   feelings to your needs

Cycling: As with Part I, you may cycle through the steps
multiple times. Also, as you are in Part II, you may also notice
more thoughts and feelings relating to unmet needs coming
up. At any point you can cycle back to Part I, and back and
forth between Parts I and II.

Part III: Learn

Emergence of New Possibilities

1. Learning from doing Parts I and II. Any new ideas,
   insights, or possibilities you now see?

2. Plan of action (specific) for how you want to meet your
   needs now that you have connected with needs met and
   not met. See if you can form a specific, action-language,
   "doable" (what you do want) request of yourself. One
   way to achieve this is to do a "post-hearsal"—imagine re-
   doing the conversation and what you might have said or
   done differently.

3. Practice: After forming an action request and a plan, you
   may want to practice whatever you came up with in order
   to make it into a new habit. One way to do this is to role-
   play a practice conversation with a practice partner or
   coach, or to do this in journaling.

CYCLING: After reaching step three, you may notice you have more learning and insights. If so, you can cycle back through the steps. You might also notice more needs (met or not met) coming up to empathize with. If so, you can go back to Parts I and II.

For a printable version, visit:
mediateyourlife.com/from-conflict-to-connection

J | FLIGHT SIMULATOR

The flight simulator is used for both the Intensity Exercise and for role-play practice of the Interpersonal Mediation (IPM) map, either the IPM role-play or the IPM Exercise.

SETTING UP THE FLIGHT SIMULATOR

1. Choose situation and clarify roles—who will play yourself working on your situation, and who will play the role of the other person in the conflict? The person whose situation it is plays the role of mediator as well.

2. Give one observation—tell the person playing the role of the "other" one thing the actual person said or did that was challenging. (Don't tell the whole story.)

3. *(For IPM Exercise/role-play only)* Dial the difficulty to be in your "learning zone":

   a. How much intensity or challenge do you want the other person to give you?

   b. What skill(s) do you want to focus on, if any?

4. Make agreements with a coach or peer support person, if one is present.

5. Timekeeper—have someone keep time.

6. Begin with SCP/self-empathy before starting.

FLIGHT SIMULATOR CONTROL PANEL OPTIONS:
FOR DURING THE EXERCISE OR ROLE-PLAY

You can pause and:

1. Perform self-connection or self-empathy.

2. Consider out loud your options and choices.

3. *(IPM Exercise/role-play)* Dial up or down the difficulty/challenge level.

4. *(IPM Exercise/role-play)* Ask yourself what skill(s) you were using and what you want to choose.

5. Ask your practice partners or coach for ideas or feedback.

6. Rewind and do over what you want to practice.

HARVESTING—"BIO-FEEDBACK"

1. Person in self/mediator role (if you want to): Start with how it was for you. What did you like?

2. Feedback from practice partner: How was it for you? Start with *needs met* feedback.

    a. What was connecting and helpful to you? *Use connection as your guide.*

    b. Try to find at least one positive thing to say, however small.

    c. Give specific observations.

    d. Share your inner experience—feelings and needs.

3. Person in self/mediator role, what further feedback, if any, would you like?

a. Choice about *needs not met* feedback.

b. Practice partner: Ask the person if they want to hear about what didn't work as well for you.

c. What could they have done differently to work better for you?

d. Give specific observations, and share your feelings and needs.

e. Keep checking to see if the person wants to hear more.

For a printable version, visit:
mediateyourlife.com/from-conflict-to-connection

ACKNOWLEDGMENTS

We thank the participants in our trainings (which we have now facilitated in sixteen countries) who, through their feedback and wholehearted engagement, have guided us in the development of our work. In a very real sense, what we have learned together and have attempted to articulate in this book, come directly from our engagement with participants in our trainings. They have told us what works and what doesn't work. We have sought not to postulate, but to discover, both in dialogue with each other and with the people who utilize what we are developing in their daily lives. They have internalized what we offered, and from this integrity of experience have given us feedback that continues to direct our path of discovery. This book is a report of this ongoing discovery process.

We would like to thank, with the deepest bow of appreciation, Julie Stiles, who has co-written this book with us. She has had the laboring oar in both writing and wrangling her co-writers. Working with her over eight years of writing projects has helped us clarify and mature our work.

We continue to appreciate Marshall Rosenberg's contributions to our lives and our work through his development and teaching of Nonviolent Communication, out of which our Mediate Your Life approach and training has grown. Marshall died on February 7, 2015. We honor his legacy and are grateful for the opportunity to have worked with and learned from him.

I, John, am particularly grateful for having had the honor and opportunity to work closely with Marshall for over a decade until his retirement, and for the close relationship that he and his wife Valentina shared with me and my family. As a result, his passing is a deeply personal loss for me. He has powerfully touched the lives of so many around the world through his incredible passion and dedication to his work over four decades. I look forward to the day his contributions will be fully recognized.

We have both had numerous teachers who have impacted our work. We thank them and acknowledge their contributions to our work and our lives.

We thank our families and loved ones for their ongoing support.

Lastly, we thank and appreciate Stacey Aaronson, who shepherded this book through the final stages of editing and design.

FOR FURTHER READING

Brown, Brené. *Daring Greatly: How the Courage to Be Vulnerable Transforms the Way We Live, Love, Parent, and Lead.* New York: Penguin Group, 2012.

Coyle, Daniel. *The Talent Code: Greatness Isn't Born. It's Grown. Here's How.* New York: Bantam Books, 2009.

Fisher, Roger and William Ury. *Getting to Yes: Negotiating Agreement Without Giving In.* New York: The Penguin Group, 1991.

Gazzaniga, Michael. *Who's in Charge? Free Will and the Science of the Brain.* New York: HarperCollins, 2011.

Grossman, Dave and Loren W. Christensen. *On Combat: The Psychology and Physiology of Deadly Conflict in War and in Peace.* Warrior Science Publications, 2008.

Kahneman, Daniel. *Thinking Fast and Slow.* New York: Farrar, Straus and Giroux, 2011.

Kinyon, John and Ike Lasater. *Mediate Your Life Training Manual, 5th edition.* Amherst, MA: Mediate Your Life LLC, 2014.

Lasater, Ike with Julie Stiles. *Words That Work in Business: A Practical Guide to Effective Communication in the Workplace.* Encinitas, CA: PuddleDancer Press, 2010.

Lasater, Judith Hanson and Ike Lasater. *What We Say Matters: Practicing Nonviolent Communication*. Berkeley, CA: Rodmell Press, 2009.

Rogers, Carl. *On Becoming a Person. A Therapist's View of Psychotherapy*. New York: Houghton Mifflin, 1961.

Rosenberg, Marshall B. *Nonviolent Communication: A Language of Compassion*. Encinitas, CA: PuddleDancer Press, 1999.

Rosenberg, Marshall B. *Speak Peace in a World of Conflict: What You Say Next Will Change Your World*. Encinitas, CA: PuddleDancer Press, 2005.

Rosenberg, Marshall B. *The Surprising Purpose of Anger: Beyond Anger Management: Finding the Gift*. Encinitas, CA: PuddleDancer Press, 2005.

Rosenberg, Marshall B. *We Can Work It Out: Resolving Conflicts Peacefully and Powerfully*. Encinitas, CA: Puddle-Dancer Press, 2004.

Sapolsky, Robert M. *Why Zebras Don't Get Ulcers*. New York: Henry Holt & Company, 1994.

About Mediate Your Life

Email: contact@mediateyourlife.com
Website: mediateyourlife.com

Facebook: Mediate Your Life
facebook.com/pages/Mediate-Your-Life/
277226242307687
Twitter: @MediateYourLife
twitter.com/MediateYourLife

About the Trainings

Mediate Your Life integrates compassion, mindfulness, and clear communication to help you learn to create and choose peace with yourself, with others, and with society at large. We offer step-by-step, highly effective processes and exercises that rewire your brain to return to presence and create connection between yourself and others.

At its core the Mediate Your Life program is about listening to—and really hearing—ourselves and others. It is about increasing our capacity for empathy so that when triggered we can overcome the body's natural "fight-flight-freeze" reaction. The process teaches how to replace conflict with true collaboration, new possibilities, and compassionate support.

We offer a variety of trainings to suit your needs. The year-long immersion program consists of three four-day in-person intensives, with practice suggestions in between.

You can take any of these workshops as a stand-alone course or sign up for the full year. We also have shorter in-person classes, and we offer the intensives as a tele-course for those who prefer.

ABOUT THE AUTHORS

JOHN KINYON

John gives workshops and trainings around the U.S. and around
the world. He is an inspirational
speaker and author who helps
people resolve conflicts peacefully
and collaboratively. John is co-
developer and founder of the
Mediate Your Life training program and company and worked

closely for over a decade with Marshall Rosenberg, founder
of the international work of Nonviolent Communication
(NVC). John has been a trainer of the Center for Nonviolent Communication (CNVC) since 2000. He co-founded
the Bay Area NVC organization (BayNVC) and has become
a leader in the worldwide NVC community.

John earned a BA from the University of San Francisco,
where he studied psychology and philosophy, and played
for USF's nationally ranked soccer team. He went on to earn
a degree in clinical psychology from Penn State University.
After graduate school, John helped launch and develop a
small commercial business before embracing communication and conflict resolution work full-time. He lives with
his wife and children in the San Francisco Bay Area.

Ike Lasater

For twenty years, Ike Lasater was a high-stakes litigation lawyer in the federal and state courts of California. In the legal context, he experienced "mediation" as a process of threatening and cajoling the parties to reach settlement. That changed when he met Marshall Rosenberg, an American psychologist and the creator of Nonviolent Communication. Ike grew to see that mediation can be an opportunity for the parties to hear each other's needs and thereby truly understand what is fueling their conflict, which typically leads to much more satisfying outcomes for the parties.

This way of approaching conflict was congruent with his values, developed through long-term practices of Zen meditation, yoga (he cofounded *Yoga Journal* in 1975), and aikido. Ike has served on the boards of the Center for Nonviolent Communication and the Association for Dispute Resolution of Northern California, and served on the mediation panel for the United States District Court for the Northern District of California. He is the co-author of *Choosing Peace* (2014), *Words That Work in Business: A Practical Guide to Effective Communication in the Workplace* (2010), and *What We Say Matters: Practicing Nonviolent Communication (2009)*. In addition to facilitating Mediate Your Life trainings, Ike coaches individuals, couples, and organizations in conflict and acts as a mediator upon request.

Julie Stiles

Besides working with Ike and John for the past ten years, Julie is a Health and Transformation Coach, ThetaHealing® Practitioner, Access Consciousness Bars Practitioner, writer, and speaker committed to empowering people to fully live their healing journey and radically alter their relation-  ship to healing and wholeness through taking back their power over their well-being. She is a graduate of the Institute for Integrative Nutrition and has an MA in Consciousness Studies from John F. Kennedy University.

Julie's work focuses on lifestyle changes, including nutrition and fitness, that promote better health, as well as on the deeper process of transformation that is often required when people step on the path of improving their overall well-being. She has supported people to eat healthier, lose weight, honor and accept their body, increase balance in their lives, create reasonable goals and reach them, move through their blocks to making change, and resolve internal conflicts. Creator and host of the podcasts Autoimmune Adventures and Being Well, Julie has also appeared on Voice America and radio shows nationwide, inspiring people to live their challenges as an adventure and create the change they'd like to see in their lives.

Julie offers private and group coaching, workshops, and webinars, and she works with people in person and worldwide via phone and the Internet. You can find her online at:

juliestiles.com and aiadventures.com

Made in the USA
Las Vegas, NV
29 January 2024

85058076R00212